Lecture Notes in Computer Science 876

Edited by G. Goos, J. Hartmanis and J. van Leeuwen

Advisory Board: W. Brauer   D. Gries   J. Stoer

B. u. Shneiderman, ... Computer
Dana Unger (eds.)

Human-Computer
Interaction

4th International Conference, EWHCI '94
St. Petersburg, Russia, August 2–5, 1994
Selected Papers

Springer-Verlag

Berlin Heidelberg New York
London Paris Tokyo
Hong Kong Barcelona
Budapest

Brad Blumenthal Juri Gornostaev
Claus Unger (Eds.)

Human-Computer Interaction

4th International Conference, EWHCI '94
St. Petersburg, Russia, August 2-5, 1994
Selected Papers

Springer-Verlag

Berlin Heidelberg New York
London Paris Tokyo
Hong Kong Barcelona
Budapest

Series Editors

Gerhard Goos
Universität Karlsruhe
Vincenz-Priessnitz-Straße 3, D-76128 Karlsruhe, Germany

Juris Hartmanis
Department of Computer Science, Cornell University
4130 Upson Hall, Ithaka, NY 14853, USA

Jan van Leeuwen
Department of Computer Science, Utrecht University
Padualaan 14, 3584 CH Utrecht, The Netherlands

Volume Editors

Brad Blumenthal
EECS Department (M/C 154), University of Illinois at Chicago
851 South Morgan St. (SEO 1120), Chicago, Illinois 60607, USA
E-mail: brad@eecs.uic.edu

Juri Gornostaev
International Centre for Scientific and Technical Information (ICSTI)
21-B, Kuusinen St., 125252 Moscow, Russia
E-mail: enir@ccic.icsti.msk.su

Claus Unger
Praktische Informatik II, Hagen University (FernUniversität)
D-58084 Hagen, Germany
E-mail: Claus.Unger@fernuni-hagen.de

CR Subject Classification (1991): D.2.2, H.1.2, H.5, I.2.7, I.7, K.3-4

ISBN 3-540-58648-2 Springer-Verlag Berlin Heidelberg New York

CIP data applied for

© Springer-Verlag Berlin Heidelberg 1994
Printed in Germany

Typesetting: Camera-ready by author
SPIN: 10479324   45/3140-543210 - Printed on acid-free paper

Preface

For many researchers, conferences are the main source of professional contacts from outside of their own local organization. Often, the contacts made at a conference are more valuable than the work reported. The East-West Conference on Human-Computer Interaction is a conference that is organized specifically to foster professional and personal contact between researchers in the former Soviet Union and researchers in the rest of the world.

The papers in this volume were all presented at the fourth EWHCI conference, held in St. Petersburg, Russia from 2 August to 5 August 1994. Approximately 80 participants attended the conference from at least 14 different countries throughout Asia, Australia, Europe, and North America. While the papers themselves are an excellent record of some of the research and ideas that were discussed at the conference, the real story of the conference is the interaction between researchers, not only during the paper sessions, but during the tutorials, poster sessions, and special topic discussion groups that were held throughout the week.

There were 13 paper sessions at the conference, running two or three in parallel. In all, about 37 papers were presented during the three days. This volume contains the best of those papers, based on the reviewers' assessments before the conference.

Three basic themes were represented at the conference: theoretical and empirical underpinnings of human-computer interaction, implemented systems, and the relationship of human-computer interaction to other fields.

The first theme included sessions on the foundations of human-computer interaction with papers on topics ranging from activity theory to Fitts' Law. In addition, the sessions on empirical studies and user diversity presented data that serve as an experimental background to interaction design.

The second theme included sessions on implemented applications, environments, and architectures demonstrating and supporting various principles in human-computer interaction design.

Finally, the third theme included sessions on the application and relationship of human-computer interaction to learning and teaching, computer-supported collaboration, hypertext, and artificial intelligence.

Of course, these papers only record a small part of the work that was done at the conference. The exchange of ideas, plans for future collaboration, and perspectives on human-computer interaction were invaluable, but the real record of the conference is in the friendships that have been built and continued over these last four years.

We express our appreciation for the help of all reviewers: Michel Beaudouin-Lafon, Stéphane Chatty, Gilbert Cockton, Allen Cypher, Prasun Dewan, Alan Dix, Michael Donskoy, Alexander Giglavy, Christian Gram, Jonathan Grudin, Keith Hopper, Anna Kamenkova, Arthur Karshmer, Rick Kazman, Jim Larson, Laura Leventhal, Allan MacLean, Scott Overmyer, Blaine Price, Eduard Projdakov, Helmut Stiegler, Dimitry Subbotin, Barbee Teasley, Julita Vassileva, and Marilyn Welles.

Special thanks go to Rachel Bellamy, Allen Cypher, and Francesmary Modugno for their assistance in editing the papers in this volume.

Brad Blumenthal
Juri Gornostaev
Claus Unger

August 1994

Table of Contents

Foundations of HCI

Empirical Studies, Applications

Environments

Architectures

Learning and Teaching

Hypertext

Ergosemiotics of User Interface Research and Design: Foundations, Objectives, Potential

Gennady Uzilevsky

Oryol Pedagogical University
Orel, Russia
Fax:: (086-00.)-9-39-28.

Abstract. Two directions of computer semiotics, structuralistic and linguo-ergonomical, are considered. The necessity in ergosemiotics, its bases, objectives and potential are discussed.

1 Introduction

It could be said that linguists and semioticians have payed attention to the appearance of computer systems during the last decades, since such systems are based on different sign systems and operate with them on various levels, beginning with machine code and ending with human-computer communication languages.

In this report we try to illuminate the achievements of semioticians in this domain. T.Winograd et al [43] considered computers as a tool for producing speech acts. J.Rassmussen [28] studied the relationship between the types of signs needed by a user and the kind of cognition that users exhibit. D.Piotrowski used the ideas of the structuralist school of glossematics as a theoretical foundation for computer systems research [26]. J.P.Decles investigated machine architecture from a semiotic position [7], and R.Boland applied methods of hermeneutics in order to investigate users' understanding of user interface (UI) [6]. We should also note M.Nadin's paper that analyzed various problems of UI design [29] including its aesthetics in terms of Ch.Peirce's conception.

It is useful to emphasize that psychologists who dealt with the construction of formal models of human-computer interaction used semiotic concepts in their work (see, for example [21;24]).

The concepts of semiotics were also used in the papers of researchers who investigated the programming aspects of UI research and design [9;10].

Especially significant are A.Marcus's papers that attempt to solve practical questions of UI, such as iconic sign construction, color choice, etc. from the standpoint of semiotics [17;18].

2 Avenus of Computer Semiotics Investigation

A number of publications that have appeared over the last few years (see, for instance, [1-2;10]) indicate the formation of a new scientific specialisation: computer semiotics. It consists of two directions:

- the first is based on the propositions of the London structuralistic school (particularly the ideas of M.Hallidays's systemic grammar [14]), U.Eco's views on the creation of different types of signs [8], and Ch.S.Peirce's conception concerning users of sign vehicles [25]. We call this direction "structuralistic";
- the second direction is based on the generalisations of computer linguistics and computer ergonomics data (we call this direction "lingo-ergonomic").

Now we briefly consider each of these directions (for a detailed analysis, see [39]).

The first scientific avenue explored by P.B.Andersen [1-2] is aimed at the investigation of computer systems and their different levels, or subsystems, in terms of semiotics. Starting the research with the UI and ending with machine code, he gives a semiotic interpretation to object-oriented programming, shows up interesting features of computer-based signs, presents a metaphoric classification of such signs, etc. Since the structuralistic avenue is primarily based on M.Hallidays's conception of language as a social event, described in terms of its functions, the highest priority is given to semantics.

We think that the usage of structuralistic propositions in the investigation of computer and HCI problems could be interpreted as a top-down approach. Merely applying semiotic ideas does not seem to be sufficient to connect them with the achievements and peculiarities of HCI. It is of real use to first consider the details of computer systems and only then to transfer semiotic ideas to various problems, including UI research, design, and implementation.

In this connection we pass on to look through the second direction worked out by U.L.Figge [10]. Computer systems and all types of signs that promote the realisation of human-computer communication are the research domain of computer semiotics. The realisations of the internal states of computer systems and their influence on users through various peripheral devices are its research subject.

The goal of this scientific avenue is the analysis and generalisation of HCI data. Computer linguistics could significantly influence the development of computer semiotics. Computer ergonomics is the other specialisation that could not only feed computer semiotics, but also serve as a field of activity for computer semiotics. This also seems to be a top-down approach.

While considering both of these directions, we came to the conclusion [39] that the fundamental questions about the nature of UI, the definitions of requirements for its design and evaluation, etc. are beyond the scope of computer semiotics.

3 Foundations of Ergosemiotics as a new Scientific Specialisation

We are prone to think that linguistics, semiotics, and ergonomics are interdependent in the investigation of computer system problems and possess common problems that may be solved from a unified position.

Therefore, it is reasonable to consider ergosemiotics as a new scientific specialisation that explores problems common to these three disciplines.

Propositions of ergosemiotics have been discussed since 1988 [33]. While investigating tendencies of engineering, ergonomics, linguistics, and semiotics, we have shown the needs both wihin these specialisations, as well the needs outside of these specialisations. The main goal of ergosemiotics consists in working out principles of effective and comfortable sign vehicle construction for humans interacting with various types of machinery, including computers [37]. This effort was undertaken to outline the ergosemiotic approach to UI research [42]. In this paper we consider the ergosemiotic foundations of UI research and design.

The first foundation stone of ergosemiotics is the systemic linguistics of W.Humboldt, I.Sreznewski, A.Potebnia, I.Boduen de Curtene, and G.Melnikov (see, for instance, [19]) that is characterized by the following system of concepts. A complex object is an object that can be decomposed into its components and elements. A system is interpreted as a complex object that fulfils a certain function in a supersystem. Elements and components of a system form its substance, i.e. they are the material of a system. The set of connections and relations represent the structure of a system. The place of an element in a structure, i.e. in a certain node of connections and relations that maintain the integrity (wholeness) of a system, characterizes the value of the element in it. A model is a set of complex object elements that are placed in certain relationships with elements of another complex object called the "original". From this, it follows that this specialisation is a product of the systemic approach and of simulation theory (see, for example, [20]).

The concepts of outer and inner determinantas of a language are considered as important elements of systemic linguistics. An inner determinanta is a main feature of a language as an adaptive system; it determines and defines the peculiarities of all concrete entities and levels of a language in their systemic interrelations [19, p. 20]. In turn, an inner determinanta is generated by outer determinanta as a function of a language in a supersystem.

It is helpful to underline the features of selforganisation of a language towards its elements and supersystem that favour the applicability of such language characteristics as structure, substance, determinanta, etc. to all levels of a language considered as a system.

Revealing the interrelations between language and speech from the perspective of systemic linguistics is of certain scientific and practical interest for HCI as an interdisciplinary scientific specialisation. Main concepts of the language include the concepts of outer form, namely, morphemes as socialized images of minimal speech entities, as well as entitites of minimal inner form, namely, the meanings of morphemes as invariant minimal elements that do not depend on morphemes.

It is useful for the investigation and design of artificial languages, especially HCI languages, to add that language signs and their meanings could not be speech elements, since a word is represented in the speech flow but not its image [19, p.26].

The propositions of this avenue of systemic linguistics can be used by ergosemiotics as the basis of a bottom-up approach to the investigation and design of human-machine interaction languages in general. .

Original ideas from Ch.S.Peirce's conception [25] forms the second foundation stone of ergosemiotics because of their break-through into the understanding of various semiotic events and signs. It should be added that the human being is in the center of this conception.

Ergonomics, especially its requirements for the design and implementation of effective, comfortable, and pleasant machinery and working environments, is the third foundation stone of ergosemiotics.

Our investigations of natural and evolutionarily developing artificial languages (EDAL) showed that their composition and structures are determined by functional asymmetries of the human brain [35]. Therefore, neurolinguistics, neurosemiotics, and neuropsychology form the fourth foundation stone of ergosemiotics.

Our experience investigating EDALs testifies to the usefulness of interpreting language as a vehicle of construction, identification, transformation, and transmission of information [23] and to the consideration of language from two perspectives:

– ontological - as a system of psychophysiological mechanisms generating texts in the form of discrete sequence of physical signs (see, for instance, [41]; and
– descriptional - as a system consisting of some interrelated levels [12].

It should be noted that language behaves as an abstract sign system with respect to the conception of text as a concrete sign system. These semiotic propositions ought to be implemented by ergosemiotics.

One of the goals of ergosemiotics is to explicate the connections between ergonomics, linguistics, and semiotics, in order to deepen and broaden the bases of this new specialisation.

4 Objectives and Potential of Ergosemiotics

Having described the foundation stones of ergosemiotics we turn to the definition of its research object and subject. Sign vehicles of human-machine interaction are the research object of ergosemiotics; various aspects of design, implementation, and functioning of semiotic formations aimed at human-machine communication are its research subject.

Because of the enormous experience accumulated in HCI research, it is usefule to apply ergosemiotic ideas to the research and design of computer systems UI. Such UI's determine the efficiency, comfort, and pleasure of users' communication with this type of machinery. Up to this time there has been no proper scientific explication of UI. The dichotomy "language - text" seems to help. Let us try to describe the problem.

While designing a UI, we should deal with the choice of peripheral devices and sign vehicles that will promote the realisation of human-machine communication. By implementing a UI we produce an operating symbolic machine that constructs concrete texts using peripheral devices, HCI languages, and software tools which form the united system.

In other words, the languages are transformed into an autonomous means for sign production. It is not difficult to arrive at the conclusion that a UI exists in two forms:

– as a generalized abstract system of physical and sign vehicles;
– as a concrete system where these vehicles are implemented and dynamically function. Ergosemiotics encourages the definition of a concrete UI as an interactive multileveled information system formed on the basis of different natural languages, artificial languages, and flexible soft- and hardware tools and distinguished by the fact that a user creatively and dynamically works with a constantly changible information massif for solving certain problems.

It is necessary to add that the ergosemiotic approach favours the analysis of different levels of UI in the context of such related semiotics aspects as pragmatics, sygmatics, semantics and syntactics (for details, see [39]). This approach is apparently more fruitful than the approach of K.Kuutti and L.J.Bannon [18] who considered the level of use situation and the conceptual and technological levels of UI analysis. To our mind, the ergosemiotic approach provides the means for creating a wholistic conception of UI that could have practical consequences. In order to explicate this proposition, we shall describe the objectives of ergosemiotics.

As noted earlier, one of the main goals of ergosemiotics is formulating the principles of comfortable and effective sign system construction for human-machine interaction, including HCI. For the implementation of effective sign systems, the following topics that concern computer system UI's must be considered:

- the study, generalisation, and usage of linguistic and semiotic facts and propositions, research data in the domain of AI, computer graphics, cybernetics, engineering psychology, ergonomics, general theory of communication, informatics, etc. We think that it would be useful to make up a special hypertext system dedicated to the data and knowledge representations for UI construction;
- the explication and investigation of various approaches to UI and HCI sign vehicle research and design;
- the study of the nature, forms and processes of HCI;
- the investigation of UI's as interactive multileveled information systems and the definition of their functions and requirements for design and evaluation;
- working out the typology of HCI languages and sign vehicles; the explication of their features, functions, peculiarities; and the determination of their structure;
- revealing principles of the optimal distribution of UI functions between different HCI languages, natural and iconic languages, etc.;
- working out the principles of HCI language construction, including the principles of information distribution on the screen;
- the explication of existing approaches to color choice by UI design and the formulation of structure-functional (ergosemiotical) approaches to proper color usage;
- the study of the use of music principles for UI formation;
- the definition of requirements for HCI languages and sign vehicle design and evaluation.

From an analysis of our definition of UI's and the objectives of ergosemiotics we have just formulated, it is easy to see that they are interrelated.

The first results we obtained working on the problems explicated above [3-5; 31-32; 34; 36; 39-40] testify to the possibility of wholistic UI conception construction. It should be said that the data we have gained are useful enough for concrete UI design. In other words, the data indicate the enormous potential of this new scientific specialisation.

Space does not permit us to reveal and discuss all aspects of the potential of ergosemiots. However, we want to shed light on some of them. First, we will consider the problem of communication. Since the days of Aristotle and Plato two approaches to the description of communication have existed:

– an object-oriented approach aimed at the examination of various types of signs that are used by communication; and

– a subject-oriented approach aimed at the examination of the processes that are involved in communication cast as thinking and knowing; believing, assuming and hypothesizing; inferring, concluding, proving, etc.

R.Posner [27] pointed out that the concept "meaning" occurred in both contexts. In doing so, he made a successful attempt to connect the hierarchy of general types of signs (signals, indicators, expressions, gestures) that describe complex configurations of believing, causing and intending, with the five types of communication (declaration, directive, assertive, expressive, commissive). This connection provided a foundation for the discovery of the conditions for achieving communication.

We think that the value of R.Posner's investigation consists in his connection of speech acts as a particular case of semiosis with all other sign processes. In our opinion, ergosemiotics can contribute significantly to the unification of these approaches and to the study of various types of communication based on different languages and codes. In our opinion, one of the objectives of ergosemiotics is the discovery of invariant structures and the transfer of these structures to the formation of HCI languages and sign vehicles for human-machine interaction.

By studying EDAL's we noticed that their outer form was characterized by two levels: abstract and concrete, that in turn are determined by functional asymmetries, which we have stated elsewhere [35]. From above it follows that any artificial language that is being constructed for human communication should consist of abstract and concrete levels.

While analyzing HCI we noticed that this abstract-concrete structure has been unconsciously introduced into the design of menu subsystem during recent years. Natural language based menus [13;29] and combinations of horizontal and vertical menus (e.g., menu bars with pull-down menus) testify to the favour of it. It is useful to add that tablet menus that do not possess an abstract level in the form of command class names are very difficult to work with [36].

We have shown that the evolution of means of communication in world cultural development have involved five periods: prevocal; vocal; vocal and written language; vocal, written language and book-printing; vocal, written language, book-printing, tele- cinema machinery, PC [39].

Most languages that are inherent in people appeared in the first period. We could name such languages and codes as languages of instruction for actions, selection, perception; languages of functional asymmetry indicators; languages of gestures, images, movements; iconic languages, color and music codes, etc. Due to the fact that these semiotic formations are weakly investigated, one of the objectives of ergosemiotics lies in the research of these sign vehicles so that we might mate features, functions, and peculiarities of the sign vehicles with new information input and output devices. It is also extremely useful and scientifically interesting to study the language of cinema. These research results will favour UI design.

Currently the indicators of the sixth period of communication exist in the form of virtual realities and computer-based prosthetics. To our mind, this period will be characterized by direct interaction of users with computers. We assume that these languages and new information devices will play a dominant role in this phase of the evolution of the means of communication. New sign vehicles based on the symbiosis of these languages are expected. It seems to us that ergosemiotics should consolidate the efforts of specialists in this direction. We are sure that the progress in new information technology design, in the construction of new information input and output devices, in the research of brain languages, functional asymmetries, and languages that are inherent in people will stimulate the discovery of non-sensory human's entries into the future and past.

Another problem that ergosemiotics should take into consideration is the use of metaphors in the research, design, and implementation of UI. We came to the conclusion that metaphors that are used in HCI, especially "user as a machine," "computer as a partner in a dialogue," "computer as a tool," "computer as a medium,"etc. do not cover all of the stages of UI and application system construction [40]. We proposed the metaphor "illusive partner" (subjectivated object or quazisubject) taken from the general theory of communication [15]; it will serve not only to maintain the process of computer system design, but also to use all other metaphors under its leadership. In our view, the choice of this metaphor in discussion has not only practical but also philosophical and theoretical significance, since engineering an artificial world should be reflexive towards humans and call forth a communicative feel in people. It is of use to add that this metaphor will collect ergonomical, psychological, and semiotic knowledge and techniques that are not covered by other metaphors.

In this connection the cognition of nature and peculiarities of the "human-human" communication process seem to assist in understanding the mapping of the new UI metaphor to the user's psychology, needs, knowledge, and tasks in the human-computer communication process. We think that the information processing model created by one of the authors of the paper [41] will also contribute to realize this intention.

5 Conclusion

Thus, we have considered the foundations, objectives and potential of a new scientific specialisation that is in the beginning of its development.

Obviously, it is of no use to oppose ergosemiotics to other scientific research directioons that deal with UI and applied programming. To our mind, the research data which were obtained by various scientific specialisations in engineering, ergonomics, linguistics, programming, psychology, semiotics etc., could be considered as requirements for the research and design of UI on the lower level addressed by ergosemiotics. In other words, we are on the threshold of the creation of a complex approach to UI research, design, and implementation in which there is a niche for many different specialisations. The paper of S.Treu [30] also seems to favour this supposition.

In our view, all of the achievements of ergosemiotics concerning human-computer systems apparently are also of use and interest to the research, design and implementation of sign vehicles for humans interacting with other types of machinery.

6 Acknowledgement

I am grateful to the anonymous reviewer for the useful comments concerning content and style of the paper. Very many thanks to Brad Blumenthal for his valuable editing of the article .

References

1. P.B.Andersen: Computer semiotics. Scand. J. of Information System, 1991 (3), 1, pp. 3-30.
2. P.B.Andersen, B.Holmquist: Interactive fiction: artificial intelligence as a mode of sign production. AI and Society, 1991 (4), 4, pp. 291-313.
3. V.O.Andreev, G.Ja.Uzilevsky: "Autograph 845-2 a low cost integrated interactive CAD/CAM workstation for mechanical design and engineering: a modified user's interface. In: International Conference on Design. ICED. Dubrownik, SFRU, 1990, pp.728-734.
4. V.O.Andreev, G.Ja.Uzilevsky: On the requiremwents to the tablet menus creation and estimation. In: 1-st Moscow International HCI'91 Workshop Proc. Moscow, 1991, pp. 86-93.
5. V.O.Andreev, G.Ja. Uzilevsky. The language of geometrical configurations as the basis of the language for computer graphics users. In: User Interface: research, design, implementation. N 2, 1992, pp. 58-71 (in Russian).
6. J.R.Boland: Information system use as a hermeneutic process. In: Information system research: Contemporary approaches and emergent traditions. Amsterdam, 1991, pp. 439-458.
7. -P.Decles: Intermediate representation in the cognitive sciences. Semiotica. 1989 (77), 1, pp. 121-135.
8. U.Eco. A theory of semiotics. Bloomington: Indiana Univ. Press, 1979, 354 p.
9. R.W.Erich, D.H.Johnson, J.W.Roach a.o.: Role of language in human-computer interfaces. Human-computer dialogue design. N.-Y., 1986, Vol. 2, pp. 165-213.
10. U.L.Figge: Computer semiotik. Zt. fur Semiotik, 1991, (13), 3, ss. 321-330.
11. J.D.Foley, V.L.Wallace, P.Chan: The human factors of computer graphics interaction techniques. IEEE computer graphics applications, 1984, (4), 11, pp. 3-48.
12. P.L.Garvin: Descriptional model of language. In: Natural Language and Computer. N.-Y., 1963, pp. 58-71.
13. A.P.Gordienko: User interface in graphical applications: object-oriented approach. In: User interface research, design, implementation, N 2, Moscow, 1992, pp. 151-160 (in Russian).
14. M.K.Halliday: System and function in language. Oxford: Oxford Univ. Press, 1976, 250 p.
15. M.S.Kagan: The world of communication. Moscow: Polytizdat, 1988, 319 p. (in Russian).

16. K.Kuutti, L.J.Bannon: Some confusions at the interface: conceptualizing the "interface" problem. In: Human job and computer interfaces. Amsterdam: Elsevier Science Publ., 1991, 19 p. (preprint).
17. A.Marcus: Corporate identity for iconic interface design: the graphic design perspective. Computer graphics and applications. 1984 (4), 12, pp. 24-32.
18. A.Marcus: Graphic design for electronic documents and user interfaces. N.-Y.: ACM Press, 1991, 266 p.
19. G.P.Melnikov: Foundations of terminology. Moscow: UFP, 1991, 115 p. (in Russian).
20. G.P.Melnikov: Systemology and linguistic aspects of cybernetics. Translated by J.A.Cooper. N.-Y. et al: Gordon and Breach, 1973, 440 p.
21. T.P.Moran: The command language grammar: A representation for user interface computer systems. Intern. J. of Man.-Mach. St., 1981 (15), 1, pp. 3-50.
22. M.Nadin: Interface design: a semiotic paradigm. Semiotica, 1988, (69), 3/4, pp. 269-302.
23. V.V.Nalimov: Probability model of language. 2-nd ed. Moscow: Nauka, 1979, 303 p. (in Russian).
24. S.N.Payne, T.R.G.Green: Task-action grammars: a model of mental representation of task languages. Human-Computer Interaction. 1986 (2), 2, pp. 93-133.
25. Ch.S.Peirce: Collected papers. Vol. 1-2. Cambridge, Mass.: Harvard Univ.Press, 1960, 535p.
26. D.Piotrowski: Structures applicatives et language naturel. Recherces sur les fondements du modele. Grammaire applicative. Ph.D. thesis. Paris, Ecole de Hauptes Etude en sciences sociales, 1990 (op. cit. 1).
27. R.Posner: Believing, causing, intending: The basis for a hierarchy of sign concepts in the reconstruction of communication. Signs, search, and communication: semiotic aspects of artificial intelligence. Berlin a.o., 1992, pp. 215-270.
28. J.Rassmussen: Information processing and human-machine interaction. Amsterdam: North Holland, 1986, 215 p.
29. H.Tennant: Menu based natural language. In: Encyclopedia of artificial intelligence, v.1, 1987, pp. 43-48.
30. S.Treu: Interface structures: conceptual, logical, and physical patterns applicable to human-computer interaction. Intern. J. Man-Mach. St., 1992, (37), pp. 565-593.
31. G.Ja.Uzilevsky: Choice of color by the construction of user interface: prerequisites and guidelines. Orel: SPE "GraphOr", 1992, 162 p. (electronic book, in Russian).
32. G.Ja.Uzilevsky: Command language and screen menu: requirements for the construction and evaluation. Applied ergonomics, 1992, pp. 41-46 (in Russian).
33. G.Ja.Uzilevsky: On the ergosemiotical approach to the construction of visual sign systems. In: Graphical signs: problems of research, design, standardisation. Kiev, 1988, pp. 13-15 (in Russian).
34. G.Ja.Uzilevsky: On human-computer communication and dialogue and approaches to their investigation. In: Ergonomics of peripheral devices and social consequences of computerisation. Orel, 1988, pp. 127-131 (in Russian).

35. G.Ja.Uzilevsky: On the structure of natural and artificial developing languages. Nauchnaja and technicheskaja informatsia, ser. 2, 1991, 9, pp. 1-7 (in Russian).
36. G.Ja.Uzilevsky: Working out of principles of tablet menu formation as the dialogue tool for PMC CAD for common machinerybuilding: report of the scientific work. Orel: OD of IPI AS of USSSR, 1989, 267 sh. (in Russian).
37. G.Ja.Uzilevsky, V.O.Andreev: Ergosemiotics as a result of engineering, linguistics, semiotics, and ergonomics development. In: Ergonomics in Russia, the other independent states, and around the world: Past, Present and Future. St.Petersburg, 1993, pp. A-32-34.
38. G.Uzilevsky, V. Andreev: Iconic signs and languages in user interface development In: Human-Computer Interaction: Third Intern. Conference, EW HCI'93, Moscow, Russia. Berlin, 1993, pp. 115-124.
39. G.Ja.Uzilevsky, V.N.Ageyev: Human-computer interaction: forms, processes, approaches. Moscow: Academy of Print, 1994 (in print, in Russian).
40. G.Uzilevsky, V.Andreev: View on the information technologies from the positions of information environment evolution. In: Information technologies and people: Proc. of Intern. Conference, p. 1. Moscow, 1993, pp. 159-164.
41. G.Ja.Uzilevsky, G.W.Eiger: On the model of analytiko- synthetical information processing in the process of communication. Nauchnaja and technicheskaja informatsia, ser. 2, 1993, 5, pp. 1-7 (in Russian).
42. G.Ja.Uzilevsky, V.P.Zinchenko: User interface research: an ergosemiotical approach. In: East-West Intern. Human-Computer Interaction Conference Proc. St.Petersburg, p.2., 1992, pp. 303-313.
43. T.Winograd, F.Flores: Understanding computers and cognition: a new foundation for design. Norwood, NJ: Ablex, 1986, 207 p.

Fitts' Law as a Design Artefact: A Paradigm Case of Theory in Software Design

Olav Bertelsen

Computer Science Dept., Aarhus University
Ny Munkegade 116, DK-8000 Aarhus C. Denmark
olavb@daimi.aau.dk

Abstract: Fitts' law is described and discussed as an example of use of theory in human-computer interaction design. The dichotomy between academic theory and applied theory is rejected and replaced by a radical pragmatic notion of theories as design artefacts. Different roles of theory in design are discussed.

1 Introduction

In the early years of interactive computing, designers relied solely on their intuition, some rules of thumb and a few guidelines. As the users of interactive systems turned from programmers to non-computer professionals, this situation became a problem —the systems were too difficult to use. Some saw in this an urgent need for a scientific foundation for HCI-design. The classical contribution to this vision is formed by the works by Card, Moran and Newell [3, 4], who believed that the future science of HCI should be based on cognitive psychology. They saw their task as one of making the bulk of academic experimental results applicable for designers. The vision was that this science had to be guided by the requirements set by the interface engineers, i.e. the theory should be operational rather than true in a more academic sense. The basic components in this applied science of the human-computer interface were task analysis, calculation and approximation. The idea was that the performance of a future human-computer system could be calculated from an analysis of the job which the system was intended to do. The special need for approximation in this field, compared to e.g. electrical engineering, was that the human system component was too complex. The implicit epistemology underlying Card, Moran and Newell's vision is formulated with great clarity in Newell's last book:

> Theories are approximate. Of course, we all know that technically they are approximate; the world can't be known with absolute certainty. But I mean more than that. Theories are also deliberately approximate. Usefulness is often traded against truth. Theories that are known to be wrong continue to be used, because they are the best available. Fitts' law is like that. How a theory is wrong is carried along as part of the theory itself. Grossly approximate theories are continuous launching pads for better attempts. Fitts' law is like that too. The scientist does the best he can with what he's got - and the engineer, who has to have answers, even more so. [13, p.14]

Newell doesn't reject the existence of a universal truth about human cognition, neither does he claim in principle that it is impossible to know this truth. The world *is* out there, but we construct approximate theories because it is too cumbersome to build an exhaustive theory, and because in many practical situations we are better off with operational rather than true theories. We can't reach the truth so we have to live with the useful. Newell's pragmatism is based on a dichotomy between applied theory (that is wrong but useful) and the truth. This position could be called methodological pragmatism.

In the field of HCI, the most prominent result from cognitive psychology is Fitts' law [6]. In this paper, I will use Fitts' law as a vehicle for a discussion of the role of theory in human-computer interaction, viewing it as a design artefact. Design artefacts are employed in the design process in order to support (or mediate) one or more of three design functions: gaining knowledge and understanding about what is to be designed, communicating during the process, and affecting the world. Examples of design artefacts are programming languages, CASE-tools, specification standards, systems development methods, and the like. Theories are thus constructed to help us master the world we are living in. Here I look at Fitts' law because it plays various interesting roles in the game of science and design.

2 Fitts' Law

The goal of Fitts' work [6] was to make sense of experimental results about human motor performance that seemed to be mutually contradictory.

> The need for a unifying concept of motor capacity is indicated by the apparent difficulty of reconciling many of the facts reported in the literature on motor skill. [6, p.382]

Thus Fitts' motivation was the purely academic one of making sense of some phenomena. Fitts' idea was that this could be obtained by realising that the capacity of the motor system (the relation between the movement-time, distance, and required precision) could be compared to the capacity of a communication channel [15], that is, a model where a sender codes signals onto a channel with a given bandwidth possibly perturbed by noise, after which a receiver gets the signal from the channel and decodes it. Fitts did not claim that mechanisms for coding etc. could be found in the motor system, but only that the limitations on performance had the same mathematical structure.

Fitts conceived the motor system as consisting of bones, muscles and nerves in the arm, as well as control mechanisms such as visual feedback. That is, the motor system consists of everything from "the signal in the brain" that initiates the movement to the resulting movement outside the subject. Fitts points out that one can only observe the total system of: receptor → neural channel (cognitive system) → effect, from the eye via the brain to the finger; you stimulates the eye and observes the resulting response in the hand. He works around this problem by applying a trick. By assuming that the neural channel consists of specific sub-channels in a chain, he sets up an experiment where everything except the motor system is eliminated. By using repetitive over-learned movements at the highest possible speed, he eliminates perception and cognitive processing from the chain, leaving the isolated capacity of the motor system (including the subjects' monitoring of the movement) to be measured. This was done in the so-called reciprocal tapping set-up.

Fitts defines the capacity of the human motor system as the ability to perform certain classes of movements in a uniform way. The time required to do a specific movement is inversely proportional to the capacity of the "motor channel". This capacity can be described by an analogy to Shannon's:

> Theorem 17: The capacity of a channel of band[width] W perturbed by white thermal noise of power N when the average transmitter power is limited to P is given by
>
> $$C = W \log \frac{P+N}{N}$$
>
> [15, p.100]

The obvious problem of this analogy is that it is impossible to get any information about the information capacity of the motor channel. Fitts does not see the information capacity of the motor system as a property of the motor system per se, but as a property of motor performance under given conditions. Thus the basis for Fitts' analysis is the amount of information required to accomplish a given movement. This quantity he denotes as the index of difficulty I_d, described by:

$$I_d = -\log_2 \frac{W_s}{2A} \ bits/response$$

where W_s is the variability of the movement, and A is the amplitude (distance). Division by the time t it takes to do the movement yields a quantity that is constant for specific classes of movements. This is called the index of performance, $I_p = I_d/t$ Consequently, Fitts' law has the following form:

$$I_p = -\frac{1}{t}\log_2 \frac{W_s}{2A} \ bits/sec$$

where I_p corresponds to Shannon's C, $1/t$ to the bandwidth of the motor system, and $W_s/2A$ to the signal to noise ratio, (P+N)/N in Shannon's formula. The interesting point is that this equation is able to describe the empirical data. From this expression of I_p, it is simple to deduce an expression for the required time t, but Fitts did not do that. He only wanted to describe the empirical data in a consistent way.

The appearance of Fitts' law is historically situated in a time when academic psychology (in the US) was on its way back from the behaviourist dark ages. The appearance of the computer had made it possible to build testable models of human cognition. The channel idea has been central in the sciences of human cognition and performance. In the behaviourist version, the channel degenerates to a black box, but the basic view of the relation between subject and object remains. In human factors engineering, human-machine relations are seen as a circular composition of channels: Machine operation → displays → sensing → data processing → controlling → controls → machine operations → ...

3   Additive Models

From the viewpoint of experimental psychology, Fitts' law is an unquestionable fact, due to the overwhelming amount of empirical evidence. When we move outside the laboratory, however, this fact appears to be questionable. The implicit assumption underlying Fitts' law is that it is possible to decompose human performance into basic tasks and add up the times for all these tasks to get the total performance time. This strategy, known as additive models, is an old idea and has been questioned for at least the last hundred years [9]. Simplistically stated, the assumption underlying additive models is that e.g. a mouse operation is the same thing no matter what context it is performed in. In HCI additive models have been widely used (e.g. the GOMS- and keystroke level models by Card et al. [4])

An experiment reported in [9] shows that additive models cannot describe even simple and controllable tasks. The subjects were solving so-called "Sterzinger lines", i.e. nonsense lines of letters and spaces. The task was to step from space to space, using the arrow keys on the computer console, until a space separating two equal letters was reached and then to indicate that by pressing the arrow-up key. In contrast to the studies by Card et al. [4], Gediga and Greif were able to monitor the performance of single keystrokes and thus discover that, although the total performance time could be described by an additive model, the time taken to perform the single key-press changed as the subject moved the cursor through the line.

The significance of these result with respect to Fitts' law is that if it is impossible to build additive models, then we may expect that the parameters in Fitts' law change according to changes in the (micro) context. Furthermore, the relevance of Fitts' law as a prescriptive tool depends on the general validity of additive performance models.

The "Sterzinger line" experiments can be seen as a critique of additive models from within experimental psychology showing that the relation between the human being and the surrounding world is dialectical and not mechanical — while the subject changes the object, the object also acts on the subject. There is no stable engine inside the subject. A more fundamental critique can be made by questioning the validity of laboratory experiments as a source of design relevant knowledge. Chapanis [5] has pointed out that, due to the complexity of human beings, it is almost impossible to keep track of the variables. This critique can be radicalised from the point of view of activity theory by stating that the human being in the controlled environment of the laboratory, is fundamentally different from the human being in "the real world" [12]. Although some aspects of human performance are evident from a laboratory experimental point of view, these aspects may not exist outside the experimental setting.

4 Fitts' Law in HCI —some Examples

Fitts' law studies expose great diversity in the way the law is used and the approach to the given (design) problem. Two general approaches can be identified. One tries to find general quantitative properties of the human motor system, constants of the human that are independent of the specific circumstances. In this group we find studies that have great resemblance to Fitts' reciprocal tapping set-up, but no resemblance to any practical situation (e.g. [11]). These studies are based on the implicit assumption that Fitts' law is part of a cognitive psychology that can form a universal framework for studies and design of HCI. At the other extreme, we find approaches more concerned with specific issues of specific (types of) interfaces, and thus more realistic in the experimental set-up (e.g. [7]), here we see studies that use Fitts' law solely as a source of inspiration. We are dealing with two fundamentally different approaches to the possibilities of a HCI-science. Either you try to establish anthropometric laws based on a "theory" about human cognition, or you can, based on specific metaphors, study specific interface classes. The classic Fitts' law study in HCI by Card, English, and Burr [2] comparing the performance of various devices in text selection, can belong to both categories. Some see these experiments as the determination of I_p in the mouse version of Fitts' law, others see the studies as a concrete, although reductionist, investigation of specific input devices. I prefer the latter interpretation.

Gillan et al. [7] report that Fitts' law can account for some of the performance variations in text selection with a mouse, but that other variations can neither be predicted nor described by Fitts' law. Two cases that theoretically should have the same I_p were examined, nevertheless the two I_p appeared to be different. Gillan et al. conclude that a general theory of mouse performance in a direct manipulation interface has to include parameters for aspects not covered by Fitts law, e.g. cognitive processes and user strategies. They point out that development of design oriented metrics has to be based upon detailed investigations of what the user does in concrete situations. Thus they give up the efforts to find the parameters in the mouse version of Fitts' law, and view their studies as dealing with some concrete properties of direct manipulation interfaces.

The applicability of Fitts' law in a practical design task is illustrated by an example regarding the placement of "soft buttons" in a hypertext browser screen layout [10]. Fitts' law was utilised to minimise the time required for mouse operation.

We probably saved tens of milliseconds per 5-minute browse. This really is not bad, as such things go; it's often not done in commercial systems, and is economical worthwhile in our expected applications, which have large multipliers. I think saving small fractions of a second by optimal button placement is probably a good illustration of the real but limited impact that traditional psychological theory can have if diligently applied. [10, p.65].

This indicates that artefacts like Fitts' law can be used to solve specific isolated design problems, whereas they are almost useless as general perspectives on human-computer interaction.

Laboratory experiments by Gediga and Wolff [8] confirm that target size influence movement time in "mousing", at the same time as the quantitative contents of Fitts' law are considered too unpredictable to be applied in design. They suggest a distinction between Fitts' law and a Fitts' effect that merely states that movement time is inversely proportional to target size, and proportional to movement length. They say that only the latter is relevant in HCI. This seems to preclude Fitts' law from being a part of the world of "task analysis, approximation and calculation".

5   Fitts' Law as a Design Artefact

Fitts made sense of a "chaotic" world by constructing a consistent predictive scheme. Although this scheme predicts and describes empirical data it provides no suggestions for an understanding of the observed phenomenon and its relations to its surroundings. Thus Fitts' law can be seen as a detached predictive metaphor. Fitts' law is basically a performance model in line with the time and motion study tradition founded by Taylor and Gilbreth. Together with this tradition it tends to reduce design of work environments, e.g. computer artefacts, to a matter of economical optimisation. No matter how much it is claimed that Fitts law is merely a useful metaphor, it will make us perceive the human being as a channel. The danger is that viewing the human being as a channel will make us treat her as a mechanical device.

The significance of these basic assumptions about the human psyche depends on the part Fitts' law plays in the game of design.

The above examples show at least three different roles. In the HCI psychology by Card et al. [4], Fitts' law was part of the *world view*. To play this role, Fitts' law must be placed in a context where human beings are seen as mechanical devices, i.e. cognitive science. Landauer [10] used Fitts' law as a *tool* for specific calculations in the design process, without adopting cognitive science as his main perspective on HCI. Gillan et al. [7] used Fitts' law as a *metaphor* for research on specific aspects of acting with a mouse. In design this amounts to the use of the Fitts' effect as a thinking tool [8]. The borders between these three roles are not clear-cut. By thinking about interface problems in Fitts' law terms (the metaphor role), other views are excluded and one is led towards mechanistic reduction. The use of a specific performance calculation serves as a thinking tool, too. Theories always play different roles at the same time.

In Newell's implicit dichotomy between true and applicable theory the metaphor role could be added as a third distinction. I would rather prefer to view the three above roles as modes of acting with and developing understanding of the world. The methodological pragmatism expressed by Newell rejects that value statements can have any relevance in the real world of design, and that differences in the overall understanding of the use of computer artefacts can have any practical significance. A simple notion of theories as design artefacts, based on this view, would state that theories are tools for prediction, calculation, and generation of visions; and that sometimes they work and sometimes they do not. Furthermore, such an idea would claim that the only valid world view should be the collection of tools for calculation, or performance models, just like the Model Human Processor [4].

In contrast to this, I will claim that value statements must be the basis for every science no matter whether they are implicit or explicit. Performance models like Fitts' law are based on specific (implicit) assumptions about the human being and her relation to her surroundings. By applying such models as tools in design we will automatically share this world view, unless we strongly specify another one. We can not avoid this ontological discussion. Our implicit or explicit choice of world view is also a choice of the world in which we want to live; disinterested sciences do not exist [1].

The absence of value statements in the methodological pragmatism of Newell [13] and Card et al. [3, 4] leads to either a position saying that any statement is valid if you like it to be so (i.e. relativism), or a position saying that only statements that can be inspected are valid in science (i.e. logical positivism). In the latter case, the scientific method is installed as a substitute/proxy/go-between for the assessment of theories, as it is seen in the idea that the psychology of the human-computer interface should be a *hard* science [14].

When designers build specific computer systems they use what they have and what they know, no matter how incompatible from a theoretical point of view. Current social- and cognitive science tend to misunderstand the strengths of science and just collect everything that seems to be right together. Scientific theories are not one-to-one reflections of the world, but artefacts mediating understanding of, and action in the world, through reduction. By stuffing everything together, nothing interesting about the world will appear, powerful theories have to be based on cruel reductions.

6 Conclusion

The fact that cognitive science is able to predict and describe many phenomena relating to HCI, should not necessarily lead to the conclusion that cognitive science must be (part of) the scientific framework for HCI. I still agree with Card, Moran and Newell that HCI design might benefit from a tighter connection between science and design, but as the use of Fitts' law in HCI indicates it is not likely that mechanistic psychology will form a fruitful basis for this connection. A pragmatic science of HCI will have to take into account the context of the use of computer artefacts, and the context of design of computer artefacts as well as the relation between science and design.

In a way it is both too optimistic and too pessimistic to state that: "Scientific models do not eliminate the design problem, but only help the designer control the different aspects" [3]. Of course, no science will ever be able to see into, or build the future. Human beings are fundamentally contingent, one is never sure of their next moves, and thus science will never fully control any aspects of the interface. On the other hand, a radical pragmatic science of HCI, a science not based on ideal natural science, can yield design-knowledge and understanding that goes beyond technical control. Such a radical pragmatic science of HCI will necessarily be based on dialectical, as opposed to mechanical materialism.

7 Acknowledgements

Thanks to Susanne Bødker, Randy Trigg, Morten Kyng, Kim Halskov Madsen, Preben Mogensen, Anders Mørch, and the anonymous reviewers for discussions, comments, and encouragement; and to Susanne Brøndberg and Janne Damgaard for last minute proof-reading.

8 References

1. Bertelsen, Olav W.: Når Uret Blir Ret... Et litteraturstudium til belysning af muligheden for teori i human-computer Interaction. [A literature study eliciting the possibilities of theory in HCI], Unpublished masters thesis, Aarhus, 1993.

2. Card, S.K.; English, W.K. and Burr, B.J.: Evaluation of mouse, rate-controlled isometric joystick, step keys, and text keys for text selection on a CRT, in Ergonomics vol.21, pp.601-613, 1978.

3. Card, Stuart K., Thomas P. Moran and Allen Newell: The Keystroke-Level Model for User Performance Time with Interactive Systems, in *Communications of the ACM*, vol. 23 pp.396-410, 1980.

4. Card, Stuart K., Thomas P. Moran and Allen Newell: *The Psychology of Human-Computer Interaction*, Hillsdale NJ, 1983.

5. Chapanis, Alphonse: The Relevance of Laboratory Studies to Practical Situations, in *Ergonomics*, vol. 10 pp.557-577, 1967.

6. Fitts, Paul M.: The information capacity of the human motor system in controlling the amplitude of movement in *Journal of Experimental Psychology* vol. 47, no. 6, 1954.

7.   Gillan, D.J.; Holden, K.; Adam, S.; Rudisill, M. and Magee, L.: How does Fitts' Law Fit Pointing and Dragging?, in *Proceeding of CHI'90 Conference on Human Factors in Computing Systems* (pp.227-234), New York, 1990.

8.   Gediga, Günter and Wolff, Peter: On the applicability of three basic laws to Human-Computer Interaction, *MBQ* 11/89, Osnabrück, 1989.

9.   Greif, Siegfried and Gediga, Günter: A Critique and Empirical Investigation of the "One-Best-Way-Models" in Human-Computer Interaction, in Frese, Ulich and Dzida (eds.), *Psychological Issues of Human-Computer Interaction in the Work Place*, Amsterdam, 1987.

10. Landauer, Thomas K.: Let's get real: a position paper on the role of cognitive psychology in the design of humanly useful and usable systems, in Carroll, J.M.,(ed.), *Designing Interaction: Psychology at the Human-Computer Interface*, Cambridge, 1991.

11. MacKenzie, I. Scott; Sellen, Abigail and Buxton, William: A Comparison of Input Devices in Elemental Pointing and Dragging Tasks in *Proceedings of CHI, 1991*, pp.161-166, ACM, New York, 1991.

12. Mammen, Jens: Menneskets Bevidsthed [Human consciousness], in Fenger and Jørgensen (eds.), *Skabelse, udvikling, samfund*, pp.73-81, 271 Aarhus, 1985.

13. Newell, Allen: *Unified Theories of Cognition*, Cambridge Ma.,1990.

14. Newell, Allen and Card, Stuart K.: The Prospects for Psychological Science in Human-Computer Interaction, in *Human Computer Interaction* 1985 vol.1, pp.209-242.

15. Shannon, Claude E.: *The mathematical theory of communication*, Illinois, 1949.

Empirical Study on the Use of a Knowledge-based System for Selecting Standard Engineering Components

Carsten Rückert and Stephan Klein
Institute for Machine Design/Engineering Design
Technical University of Berlin
Berlin, Germany

Abstract

In a study on computer-aided design work, 13 mechanical engineers performed a design task. Seven subjects used conventional tools (e.g. drawing board, calculator and catalogues), while six others used the computer-based design system KALEIT, including the knowledge-based system WIWENA. All subjects were videotaped, their actions categorized, and strain measurements were continuously recorded. Directly after the experiment, phases with high strain measurements were shown to the subject on video. The subject was asked to identify possible stress factors. This videoconfrontation indicated stress factors caused for example by the software's user interface, and allowed us to improve the software. An analysis of the knowledge-based system WIWENA has resulted in recommendations to change the information flow between the user and the system.

1   Introduction

At the Technical University of Berlin, computer-aided and conventional design work has been compared in a laboratory study[*]. The goal was to provide specifications for design methods and for computer-based design-systems. For that purpose, 13 mechanical engineers had to solve a design task which they performed within a controlled laboratory setting. During the experiments, strain measurements of the subjects were recorded. After an experiment, a strain-induced videoautoconfrontation was conducted to identify possible stress factors. This enabled us to improve the software used in the study and to give recommendations for knowledge-based systems.

---

[*] This project is part of the research group "Non-technical components of design work during increasing use of CAD-systems", funded by the German National Science Foundation (DFG). Principal investigators: Prof. Dr.-Ing. W. Beitz, Institute for Machine Design, Technical University of Berlin, Germany; and Prof. Dr.-Ing. H. Luczak, Institute for Human Factors, Technical University of Aachen, Germany.

2   Working Environment

2.1   The design-system KALEIT

Most commercially available CAD-systems support only drawing and not the whole design process. To allow a comparison between computer-aided and conventional design work, KALEIT was chosen for the experiments because it provides the engineer with a computer-aid during every design phase**) [Beitz 1992]. The system was developed at the Institute for Machine Design of Technical University of Berlin. It consists of several modules - each module for one design step - beginning with editors for the design task, the specifications and the function-structure [Kuttig 1993]. The preliminary and the definitive layouts can be draughted using GEKO, a program based on the CAD-system CATIA. For the selection and sizing of standard components, the designer can use the knowledge-based system WIWENA at every design stage. With the exception of WIWENA, all modules are integrated into X-windows with a common menu and can be handled in parallel. This paper discusses results concerning WIWENA.

Seven engineers worked with conventional tools, i. e. drawing board, calculator and catalogues. A second group of six engineers worked using the design-system KALEIT.

2.2   Concept of the knowledge-based system WIWENA

The "WIWENA"-system (Wissensbasiertes Auslegungssystem für Welle-Nabe-Verbindungen/Knowledge-based system for determination of shaft-hub-connections) is based on the WIKON-shell (Wissensverarbeitendes System für die Konstruktion/Knowledge-based system for Engineering Design) which was developed at the Institute for Machine Design (fig. 1) [Groeger 1990]. Among auxiliary functions two important operations are possible [Klein 1992]:

-    Development of the knowledge base, meaning building hierarchies, object definition and handling, and defining rules as well as
-    consultation of the knowledge base, meaning determination of the most fitting connection.

Determination of shaft-hub-connections is usually carried out in six steps (fig. 2), "Analysis of constraints", "selection of suitable connections", "evaluation of chosen connections", "sizing", "calculation", and "embodiment design" [Groeger et al. 1992].

**)This project is part of the research program SFB 203 "Computer-aided Design Models in Machine Engineering", funded by the German National Science Foundation (DFG). Principal investigator: Prof. Dr.-Ing. W. Beitz, Institute for Machine Design, Technical University of Berlin, Germany.

An interface to the geometric modeler is necessary for analyzing the given design (1st step) and adding the data of the chosen connection to the product model (final step).

The system is flexible in that it does not force the design engineer to proceed in an obligatory way. He has the option to choose among steps and activities as required. The six possible steps are now explained briefly.

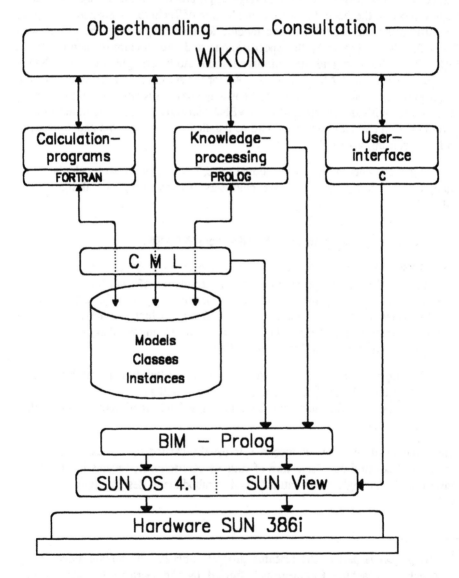

Fig. 1: Concept of the WIKON-Shell

Analysis of Constraints. This step is necessary for analyzing the constraints (e.g. shaft-diameter, torque) of the determination. For that purpose selected data can be taken from the geometric modeler. Links to the product model stored in a database allow the use of non geometrical information.

Selection of Suitable Connections. Selection of connections results from the stored property values which represent the capabilities of the connections. These property values can be words as well as numerical data. To use the list of the roperties they have to be defined before. Pop-up menus support the engineering designer in defining his textual requirements. He can narrow down the requirements gradually and observe the consequences of changes made. The system looks up the knowledge base for those connections which fit the given requirements and lists these in a window. The resulting unsorted list provides the basis for further work (fig. 3). When selecting the connections torque-strength is considered by sizing equations.

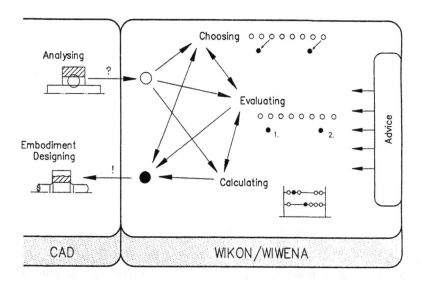

Fig. 2: Integration of the determination of shaft-hub-connections into the design process

Evaluation of Chosen Connections. The unsorted list must be graded to find the best solution. This is done by an evaluation of the properties of the connections which considers the meeting of requests and overcompliance with requirements. It is therefore necessary to rank the property values independently of their data format. Each connection gets points for each of its property values (strings or numerical data). According to user specified weighting factors and based on these points, the relative value of the connections is calculated and the elements in the list are rank ordered.

Sizing. For a rough calculation of the load capacity of the chosen connection has to be estimated.For that purpose the calculation equations had to be simplified to the form d = f(T) with d: diameter, T: torque. Based on standard parameters defining all geometrical data depending on d, the more complex calculations could be simplified. The equations were used to display a graph of given torque and required shaft-diameter. The user can change the standard parameters and see the changes in the graph. The required diameter is then roughly calculated based on the user's inputs.

Fig. 3: Consultation: selection of suitable connections

Calculation. Calculation is the final step of fixing geometrical requirements of the connections for given material properties. For that purpose separate programs are integrated which can be started by the WIKON-system via an interface. Changes of input data which are necessary during this step are stored and taken into account when forming the geometric model. As most calculation methods reduce the complex form of shafts and hubs to simple models, the designer must be supported when doing the embodiment design.

Embodiment Design. The system offers design hints consisting of textual and graphical information. These hints are depending on selection parameters the user has to input. Selection parameters can be all forms of requirements. Thus, only research has been made and published on loads, manufacturing, and testing of shaft-hub-connections. Using toggles the user can give free combinations of static or dynamic torque, bending moment, shearing and axial force. For displaying the design hints we use a hypermedia concept, where textual and graphical hints are connected by links. For user information the selection parameters are shown in an extra window. The source of each design hint can be shown on request.

2.3 Realization of the WIWENA system

The connections are represented declaratively as objects in frames. Properties of these objects can be defined and property values can be allocated to these properties. Different data formats are permitted for property values. In addition to numerical data up to five words can be used as property values. It is possible to assign more than one value to the defined properties.

The knowledge base of shaft-hub-connections was set up based on a thorough study of the literature. The connections were classified in a schema which was established according to German Standard DIN 32705. Properties were defined for the connections and property values were fixed. A careful preparation of the knowledge domain before computer implementation is of greatest importance. A part of the knowledge base is shown in figure 4 [see Groeger et al. 1992]. Dotted spaces refer to property values which cannot be assigned definitely and which depend on special constraints or on other property values.

SHAFT–HUB–CONNECTIONS			LOAD						TRANSMISSION FEATURES							
			Torque variation	Axial force variation	Shearing force variation	Bending moment variation	Axial force transmission (ext. parts req.)	Load transmission	Centering	Axial relocatability	Speed influence	Transmission with backlash	Tangential adjustable mounting	Axial adjustable mounting	Axial exact fixing	Shaft diameter in mm
Interference fits		Shrink fit	4	4	4	3	no	fric.	4	no	2	no	4	4	4	10-1000
		Axial interfer. fit	4	4	4	3	no	fric.	4	no	2	no	4	4	4	10-1000
		Coned interference fit	4	4	4	3	no	fric.	4	no	2	no	4	4	0	10-1000
		Oil shrink fit	4	4	4	3	no	fric.	4	no	2	no	4	4	4	10-1000
		Stepped shrink fit	4	4	4	3	no	fric.	4	no	2	no	4	4	4	10-1000
Coned connections		Shrink disk	4	4	4	3	no	fric.	4	no	2	no	4	8	4	10-440
		Expanding bolt	4	4	4	3	no	fric.	4	no	2	no	4	4	4	95-530
Clamping joints		Solid clamping joints	4	4	4	3	no	fric.	4	no	0	no	4	4	4	5-800
		Divided clamping joints	4	4	4	3	no	fric.	4	no	2	no	4	4	4	5-500
Firm keying		Hollow key DIN 6881	3	3	2-3	2	no	fric.	2	no	0	no	4	4	0/4	22-130
		Hollow gib key DIN 6889	3	3	2-3	2	no	fric.	2	no	0	no	4	4	0/4	22-130
Bolted connections		Radial bolted connection	3	3	3	2-3	no	fric.	2	no	0	no	4	4	4	5-500
		Axial bolted connection	3	3-4	3	3	no	fric.	2	no	4	no	2	0	4	5-500
Disk connections		Star disk connection	3	0/2	1-2	1-2	yes/no	fric.	2	no	2	no	4	4	0/4	3-100
		Disk connection	3	0/2	1-2	1-2	yes/no	fric.	2	no	2	no	4	4	0/4	2-170
Spline profile		Spline profile DIN ISO 14	1-3	0-3	1-2	1-2	yes	pos.	0-2	x load	0/4	yes	2	0	4	11-112
		Spline profile DIN 5464	1-3	0-3	1-2	1-2	yes	pos.	0-2	x load	0/4	yes	2	0	4	20-125
		Spline profile DIN 5471	1-3	0-3	1-2	1-2	yes	pos.	0-2	x load	0/4	yes	2	0	4	15-70
		Spline profile DIN 5472	1-3	0-3	1-2	1-2	yes	pos.	0-2	x load	0/4	yes	2	0	4	25-154
		Involute spline profile DIN 5480	1-3	0-3	1-2	1-2	yes	pos.	0-2	x load	0/4	yes	2	0	4	8-500
		Serration profile DIN 5481	1-3	0-3	1-2	1-2	yes	pos.	0-2	no load	0/4	yes	2	0	4	8-125
Polygonal spline profile		P3G DIN 32711	1-4	0-3	1-3	1-3	yes	pos.	0-2	no load	0/4	yes/no	2	0	4	14-100
		P4C DIN 32712	1-4	0-3	1-3	1-3	yes	pos.	0-2	x load	0/4	yes/no	2	0	4	14-100
		P3G-coned	4	3	3	3	yes/no	pos.	4	no	4	no	2	0	0	14-200
Hirth serration			3	3-4	3	3	yes	pos.	0/4	no	4	no	2	0	4	30-900

Fig. 4: Part of the knowledge base

The WIKON-shell allows different ways of fixing property values for the connections:

- single input of property values for each instance and property,
- fixing and limiting property values by rule for instances and entire classes, and
- fixing property values by rule for special instances or classes depending on special constraints.

Fixing property values by rule is quite efficient because fixings can be made for entire classes and can be inherited by subclasses. For example, frictionally engaged connections are transmitting torque free from backlash. This fact is fixed only once in the class of frictionally engaged connections and valid for all subclasses of this class. Compared to discrete fixing of property values the likelihood of making errors is less than it is when using rules.

When using minimum requirements those problem solutions which exceed these requirements have to be found, too. A rule for all connections defines that meeting a requirement at the level of "very good" includes meeting it "good" which includes "medium" etc. So all problem solutions meeting a requirement at the level of "very good" are found even if simply "good" was required.

Load capacity of the connections is taken into account by sizing them on the basis of standard values for geometry and materials. These standard values can easily be changed and the consequences are shown in a torque/shaft-diameter graph. Changes made of the input data when sizing a connection are retained for further work. During consultation a special menu offers advice which is adapted to the current design phase and activity.

3   Experiments

3.1   Persons Studied

To study KALEIT and WIWENA in a laboratory setting resembling industrial working processes, the subjects for this study were chosen among male engineers graduated in mechanical engineering at the Technical University of Berlin. They all had an education in design methodology, and those using KALEIT knew at least one KALEIT module in advance. During sessions prior to the experiments, they were trained to use the other modules.

3.2   Design Task

Each subject had to solve the same design task, which consisted of designing a device to rotate a table in a washing machine. The subjects got a drawing (fig. 5) and a textual description of the task as well. This design task was specifically tailored to allow the use of GEKO's macros, and required the selection of at least one shaft-hub connection, so that WIWENA could be used. A time of six hours was permitted to perform the task. Thus one experiment including the videoconfrontation took about eight hours and was always conducted on a single day.

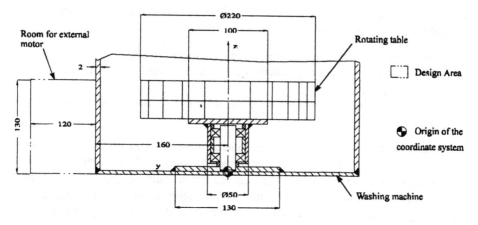

Fig. 5: Design task

3.3 Data Analysis

To analyse the interaction between user and system, the stress-and-strain-concept was used [Luczak 1975] (fig. 6).

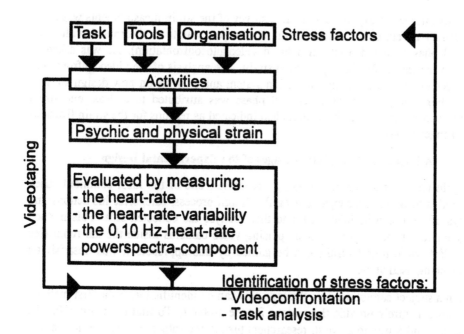

Fig. 6: The stress-and-strain-concept

In this context, stress is an exterior influence on the subject, e. g. a work-load such as a difficult design task. The subject's activities to manage stress generate strain experienced by the subject. Several parameters to evaluate strain were developed by human factors science. In this study the following variables were continuously measured [Springer et al. 1990]:

-   the heart-rate, which increases under most forms of stress,
-   the heart-rate-variability, which decreases in case of informatorical or physical stress, and
-   the 0,10 Hz heart-rate powerspectrum, which indicates stress on the short-term memory.

To evaluate the strain experienced by the subjects while working on the design task, the heart-rate of the subjects was continuously measured. In addition every experiment was videotaped, so that the recorded strain could be used to identify the stress factors. To avoid outside influence on the subjects, the devices needed for interpreting and recording the measurements were located in a room adjoinig the lab. Only the subject and his tools, the video cameras and the experiment manager were present in the lab room. The experiment manager answered questions and adjusted the video cameras when necessary.

During the experiment, the subject's actions were categorized into a schema. The tools used by the subject and the representation mode of the design were categorized later using the videotapes.

Directly after every experiment, a quick survey of the strain measurements was made to identify exceptional, critical strain. The subject was then confronted with these critical phases on video (strain-induced videoautoconfrontation). He was asked to explain the causes for the experienced strain. The analysis of the videoconfrontation provides hints for improving the design-system and informs on how design work is done. For that purpose, every critical phase was attributed to at least one stress factor, according to what the subjects had indicated as reasons for the strain [Rückert & Springer 1994].

3.4   Advantages And Disadvantages of the Experimental Design

To gain results from studies on design processes, one of the most commonly used method is to watch the subject during the design process, categorize his actions and errors, if these can be identified, and then analyse the collected data. This method was applied in our experiments by placing video cameras inside the lab room (see 3.3). Yet while useful results can be gained by this approach, it was unsatisfying when being used alone.

When a subject cannot perform the task, this can be identified with the first method, but this can rarely provide the reasons for the problem. To find the reasons for the problem, and a way to solve it, researchers turn to the subject for more information. The information can be gathered during or after the experiment itself.

When the information is gathered during the experiment, the subject must verbalize his thoughts during the design process. We did not use this method, because the influence of verbalizing thoughts on the design process cannot be calculated.

Instead, we conducted an interview after the experiment, confronting the subjects with their own design processes on videotape. Since showing the subjects the whole six hours of the experiment would have imposed to much stress on most subjects, we had to reduce the amount of videotape to be shown. The stress-and-strain-concept enabled us to focus only on videophases where high strain had been measured, and where problems or decision making processes could be expected. In our experience, this method worked quite well. Yet there are a few drawbacks on this method which have to be taken into account when judging our results.

The delay between the experiment and the videoconfrontation was kept as short as possible, but it cannot be excluded that the subjects' memory was altered in the meantime. Also, some subjects might be tempted, conciously or unconciously, to present themselves and their design work in a way different from reality. Since our society values reasoned decisions, subjects might give reasons for decisions even though they had not figured these out when the decisions were made. Nevertheless, all methods we contemplated had similar flaws, and we found that subjects had plenty of ideas on improving KALEIT and WIWENA, some of which were valuable and have been used to improve the system.

4   Results

4.1   Checking WIWENA

At a first look, WIWENA met its planned function quite well. We compared the use of the system with the use of a technical book on construction components [Niemann 1981], that was available to the subjects during the experiments. The book's content is similar to WIWENA's, including information on shaft-hub-connections and their calculation, and is thus suited for a comparison with WIWENA. Obviously subjects using WIWENA used the book only marginally, in contrast to the other subjects (fig. 7).

Moreover, our subjects strain measurements were lower during the use of WIWENA than during the use of the book, indicating that the system relieved the subjects of information search and decision making processes (fig. 8). Though this result has to be considered with caution because of the small number of subjects involved, the low strain measurements of the system users are remarkable. Previous research had shown that handling computer user interfaces is an additional stress factor [Luczak et al. 1991]. The different result in this study can be attributed to the fact that the subjects using WIWENA were all experienced computer-users familiar with WIWENA's SunView interface.

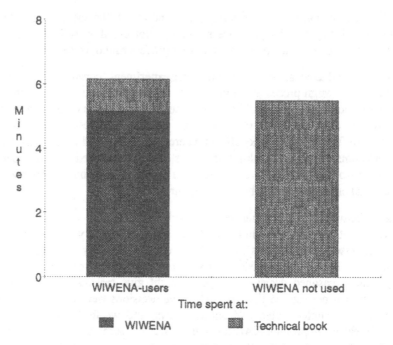

Fig. 7: Amount of time spent on using WIWENA, compared to the use of a technical book (average of all subjects)

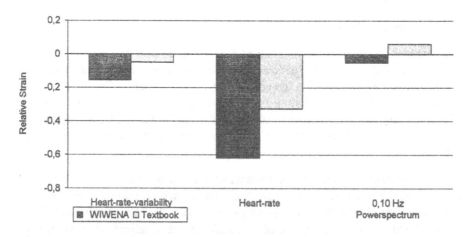

Fig. 8: Mean strain measurements of the subjects when using WIWENA, compared to the use of a technical book

In addition the videoconfrontations provided valuable hints for improving the knowledge-based system. For example, WIWENA did not list any adequate standard component if no component meets the requirements entered. The user was then left without indications about his possibilities to change the requirements or to find a component anyhow. To change this, we propose to check the requirements for compatibility when they are entered, and to refuse unrealistic requirements.

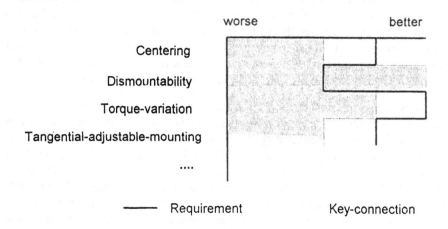

Fig. 9: Capability bars

A second possiblity is to list construction components that do not meet the requirements exactly, but nearly meet them. Such components should be listed in a different colour or font than components meeting the requirements. To give the user information on the violated requirements, we have conceived capability bars (fig. 9). Contemplating a construction component which violates a requirement, the engineer has two possiblities: either to choose an other component, or to change the design environment in a way that eliminates the violated requirement. Furthermore, the capability bars are a good way to represent information that initially was available as text only.

4.2   User acceptance

The videoconfrontations showed that the user acceptance of WIWENA was different from the other programs of the design-system. Mainly the acceptance of the module for selecting construction components was important for the acceptance of the whole system.

At the selection-module, the user must first enter the requirements to be met by a construction component. WIWENA then consults its knowledge-base, and provides a list of components adequate for the given requirements. After an evaluation, the user can select a component he deems best for his application. Two groups of users can be identified.

One group of subjects was satisfied with WIWENA, because it shortened the time needed to find a shaft-hub-connection. WIWENA presented a components list where they found an applicable component they had not thought of.

A second group was less satisfied with WIWENA. In relation to the system's knowledge-base, the subjects are not only users but also experts themselves. While giving the requirements for the construction component, they already developed possible solutions in their mind. When the list presented by WIWENA did not match their own solutions, they usually did not try to find out the reason for the difference. Since the subjects worked under time pressure, they preferred to select a component from their own solution list. When interviewed about this problem, they claimed that WIWENA is not a competent expert and that they would not use it again.

The problem can be symptomatic, for a meeting of experts. When human experts convene, it is normal for them to profess varying opinions. Usually these differences are resolved within a discussion. Such a discussion should also be possible with a knowledge-based system. To provide WIWENA with this capability, we have developed a scenario in which the user can enter his own solutions. These are checked by WIWENA for errors and omissions (see also [Langlotz & Shortliffe 1984]). WIWENA can also present its own solutions on the user's demand. The explanation component of current expert-systems thus becomes a discussion component.

Since the project's funding ended in 1993, it was not possible to adapt WIWENA's user interface to the proposed scenario. Instead the figures 10 and 11 show a future user interface as it could be. As before, the user has to enter the requirements the shaft-hub connection has to meet (fig. 10, left side). In the future, the system may analyse the design situation automatically, so that this step can be omitted.

Fig. 10: Proposed user interface for entering the user's solution proposals

In compliance with our proposal, the user may now enter his own solution to the shaft-hub-connection problem. She or he can directly enter a connection, or choose one from a list presented by WIWENA (fig. 10, right side). After this, WIWENA checks the user's solutions for compliance with the requirements, and presents the results of the check (fig. 11, upper part). The connections in the list are ordered according to an unweighted evaluation, i. e. the best connection meeting the requirements is listed in the first place. Also, WIWENA's own solutions are listed on the lower left side of the window. If a solution preferred by the user does not meet the requirements (e. g. the connection "Disk_connection" in fig. 11), he can look at the corresponding capability bars (fig. 11, lower right side). Then the user may decide to change his design in a way that the violated requirement can be dropped, or he may decide to select an other connection.

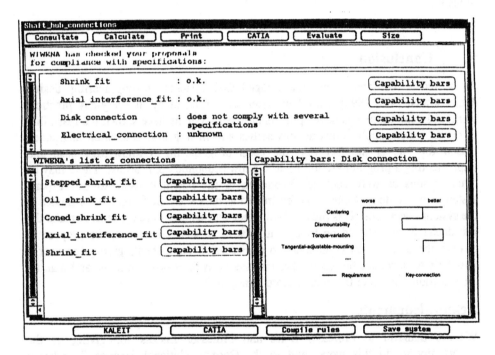

Fig. 11: Proposed user interface: Checking the user's solutions

The systems selection mechanism should be more transparent with this interface than with the old interface, and we hope it will become an efficient information system. This should be verified in a further study.

4.3 Limitations of the Study

To interprete the results of this study correctly, the following restrictions have to be taken into account:

- The study was done in a laboratory. All engineers graduated in mechanical engineering at the Technical University of Berlin and were educated in design methodology.
- The aim of the study was to identify and to reduce stress factors at design work. The design processes in this study may not be representative of design processes found in industry.

Thus it is not possible to transfer the results directly to design processes in the industry.

5 Conclusion

As a recent conference on knowledge-based systems in engineering design demonstrated [VDI 1993], only few systems are used today in every-day practical work, although numerous developments of expert-systems have shown the feasibility of expert-system applications at universities and in industry. One often mentioned reason for this is the fact that the costs of gathering a knowledge base and implementing a program are too high to allow economic applications. There may be other reasons as well, such as skepticism of the potential users toward expert-systems. In our study, some users felt treated as data entry clerks and subordinates to the system's decisions. This proved fatal, since the subjects were the ones to make the last decision, and should be treated at least as equals. To do this, we propose to change the explanation component to a discussion component, giving the user a possiblity to introduce his knowledge into the decision making process, and making the selection process of the system more transparent.

Acknowledgments

We are thankful to Professor Beitz and Professor Luczak for giving us the opportunity to do this work, and to the German National Science Foundation (Deutsche Forschungsgemeinschaft DFG) for funding it. We would like to thank our student coworkers Udo Grätzel and Georg Eispert for their support in the experiments, and Dr. Bernd Groeger and Geza Lakatos for developing the expert-system shell WIKON.

References

Beitz, W.; et al.: Strukturen rechnerunterstützter Konstruktionsprozesse. Abschluß-bericht des Teilprojektes B2 des Sonderforschungsbereichs 203: Rechnerunterstützte Konstruktionsmodelle im Maschinenwesen. Berlin: TU Berlin 1992.

Groeger, B.: Ein System zur rechnerunterstützten und wissensbasierten Bearbeitung des Konstruktionsprozesses. Konstruktion 42 (1990), pp. 91-96.

Groeger, B.; Klein, St.; Suhr, M.: Auslegung von Verbindungselementen am Beispiel Welle-Nabe-Verbindungen mit Hilfe der Wissensverarbeitung. Konstruktion 44 (1992), pp. 145-153.

Klein, St.: An Example of Knowledge-based Decision Making when Selecting Standard Components: Shaft-Hub-Connections. Proceedings of the 4th International ASME Conference on Design Theory and Methodology DTM '92, Phoenix/ Arizona. ASME 1992, pp. 149-156.

Kuttig, D.: Potential and Limits of Functional Modelling in the CAD-Process. Research in Engineering Design (1993) 5, pp. 40-48.

Langlotz, C.; Shortliffe, E.: Adapting a consultation system to critique user plans. In: Coombs, M. (Editor): Developments in expert-systems. London: Academic Press 1984.

Luczak, H.: Untersuchungen informatorischer Belastung und Beanspruchung des Menschen. VDI-Fortschrittberichte, Reihe 2, No. 10, Düsseldorf: VDI-Verlag 1975.

Luczak, H.; Beitz, W.; Springer, J.; Langner, Th.: Frictions and Frustations in Creative-Informatory Work with Computer-aided Design - CAD-Systems. In: Bullinger, H.-J. (Ed.): Human Aspects in Computing: Design and Use of Interactive Systems and Work with Terminals. Amsterdam, Elsevier: 1991, pp. 175-179.

Niemann, G.: Maschinenelemente. Band 1: Konstruktion und Berechnung von Verbindungen, Lagern und Wellen. Berlin, Heidelberg, New York: Springer-Verlag 1981.

Rückert, C.; Springer, J.: Konstruieren unter arbeitswissenschaftlichen und konstruktionsmethodischen Gesichtspunkten. Konstruktion 46 (1994) pp. 33-40.

Springer, J.; Müller, Th.; Langner, Th.; Luczak, H.; Beitz, W.: Stress and strain caused by CAD-work - Results of a laboratory study. In: Berlinguet, L.; Berthelette, D. (Eds.): Proceedings of the Work with Display Units Conference, Montreal 1989. Amsterdam: Elsevier 1990.

VDI-Berichte 1079: Rechnerunterstützte Wissensverarbeitung in Entwicklung und Konstruktion '93: Tagung in Heidelberg, 28./29. September 1993 / VDI-Gesellschaft Entwicklung, Konstruktion, Vertrieb. Düsseldorf, VDI-Verlag 1993.

Positive Effects of Sound Feedback During the Operation of a Plant Simulator

Matthias Rauterberg and Erich Styger

Usability Laboratory, Work and Organisational Psychology Unit,
Swiss Federal Institute of Technology (ETH)
Nelkenstrasse 11, CH-8092 ZURICH
Tel: +41-1-632-7082, email: rauterberg@rzvax.ethz.ch

Abstract

An experiment was carried out to estimate the effect of sound feedback on the work of a plant operator. Eight students of computer science operated a process simulation program of an assembly line with computer numeric controlled (CNC) robots. Relevant information of disturbances and machine breakdowns was given only in a visual (test condition 1), and in visual and audible form (test condition 2). The results indicate, that the additional sound feedback improves significantly the operator performance and increases positively some mood aspects.

KEYWORDS: Audible feedback, non speech sound generation, human - computer interaction, visual strain.

1 Introduction

Using non speech sounds to provide system information is appealing for several reasons. First, by adding sound to the interface the bandwidth of communication can be significantly increased. Second, the information conveyed by sounds is complementary to that available visually, and thus sound can provide a mean for displaying information that is difficult to visualise, especially with limited screen real estate. Sound feedback can help to improve the usability of interfaces in the following ways:

User Interface Design – Most of all user interfaces stresses the visual perception. Sound feedback can help to reduce eye strain.

Multimedia – New possibility for the interactive representation of complex sound generating events and processes.

User interfaces for people with impaired vision – Simulations with the utilisation of audio data will in future also have their application in the training of people with impaired senses, in particular of people with damaged vision.

The hearing of sounds in everyday life is based on the perception of events and not on the perception of sounds as such [Rauterberg-94]: For this reason, everyday sounds are often described by the events they are based on. Sound is a familiar and natural medium for conveying information that we use in our daily lives. The following examples help to illustrate the important kinds of information that sound can communicate [Mountford-90]:

Information about physical events – We can hear whether a dropped glass has bounced or shattered.

Information about invisible structures – Tapping on a wall is useful in finding where to hang a heavy picture.

Information about dynamic change – As we fill a glass we can hear when the liquid has reached the top.

Information about abnormal structures – A malfunctioning engine sounds different from a healthy one.

Information about events in space – Footsteps warn us of the approach of another person.

The textual representation of information is of most use when the user is familiar with the domain area and can demonstrate much experience and knowledge in that domain area [Marmolin-92]. In comparison, more concrete (visual and auditory) representations of information that the user can query are of most use when the domain area is new and unknown.

The parallel use of different media and the resulting parallel distribution of information, for example by simultaneously showing a predecessor through a concrete representation and its explanation through audio distribution, leads to a denser sharing of information. In this case, the user can dedicate his attention solely to the visual information, which has parallel audio support. This reduces the need to change the textual or other visual delivery and prevents the overflow of visual information [Edwards-88].

Sounds and music can be utilised to improve the user's understanding of visual predecessors or can stand alone as independent sources of information. Gaver et al [Gaver-91] used sounds as diagnostic support applied with the direction of a process simulation in a collaborative environment. But, he did not prove the hypothesis that an interface with sound is superior to an interface without sound feedback. Gaver et al [Gaver-91] describe only some global impressions of different user reactions to sound feedback.

Our main interest was to test the hypothesis of [Buxton-89] and [Gaver-91], that people in the real world monitor multiple background activities simultaneously through sound. So, we use auditory cues to help users to monitor the status of ongoing processes. Diagnosing and treating problems with the plant were aided by alert sounds (see also [Gaver-91]). In difference to [Gaver-91] we used individual sessions, and not a collaborative environment. We carried out an experiment, that allows us to test our hypothesis with the methodology of applied statistics.

2   Method

2.1   Subjects

Eight male students of computer science at the ETH took part in the experiment (mean age of 24 ± 1 years).

2.2   Simulator

The simulation is based on a flexible manufacturing system, that produces cases made of aluminium (see 'work pieces' in Figure 1). The whole system consists of eight computer-numeric-controlled (CNC) manufacturing centres and eight loading robots for these centres. In the input directing station all work pieces are automatically directed on the assembly line. The assembly line transports each work piece through different stations to the CNC manufacturing centres and back to the output directing station. The whole plant was deliberately designed to be too large to fit on the computer screen, so users could only see about half the CNC machines at any time (see 'actual screen clipping' in Figure 1).

We designed our simulator so that each of the machines made sounds to indicate its status over time. Each sound was designed to reflect the semantic of the actual event. For instance, a splashing sound indicated that cooling liquid was being spilled. Because of the complexity of our system, as many as 38 sounds made be placed at once. We attempted to design the sounds so that none would be masked (rendered in-audible) by other sounds. [Gaver-91] describe two strategies to be useful in avoiding masking. First, sounds were spread fairly evenly in frequency, so that some were high-pitched and others lower. Second, we avoided playing sounds continuously and instead played repetitive streams of sounds, thus maximising the chance for other sounds to be heard in the gaps between repetitions. CNC 0 and CNC 4 are characterised by a high-pitched sound. CNC 3 and CNC 7 are low-pitched.

A work piece could have one of the following status: (1) loading on the assembly line at the input directing station, (2) transportation on the assembly line, (3) fixation on the carrier at the reset station, (4) final fixation and twist on the carrier, (5) fixation on a pallet with three other work pieces at the robot, (6) processing one of two sides in the CNC station, (7) change from one side to the other at the reset station, (8) to be provided with a serial number at the labelling station, (9) loading off the assembly line at the output directing station. Steps (3) to (7) are carried out twice, once for each side of the work piece.

Table 1: Sound types, duration, and size.

machine	sound	duration	size
CNC 0-7	normal	1.20 s	51 KB
CNC 0-7	no cooling	1.08 s	46 KB
CNC 0-7	jammed pipe	1.38 s	59 KB
robot 0-7	normal	0.39 s	16 KB
robot 0-7	lost piece	1.04 s	44 KB
robot 0-7	tear off pipe	1.04 s	44 KB
input station	normal	0.41 s	17 KB
output station	normal	0.78 s	33 KB
reset station	normal	1.40 s	60 KB
twist station	normal	0.40 s	17 KB
labelling station	normal	0.49 s	21 KB
control station	global alarm	0.24 s	10 KB

Normal running of a machine was coupled with a characteristic sound pattern. Each machine breakdown generated instead of the normal sound a specific alert sound (see Table 1). If a robot or a CNC centre breaks down, then this centre can not process the pallet of four work pieces further on. The first consequence of a breakdown is a jam on the assembly line. The second consequence is the productivity of the plant decrease.

2.3 Task

Subjects were instructed to operate a plant simulator and to take care for a high productivity rate. The task was to trouble-shoot the whole manufacturing system. First, each subject had to detect that a breakdown happened. Then he has to find the interrupted machine (robot or CNC machine). The actual breakdown event shows the operator how to repair the machine. The operator can get this information visually in a modal dialogue box with the status report at the control station or in an auditory form through sound feedback.

A CNC machine could have two breakdown events ('jammed outlet pipe of cooling agent', 'empty cooling agent'). A robot could breakdown with two different events ('lost work piece', 'tear off a pressure pipe').

Table 2: Machine, breakdown type, and repair code.

machine	breakdown	code
CNC 0-7	no cooling	3713
CNC 0-7	jammed pipe	8319
robot 0-7	lost piece	1731
robot 0-7	tear off pipe	1733
control station	status report	8700

Each interrupted machine could be repaired by entering an appropriate repair code (a four-digit number, see Table 2) in a repair dialogue box at the machine. The operator sees only a part of the whole plant (see 'actual screen clipping' in Figure 1). He moves the actual screen up and down by clicking with the mouse in the scrollbar area to 'go to' the interrupted machine. A mouse click on the machine symbol pops up the repair dialogue box. Entering the correct repair code transfers the interrupted machine in the normal state. If an incorrect repair code is entered, then no internal state change happens and the user could hear only a short beep.

Users' view of the plant behaviour was that robots and CNC centres breakdown accidentally. Our simulation program was programmed so, that all breakdowns appeared in the same sequence. This approach guarantees that the trials between users are maximally comparable.

2.4 Procedure

We run the experiment with a two-factorial test design. Factor A was 'with' or 'without' sound feedback. Test condition 1 was only visual feedback with a warning flasher and a modal dialogue box with status information of each manufacturing system at the operator control station. Test condition 2 was visual and audible feedback of each machine breakdown.

Factor B was a repeated measurement design. Four subjects started the experiment with sound feedback (test condition 1) and repeated the same task without sound feedback (test condition 2). The other four subjects started without sound feedback (test condition 2), and repeated the task with sound feedback (test condition 1).

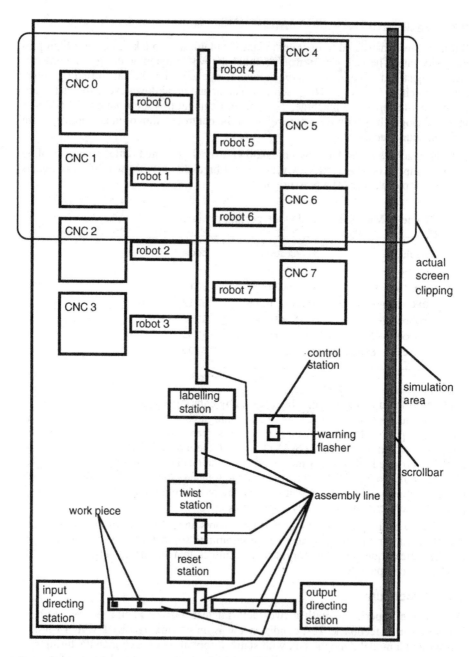

Figure 1: The schematic view of the plant simulator shown to the users. The rectangle shows the actual screen output each user sees at a given time. The whole system consists of eight computer-numeric-controlled (CNC 0..7) manufacturing centres and eight loading robots (robot0..7). In the input directing station all work pieces are automatically directed on the assembly line. The whole plant was deliberately designed to be too large to fit on the computer screen, so users have to scroll.

Each subject filled out a questionnaire to estimate the individual experiences with computers (about 10 minutes). The subjects were introduced in operating the simulation tool through 'learning by using' (about 15 minutes). The simulation ran for the trouble-shooting task exactly 20 minutes. Before and after each trouble-shooting task the user has to answer a mood questionnaire (eight scales with overall 36 items as monopolar rating scales [Apenburg-86]). After each trouble-shooting task we measured the subjective satisfaction with a semantic differential (11 bipolar items). Each individual session took about 90 minutes.

2.5   Material

We ran the experiment on an IBM compatible PC (Olivetti® i386, 25 MHz, 6 MByte main storage, 17" VGA colour screen) with an extra sound card (Logitech® 16 Bit, 44 kHz, stereo). A special simulation program was developed in Turbo Pascal® 1.0 to present the signals on the screen. Users heard the sound out of two small active speakers (maximal 3 watt). All machines at the left side (see Figure 1) could be heard out of the left speaker. The right speaker gave out the sound of all machines at the right side.

2.6   Measures

Our first dependent variable is a point scale that measures the productivity of the plant. Each work piece, that entered the assembly line at the input direction station, counts one point. One point is counted for each side, that was processed at a CNC machine. Each work piece, that left the assembly line at the output direction station, counts an extra point. Each work piece on the assembly line counts one to four points. The productivity score after 20 minute's simulation time is the sum over all work pieces that entered the assembly line.

The second dependent variable is the number of requested status reports at the control station.

The third and fourth dependent variables are number of correct and number of incorrect repairs.

The eight scales of the mood questionnaire and the 11 items of the semantic differential are dependent variables to measure users' satisfaction.

3   Results

First, we present the results of the four dependent variables that measure users' trouble-shooting activities. We find a significant difference between the two test-conditions for the productivity score (see Table 3).

Without sound feedback users moved to the control station and requested the status report significantly more than in the test condition with sound feedback (see Table 3). We could observe, that most of the users in test condition with sound go first to the control station to look for all breakdowns, and go after that through the whole plant to repair machine by machine. During this walk-through they could remember all not repaired machines listening to the sound pattern.

On one side, we can observe a significant improvement through sound feedback, on the other side we can find, that users perceive the simulation with sound more non-transparent and feel more confused than without sound (see Table 4).

Table 3: Results of the four dependent variables that measure users' trouble-shooting activities.

Variable	With sound	Without sound	P sign
productivity score	70 ± 5.6	65 ± 5.3	.052
# of status reports	17 ± 5.8	23 ± 4.0	.043
# of correct repairs	36 ± 2.5	36 ± 2.3	.550
# of incorrect repairs	16 ± 11.0	9 ± 7.1	.113

Table 4: Results of the eleven items of the semantic differential (bipolar rating scale: -2, -1, 0, +1, +2).

Variable (-)...............(+)	With sound	Without sound	P sign
time time			
consuming.......saving	-1.1 ± 0.7	-1.0 ± 0.9	.791
rigid.........flexible	-0.9 ± 1.3	-0.8 ± 0.8	.735
circumstantial..simple	+0.5 ± 2.3	+0.4 ± 3.1	.889
intransp...transparent	+0.4 ± 1.1	+1.4 ± 0.6	.064
confuse....unequivocal	+0.1 ± 2.7	+1.1 ± 1.0	.179
unclear..........clear	0.0 ± 2.6	-0.4 ± 1.4	.596
complicated..uncomplic	0.0 ± 1.1	-0.3 ± 1.9	.712
prescribed........free	-0.5 ± 0.9	-0.4 ± 1.1	.816
unforesee..foreseeable	0.0 ± 2.3	+0.1 ± 1.8	.871
unsuscept..susceptible	-0.8 ± 1.1	-0.9 ± 1.0	.781
angry.........pleasing	-0.4 ± 1.7	-0.1 ± 1.3	.709

Table 5: Results of the differences (after - before) of the eight scales of the mood questionnaire (monopolar rating scale).

Variable	With sound	Without sound	P sign
readiness of endeavour	+2.4 ± 4.1	-0.5 ± 4.1	.199
restfulness	+1.3 ± 2.7	+0.4 ± 3.3	.589
readiness for contacts	+0.9 ± 2.5	-0.8 ± 2.2	.219
drowsiness	-1.1 ± 2.4	-1.5 ± 3.2	.801
self-assurance	+1.8 ± 2.0	-0.6 ± 1.7	.022
social acceptance	+0.1 ± 1.0	-1.1 ± 1.0	.031
to feel excited	0.0 ± 6.1	-1.0 ± 5.9	.738
mood-laden	+1.3 ± 2.2	-0.3 ± 1.0	.128

Users felt significantly more self-assure and more social accepted after working with sound feedback than without sound (see Table 5). Their readiness for endeavour, restfulness, and mood increased in the test condition with sound.

The results of this experiment showed, that the performance of operating a plant simulator could be significantly improved, when feedback of machine break downs and other disturbances was given in an auditory form, too. We can also observe a significant increase of different aspects of users' mood. Overall, we can say that users feel better and less stressed with sound feedback, than without sound.

We found that sound feedback was effective in the following way. Sound feedback helped users keep track of the ongoing processes. Sounds allowed users to track the activity, rate, and functioning of normally running machines. Without sound feedback, users overlooked machines that were broken down. With sound feedback these problems were indicated either by the machine's sound ceasing or by the various alert sounds. Continuous sound feedback allowed users to hear the plant as an integrated complex process. The sounds merged to produce an auditory pattern, much as the many sounds of everyday machines.

4 Discussion

The sense of hearing is an all-round sense. This aspect is an important difference to visual perception, that is a directional sense. An auditory interface can be much larger than the visual interface (screen). Visually hidden aspects of parallel processes in the background can be made perceptible with auditory feedback [Cohen-93]. The results of our experiment support this design approach. Sound feedback of concurrent processes, that are important for task solving, improves the usability of interfaces.

Audition is a spatial sense; we can be aware simultaneously of many sounds coming from different locations. But spatial patterns in audition are much more limited than those of vision. It is primarily a time sense, for its main patterns are those of succession, change, and rhythm. Auditory feedback typically arrives sequentially in time, whereas visual pattern my be presented either sequentially or simultaneously. Of course many perceptual experiences depend on the operation of several senses at once; then the prominence of sense over another becomes a matter for study [Hartman-61].

Sound feedback has poor 'referability', meaning that they usually cannot be kept continuously before the user, although they can be repeated periodically. Visual patterns offer good referability, because the information usually can be 'stored' in the display. The most important advantage of sound feedback is its 'attention-demanding'; it 'breaks in' on the attention of the user. Visually stimuli, however, do not necessarily have this captive audience. The user has to be looking toward the display in order to perceive the stimulus [Rauterberg-93]. Hearing is somewhat more resistant to fatigue than vision [McCormick-57, p. 427].

How many different concurrent sounds can be discriminated? Users reacted up to 38 different sounds in our simulation study. Momtahan et al [Momtahan-93] could show that staff in operating rooms was able to identify only a mean of between 10 and 15 of the 26 alarms. Nurses were able to identify only a mean between 9 and 14 of the 23 alarms found in their intensive care unit. Momtahan et al explain their results with the poor design of auditory warning signals. Standardisation of sound feedback can minimise this perceptual problem.

Cohen [Cohen-93] found that it is a difficult task to design sound pattern "which tell the right story and are also pleasant and emotionally neutral." Good sound feedback needs sound patterns that are interpretable without visual redundancy (e.g., door creaks open, door slams [Cohen-93]). We have to look for everyday sounds that 'stand for themselves'. Given these sounds we have to map them in a metaphorical sense to new events introduced by technology (e.g., door creaks open => login, door slams => logout [Cohen-93]). For simulation tools, that deal with real world events, we can easily use the corresponding real world sounds. The results of our study support this 'real sound' approach.

To avoid disturbances at the workplace we need empirical studies with earphones -- or other possibilities -- to restrict the auditory feedback space to the user's location. Everyday sounds are mostly soft and slight, so, maybe soft sound feedback is an appropriate approach to avoid unintentional effects in a collaborative environment.

5 References

[Apenburg-86| Apenburg, E. (1986) Befindlichkeitsbeschreibung als Methode der Beanspruchungsmessung. *Zeitschrift für Arbeits- und Organisationspsychologie* 30(N.F. 4):3-14.

[Buxton-89] Buxton, W. (1989) Introduction to this special issue on non speech audio. *Human-Computer Interaction* 4(1):1-9.

[Cohen-93] Cohen, J. (1993) "Kirk Here:" Using Genre Sounds To Monitor Background Activity. in S. Ashlund, K. Mullet, A. Henderson, E. Hollnagel and T. White (eds.) INTERCHI'93 Adjunct Proceedings. (pp. 63-64), New York: ACM.

[Edwards-88] Edwards, A. (1988) The design of auditory interfaces for visually disabled users. In E. Soloway, D. Frye and S. Sheppard (eds.) Conference Proceedings "Human Factors in Computing Systems" CHI' 88. (pp. 83-88), New York: ACM.

[Gaver-89] Gaver, W. (1989) The Sonic Finder: an interface that uses auditory icons. *Human Computer Interaction* 4(1):67-94.

[Gaver-91] Gaver, W., Smith, R. & O'Shea, T. (1991) Effective sounds in complex systems: the ARKola simulation. In S. Robertson, G. Olson and J. Olson (eds.) Conference Proceedings "Reaching through Technology" CHI'91. (pp. 85-90), Reading MA: Addison-Wesley.

[Gaver-93] Gaver, W. (1993) Synthesizing auditory icons. S. Ashlund, K. Mullet, A. Henderson, E. Hollnagel & T. White (eds.) Conference Proceedings on "Human Factors in Computing Systems" INTERCHI'93. (pp. 228-235), Reading MA: Addison-Wesley.

[Hartman-61] Hartman F. (1961) Single and multiple channel communication: a review of research and a proposed model. *Audio-Visual Communication Review* 9(6):235-262.

[Marmolin-92] Marmolin, H. (1992) Multimedia from the perspective of psychology. In L. Kjelldahl (ed.) Multimedia: Systems, interaction, and applications. (pp. 39-52), Berlin, Heidelberg: Springer.

[McCormick-57] McCormick, E. (1957) Human Engineering. New York: McGraw-Hill.

[Momtahan-93] Momtahan, K., Hetu, R. & Tansley, B. (1993) Audibility and identification of auditory alarms in the operating room and intensive care unit. *Ergonomics* 36(10):1159-1176.

[Mountford-90] Mountford, S. & Gaver, W. (1990) Talking and Listening to Computers. In B. Laurel and S. Mountford (eds.) The Art of Human-Computer Interface Design. (pp. 319-334), Reading, MA: Addison-Wesley.

[Rauterberg-93] Rauterberg, M. & Cachin, C. (1993) Locating the primary attention focus of the user. in T. Grechenig & M. Tscheligi (eds.) Human Computer Interaction. (Lecture Notes in Computer Science, vol. 733, pp. 129-140), Berlin: Springer.

[Rauterberg-94] Rauterberg, M., Motavalli, M., Darvishi, A. & Schauer, H. (1994) Automatic sound generation for spherical objects hitting straight beams based on physical models. In T. Ottmann and I. Tomek (eds.) Educational Multimedia and Hypermedia: ED-MEDIA'94'. (pp. 468-473), Charlottesville (USA): Association for the Advancement of Computing in Education.

Retail User Assistant: Evaluation of a User-Adapted Performance Support System

Beth Meyer

AT&T Global Information Solutions
Human Interface Technology Center
500 Tech Parkway, NW
Atlanta, GA 30313
U.S.A.
(404) 853-2935
Beth.Meyer@AtlantaGA.ncr.com

Abstract

This paper describes the Retail User Assistant (RUA), a prototype system that provides continual adaptive help for the use of an existing retail point-of-sale device. A preliminary study compared performance of three groups: one using the retail device alone, one using the device with a nonadaptive version of the RUA, and one with the adaptive RUA. Trends in the results imply that performance support, both adaptive and nonadaptive, improved accuracy but slowed performance. The RUA's adaptation, which gave less detailed help as users learned the task, was readily accepted by users and seems to have improved users' performance times. This result is discussed in the context of previous research on adaptive help and adaptive interfaces.

1 Introduction

This paper describes an adaptive performance support system prototype developed at the NCR Human Interface Technology Center. This prototype, called the Retail User Assistant (RUA), provides assistance to users of the NCR 7052 retail point-of-sale system, a computerized cash register system that is used in several large chains of department stores. The NCR 7052 system by itself includes a keyboard, scanner, receipt printer, and a two-row by 20-character text display. The RUA provides assistance on a full personal computer display that was added to this existing system. (Since a design constraint was that the existing NCR 7052 system be able to operate regardless of the condition of the RUA, it was not possible to integrate the two displays on a single device.)

The RUA provides multimedia help displays that are relevant to the current state. The RUA software includes a task model; at each step in a transaction, it uses this model to interpret the current state and select the appropriate display to guide the user. For example, immediately after a user enters a check amount, he or she must insert the check into the printer. At that point, while the 7052 only displays a two-word prompt, the RUA might display a video showing exactly how to insert the check. (Of course, the user would be free to begin the next step at any time, even if the video was still playing.) The RUA software is also designed to detect common errors as early as possible, and to guide users through the process of correcting these errors.

The most interesting feature of the RUA, however, is its capacity to adapt to the changing support needs of its users. The RUA keeps records of each user's performance history in each task, so that users who have performed a task very infrequently or with many errors are given more detailed information than more consistent performers. It is able to keep individual performance records because the user enters an identification number at the beginning of each transaction, as part of the normal use of the 7052 system. As a new user learns to perform a task reliably, the RUA decreases the level of detail in the displays it presents to him or her. For example, the first time that a user performs a layaway transaction, the RUA shows the user a slip insertion video when it is necessary to insert the slip. If this user performs several layaways correctly (usually around five, but it depends upon the individual pattern of performance), and if the time intervals between the layaways are not extremely long, the RUA begins to simply prompt the user to insert the slip rather than showing the video. Conversely, if an experienced user begins to develop consistent problems with a task, the RUA increases the amount of assistance presented.

2 Design Issues and Constraints

A number of constraints and issues surrounded the RUA development. A test of the RUA in a live retail environment, in addition to lab testing, was planned from the beginning of the project. Because of this, preventing negative transfer during or after the field test was a major concern. Hence, the RUA could not change any existing procedures for operating the NCR 7052 system.

This requirement reduced the ways in which the RUA could act as an intelligent agent. For example, the RUA could provide information to help the users detect errors, but could not automate the process of correcting them; if the latter feature were provided, the removal of the system after a few weeks of use would cause problems for the users.

Similarly, the system could not interrupt users at work to request their permission to adapt the displays, since this interruption could cause problems in the real working environment. The system also could not add any significant tasks to the users' working environment. Therefore, all adaptation could be classified, using Malinowski et al's taxonomy [4], as "Self-adaptation" -- it was controlled and implemented entirely by the system, with no input from the user. Clearly, this was a risky design decision, since pure self-adaptation by the system can often cause users to feel frustrated and out of control [3, 5, 6].

It became clear during the planning and execution of the laboratory evaluation of the RUA that adaptive systems pose special testing challenges. Most of the adaptations of the RUA were designed to take place over a long period of use.

Hence, testing the adaptive features required a rather long testing period; for most subjects, the test session was around two hours. While a longer session could have provided more data, the additional data would have surely shown effects of subject fatigue. Also, there were problems in testing the fully adaptive RUA against a version that did not adapt but that remained at the highest level of assistance. Since for new users it was not appropriate for the system to start giving less detailed assistance until well past halfway through the test, the two conditions were identical for much of the test. This made effect sizes smaller and limited to the latter trials of the test. (Issues of evaluating adaptive interfaces are discussed further in [8].)

3 Evaluation results

The RUA was evaluated in laboratory usability tests, and was demonstrated in a store training room. Ironically, after the prototype was designed specifically for field use, changes in the planned field testing environment made the actual field test impossible. The laboratory testing involved observing new 7052 users as they performed 48 transactions (eight trials each of six different transaction types). Each subject was assigned to one of three conditions:

* 7052 only; no aiding
* 7052 and RUA with aiding fixed at the level of greatest detail
* 7052 and RUA with fully adaptive aiding

There were five subjects per condition. Subject demographics were relatively diverse, in order to replicate as much as possible the diversity of the intended user group (retail salespeople). Each group consisted of around three men and two women, with ages ranging from under 20 to the mid-30's. Many of the subjects, but not all, were students in area universities.

The experimenter trained each subject to criterion performance of the following types of transactions:

* Cash sales with dollar amount markdowns
* Cash sales with percentage markdowns
* Cash sales to employees
* Check sales
* Cash returns
* Layaway sales

To initially train each subject, the experimenter explained how to perform each task, demonstrated each task on the 7052, and then allowed the subject to try the task with coaching as necessary. The content of the training was determined by a prepared script, and the same script was used for all subjects. After all of the material was explained, the subject would begin performing exercises for each of the transaction types, and would continue performing exercises until reaching the training criterion for each type. Once subjects reached the training criterion for any one transaction type, they would not perform any more exercises for that type.

The criterion to which subjects were trained was at least one error-free performance of each type of transaction within a time limit. The time limit for each type of transaction was obtained by doubling typical expert performance times for the same transactions. To reach this criterion for all of the transaction types, subject usually required about an hour of training.

After the training period, subjects then performed eight trials each of the same types of transactions, for a total of 48 transactions. As the subjects performed these transactions, the experimenter would watch from a control room to record performance times and number of errors. (Recording errors in this way required that the experimenter work from an additional copy of the task specifications, so that the experimenter could determine which actions were correct and which were not.) These trials were given in blocks of the six transaction types; subjects would perform one trial each of the six different types, then the second trial of each of these types, and so forth. The order of the transactions was the same for all subjects, largely to ensure that the experimenter would always know the subject's current task assignment. Different trials of the same type of transaction would vary in terms of the merchandise items being sold or returned, the discount amounts if any, and the total amount of the transaction.

The results of the laboratory test were interesting, if not conclusive nor usually statistically significant (due to very high variability within conditions and relatively small number of subjects).

To evaluate the effect of the performance support features (the presence of instructions and error detection), one can compare overall performance data of the two RUA groups against that of the 7052-only group. In general, performance times of the 7052-only group were faster than those of the two RUA groups. For the especially error-prone employee sale transaction, this effect was significant (see Figure 1).

While it may be surprising that additional help slowed users, a probable cause for this effect is the effectiveness of the error detection features. As discussed previously, the RUA could help users detect errors and instruct users in correcting them, but could not actually make the process of correcting them easier. Hence, the RUA users were better able to detect errors, but then would spend time correcting them, while users in the 7052-only group would continue on without being aware that they made a mistake. In the employee sale transaction, adaptive RUA users corrected on average about 85% of their errors, fixed-level RUA users corrected about 60% of their errors, while users in the 7052-only group corrected only about 20% of their errors (see Figure 2). In general, subjects in the two RUA groups made fewer errors than subjects in the 7052-only group (see Figure 3). Therefore, the performance support features of the RUA appeared to improve subjects' accuracy, but at some cost to their speed.

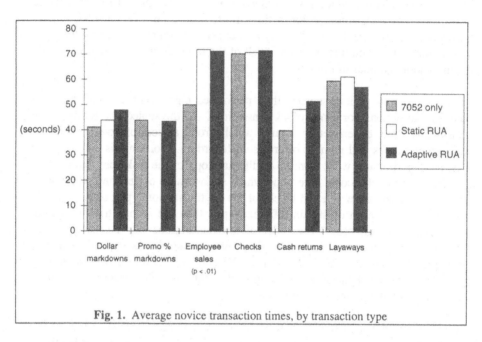

Fig. 1. Average novice transaction times, by transaction type

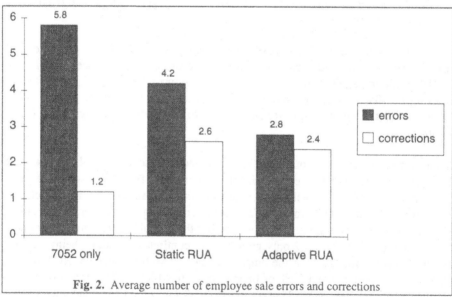

Fig. 2. Average number of employee sale errors and corrections

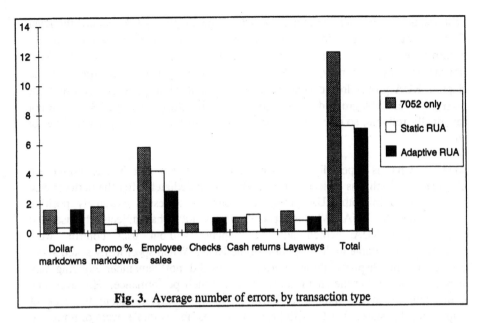

Fig. 3. Average number of errors, by transaction type

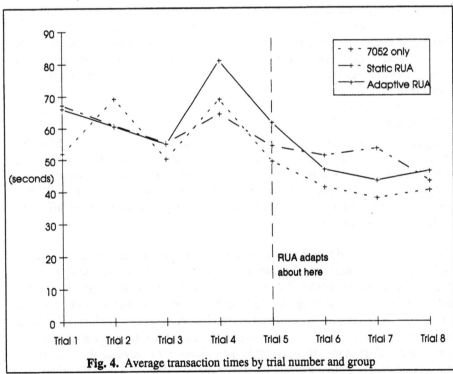

Fig. 4. Average transaction times by trial number and group

The ability of the RUA to adapt to users' growing expertise may have reduced this cost. Figure 4 shows average performance times for the three groups across the eight practice trials. While the point at which the adaptive RUA reduced the level of help was different for different subjects (depending on each subject's performance record), it tended to do this around practice trials 5 or 6 for most subjects and transaction types. As Figure 4 shows, performance times for the adaptive RUA group drop dramatically at this point while performance times for the fixed-level RUA group decrease more gradually. Again, these effects were not statistically reliable, so one cannot base firm conclusions on this particular set of data.

However, what is especially interesting and significant is the user preference information, which was collected from each user immediately after the performance test. Subjects in both RUA groups consistently expressed extremely positive opinions about the RUA. What is especially important is that subjects who used the fully adaptive RUA, which adapted displays without user control, were unanimously favorable in their opinion of the RUA. When specifically asked about changes in the displays, these subjects either did not remember noticing any changes or stated that the changes did not affect their performance. However, one of the subjects in the fixed-level RUA group did complain about the *lack* of adaptation. He stated that the slip insertion videos, for example, were of no use to him once he had learned how to do the task.

This information is especially interesting because, in previous experiments with adaptive interfaces, self-adaptation by the system without any user control has caused most users to react very negatively [3, 5, 6]. Clearly, this was not the case in this instance.

4 Discussion

This data is very exploratory; further research, using more subjects observed over a greater number of trials, is needed to confirm the quantitative trends. However, the adaptation of the RUA clearly did not disrupt performance and was quite readily accepted by users. This result departs from previous research on adaptive interfaces which do not give the user control over the adaptation. This difference requires some explanation.

First of all, one should not conclude from this data that systems should not give the user control over interface adaptation! Previous research clearly shows both the costs of a lack of user control [3, 5, 6] and benefits for greater user control [7]. The primary reasons for designing the RUA with this sort of adaptation were practical constraints; for example, we were not allowed to give users significant additional tasks to perform. It clearly is preferable, most of the time, to give the user control over system adaptation. However, this data along with previous research shows that user control is more important for some types of adaptation than for others.

The question arises: Why was self-adaptation acceptable to RUA users when it was not acceptable to users of other systems? To answer this question, one must examine the properties of previous self-adapting systems that were not well accepted by users, as well as the properties of the RUA.

4.1 Previous Evaluations of Self-Adapting Systems

In the study by Maskery [5], the system being evaluated would change from a system-led dialogue style to a user-led dialogue style after a certain number of uses. This change would involve a significant change in actions and strategies required of the user. While learning with the system-led dialogue style, the users would develop a strategy of attending to a system display and basing their actions on that information. When the dialogue style changed to a user-led style, the existing strategy suddenly became useless and a new strategy had to be learned. In other words, when this system adapted, the stimulus-response relationship that users had been practicing no longer applied.

Users' actions also had to change when the system in the Morris, Rouse, & Ward study [6] adapted. In this case, the adaptive system would detect high-workload conditions. When these conditions occurred, the system would automatically begin performing one of the users' multiple tasks. Rather than requiring users to learn a new response to a different display, this adaptation required users to *not* use the responses they had already learned for the same displays. Users in this case did not need to do the same degree of learning as in the Maskery study, which may explain why the adaptation in this case did not decrease performance.

However, the adaptation in this study still significantly changed the stimulus-response relationship; users were required to stop performing certain actions that they had learned to perform. The transfer of the task from the user to the system disoriented some users. The fact that users still had to make changes in their patterns of actions may be why they reacted so negatively to the adaptive aid, even though it did not hurt their performance.

In the study by Hockley [3], the primary type of adaptation was that of "guidance level." The command-based interface provided six different levels of guidance, which differed in amounts of feedback and prompting that the system gave the user. The system would adapt the guidance level for each user and each command according to prior performance. Hockley explains the negative user reactions to the adaptive system by stating that system responses to individual commands could change markedly from one command to another. This statement implies that at least some levels of guidance showed very different displays from other levels. These differences may well have been dramatic enough to change the stimulus-response relationship. The user who had learned a correct command sequence at one level of guidance might not have been able to construct a related command sequence with another guidance level that provided very different information.

One explanation, then, for the negative user reactions to these three adaptive systems is that the adaptations changed the stimulus-response relationship, thereby forcing the user to do some additional learning. Users may always prefer to have control over such changes.

4.2 Properties of RUA Adaptation

However, this hypothesis raises a question. Why did users so readily accept the adaptation of the RUA system? While the RUA adaptations did not require users to change their actions, they did cause changes to the instructional displays. Would not those changes also significantly change the stimulus-response relationship?

The answer may lie in the effects of experience with a task. One common observation in the study of experts is that of "chunking" of tasks. What novice performers perceive as a sequence of independent actions, experts may perceive in a more unitary way [2]. A proposed mechanism that predicts this observation is "composition," a component of Anderson's ACT* theory of learning [1]. According to this theory, knowledge about how to perform a task may be represented by a sequence of production rules, each of which links an external condition (such as a display) or knowledge derived from a previous action (such as a subtotal in addition) to a required action. When a set of actions is performed together repeatedly in response to equivalent conditions, the multiple rules are "composed" into a single rule that only requires the external conditions.

This theory was applied in the design of RUA adaptation. All displays included summary information that would be sufficient to begin the correct actions. The displays given to newer users and lower performers, however, also included information that might prompt actions required later in the task. For example, new users might see a prompt to do a task, along with a video showing them how; this display would demonstrate each step of the task. More experienced users would only receive the prompt. (The overall characteristics of the display, such as background and color scheme, always remained the same.)

This adaptation seemed to fit well with users' work. As users first learned their tasks, they appeared to attend carefully to all parts of the displays. They would sometimes replay videos to repeat information about later steps of the tasks. However, as they repeated the tasks, users appeared to spend less time viewing the displays. It may have been that, by the time the system removed the detailed information, users were no longer attending to this information and thus did not consider the change to be significant (or even noticeable).

It may also be that the process of initially learning a task lends itself to the sort of adaptation used with the RUA. Again, the ACT* theory [1] may provide some insight. In addition to the knowledge of how to perform skills mentioned earlier, which can be represented as production rules, there is also knowledge of facts and relationships. A better representation of this sort of knowledge might be a network

4

of concepts with links indicating the relationships between them. This sort of knowledge is called *declarative knowledge,* while the ability to perform a task is called *procedural knowledge.*

According to the ACT* theory [1], when a person first receives instructions about how to perform a task, that knowledge is first stored as declarative knowledge. When people attempt to actually perform a task for the first time, they may use general problem-solving productions to generate actions (and hence, procedural knowledge) from their memory of the instructions. After they have done this, and have strengthened the procedural knowledge through one or more practice tasks, they can then use the procedural knowledge directly without having to refer to the declarative knowledge representing the instructions. Hence, some declarative information may be needed for the user to be able to generate the initial actions, but may not be needed once the user has constructed a working set of production rules by performing the task correctly once or twice. Again, the fact that users spent less time viewing the RUA displays as they learned the tasks seems to support this theory.

Another factor that may have contributed to the user acceptance of the RUA was the cost of continued detailed help. The screen clutter of unnecessary instructions, as well as the potential of video instructions to distract from the task, may have hurt performance once the task was sufficiently learned. The subject's complaint about continued videos and the drop in performance time for the adaptive group in the later trials support this claim. If users even vaguely perceive a performance improvement after the adaptation, it would improve their acceptance of the system.

In conclusion, while it is preferable to give users as much control over adaptation as possible (and as is convenient for the users), this research suggests guidelines for designing adaptation when user control is not possible. Adaptive systems which do not require users to change their actions, which change displays only in accordance with probable changes in user attention, and which reduce performance costs of static interfaces may have the greatest chance of success. Conversely, this analysis implies that for adaptations that will change user actions or involve new learning -- for example, providing a new icon to automate a common task -- it is important to give the user control over the adaptation.

Acknowledgments

The author wishes to thank Haila Darcy, Clarkson Jones, Marna Elyea, Michael Harris, K.C. Burgess Yakemovic, and Dick Henneman for their assistance with this research. Thanks also go to Tom MacTavish of NCR HITC and Lee Hoevel of NCR Technology & Development Division for their permission to publish this research.

References

1. Anderson, J.R. (1982). Acquisition of cognitive skill. *Psychological Review, 89,* 369-406.

2. Chase, W. G. & Simon, H. A. (1973). Perception in chess. *Cognitive Psychology, 4,* 55-81.

3. Hockley, A. T. (1986). Adaptive user interfaces for information systems: an evaluation. In P. Zunde & J. C. Agrawal (Eds.), *Empirical Foundations of Information and Software Science IV: Empirical Methods of Evaluation of Man-Machine Interfaces* (pp. 149-161). New York: Plenum Press.

4. Malinowski, U., Kühme, T., Dieterich, H., & Schneider-Hufschmidt, M. (1992). A taxonomy of adaptive user interfaces. In A. Monk, D. Diaper & M. D. Harrison (Eds.), *People and Computers VII: Proceedings of the HCI '92 Conference, September 1992* (pp. 391-414). Cambridge: Cambridge University Press.

5. Maskery, H.S. (1985). Adaptive interfaces for naive users -- An experimental study. In B. Shackel (Ed.), *Human-computer interaction -- INTERACT '84* (pp. 343-349). Amsterdam: Elsevier Science Publishers (North-Holland).

6. Morris, N. M., Rouse, W. B., & Ward, S. L. (1988). Studies of dynamic task allocation in an aerial search environment. *IEEE Transactions on Systems, Man, and Cybernetics, 18,* 376-389.

7. Oppermann, R. (1992). Adaptively supported adaptability. In G. C. van der Veer, M. J. Tauber, S. Bagnara, & M. Antalovits (Eds.), *Human-Computer Interaction: Tasks and Organization. Proceedings of the Sixth European Conference on Cognitive Ergonomics (ECCE 6)* (pp. 255-268). Rome: CUD.

8. Totterdell, P. & Boyle, E. (1990). The evaluation of adaptive systems. In D. Browne, P. Totterdell, & M. Norman (Eds.), *Adaptive User Interfaces* (pp. 161-194). London: Academic Press.

Growing an Icon Set: User Acceptance of Abstract and Concrete Icon Styles

Leslie G. Tudor

User Interface Design Group
AT&T Bell Laboratories
200 Laurel Ave., Room 4F-509
Middletown NJ 07748 US
(908) 957-6448, lgt@mtqua.att.com

ABSTRACT

This research was conducted in order to evaluate 69 icons, which were designed to represent 23 telecommunications referents. Seven of these icons were previously proposed by the CIAJ (Communications Industry Association of Japan) Design Committee and the remaining 62 were designed by IDEO of London. Icons were tested via recognition and evaluation tasks. The data revealed that the icons with the highest mean recognition scores and evaluation ratings were usually those which tended to look like the item(s) that they were designed to represent. Icons that communicated their meaning through symbolic representations did not fare as well. Mean recognition scores and evaluation ratings for the 7 CIAJ icons varied.

1 Introduction

In the telecommunications arena, researchers, engineers, and designers have attempted to design and test icons that are destined for both personal and business products. A variety of methodologies and statistical analyses have been used. In response to wide variations in testing procedures, Whitten (1992) in his submission to CCITT, suggested that future studies use specific testing procedures. Specifically, Whitten suggested that a recall and recognition-matching test should be used, as well as subjective rating tests that utilize referent descriptions which are presented in scenario form. Bocker (1992) felt that explaining the functions in the context of a typical usage scenario was helpful, but that a "complete matching" recognition task was not advisable; in a real-life scenario, the user would most probably be trying to match only one cognitive representation to one out of several icons. In our view, this method is further complicated by the fact that this kind of task is relatively easy, in that the most difficult representation-icon matches are isolated as less difficult matches are completed.

Bocker (1992) tested 7 set of icons, each of which were generated by designers who hailed from 7 different European countries. Each icon set contained 7 videophone icons. The subjects, who represented 8 European countries, participated in a variety of tasks. Specifically, for each icon family, subjects were asked to select the icon that best represented each of the 7 referents, and to then indicate how certain they were of their selection and how well they thought the icon represented the referent. Subjects also viewed each referent name paired with the 7 icons designed to represent it, and selected the best one. Finally, subjects selected the icon set that they preferred the most.

Bocker used a multiple index approach, which took each icon's number of hits, misses, and false alarms into account, as well as preference scores, certainty and representation ratings. This statistical approach was interesting in that it not only provided data about individual icons but also gave insight into the usefulness of icons in their respective families, i.e. their confusability factors. However, what Bocker did not do was to provide the reader with knowledge about statistically significant and non-significant differences between recognition (% hits) scores. This information would have undoubtedly lent greater credence to Bocker's conclusions.

Relatively recently, the Communications Industry Association of Japan (CIAJ) issued a paper (1991) describing the design and testing of 12 telecommunications icons. However, it was not clear what methodology was used in obtaining the data. Furthermore, usability testing included both engineer and design staff members, as well as other communication employees. The use of these relative "experts" and "inside users" is questionable; doing usability testing with prospective users who are also novices is always preferable, if not mandatory.

The current project was motivated both by AT&T's desire to develop a full line of icons for both its personal and business products, and as a response to the CIAJ report. Seven of the CIAJ icons were of great interest to us, as standardization of these icons meant that they would likely appear on AT&T future products. Therefore, it was felt that the CIAJ icons should be tested using an American subject pool which also represented a prospective customer base. In developing an appropriate methodology, Whitten's (1992) recommendations, as well as Bocker's (1992) comments were considered.

2 Method

2.1 Subjects

A total of 216 subjects participated in the study. Subjects from large and small businesses were used, as well as consumers who were also computer literate. For each of these groups, equal numbers of subjects were drawn from the East, South, and West Coasts of the United States.

2.2 Materials

Twenty-three icon referents were used (see Table 1, Column 1). Each of these referents were matched to 3 icons, for a total of 69 icons (see Table 1, Columns P, A, and C). IDEO of London designed 62 of the 69 icons. The remaining 7 icons were proposed by the CIAJ-Design Committee (see Table 1, Family P icons = "Volume". "Achieve Dial Tone", "Hold", "Music on Hold", "Mute", "Store", "Speakerphone"). The Family P icon for "Volume" was tested in isolation, apart from its use in combined representations, such as "Receiver Sound Volume". Each of the 69 icons was assigned to an icon family, based on their respective characteristics. The icon families were those of "Concrete", "Abstract", and "Proposed". Icons assigned to the Concrete family (Family C) were those which depicted the physical analogs that they represented, whereas Abstract family

(Family A) icons communicated their meanings through the use of symbolic representations. Finally, the icons assigned to the Proposed family (Family P) included the 7 icons proposed by the CIAJ-Design Committee. The rest were designed so as to be stylistically consistent with the existing Japanese icons, although some of these could have also been allotted to Families C or A, based on their respective characteristics. Icons were presented as illustrations, as part of a questionnaire. The questionnaire was comprised of 2 sections: recognition/subjective certainty, and preference/evaluation. The recognition and subjective certainty tasks were combined and presented first. During these tasks, subjects were first presented with a list of 23 referents, along with their respective descriptions. Referent descriptions were presented in the form of scenarios. Subjects were presented with 3 family sets of 23 icons each. Each of the 23 icons in each family set was designed to represent one of the 23 icon referent descriptions. The subjects task was to read an icon referent description, look at the icons in a specific family set, and select the most appropriate icon for that referent. Subjects were required to select both a first and a second choice. As part of this task, subjects also had to provide a certainty rating for each of their choices by using a 7 point rating scale (ranging from "not at all confident" to "completely confident") Subjects repeated this task for all 23 referents, selecting icons from the same family. Only after the icons from a particular family were tested did the testing of another icon family begin. Again, for each referent, subjects selected a matching icon from a specified family set and provided certainty ratings. The 23 icon referents combined with the use of the 3 icon families, having 23 icons each, resulted in a total of 69 recognition/subjective certainty trials.

During the evaluation/preference task, each referent was paired with 3 appropriate icons. Subjects were asked to evaluate how well each icon represented its respective referent by using a 7 point rating scale (ranging from "not at all" to "completely"). An optional comment area was provided after each trial. As there were 23 referents, each having 3 appropriate icons (one from each family), there were 23 icon evaluation/preference trials.

2.3 Experimental Design

A 3 x 3 x 3 (Location (L) x Subject Type (S) x Family (F)) repeated measures design was used, consisting of 2 between and 1 within factors. Between factors consisted of location (East Coast, West Coast, and South Coast) and subject type (small business, large business, and consumers who were also computer literate.) Subject type combined factorially with location resulted in a 9 cell matrix, with 24 subjects per cell. The within factors consisted of family (concrete, abstract, and proposed). Each family was comprised of 23 icons, each of which pictorially represented a telecommunications referent. During the recognition/subjective certainty task, order of family presentation was counterbalanced across subjects. Specifically, 6 orderings of family presentation were generated and each order was assigned to 4 subjects in each subject cell. Additionally, order of icon referents was counterbalanced across subjects. Half of the subjects in each subject cell received a random ordering of icon referents. For the remaining subjects, the first half of the icon referents were switched with the second half. After the orders were switched, order of icons within each half were randomized. For the preference/evaluation task, half of the subjects received a randomly generated list of referents, paired with their respective icons. For the remaining subjects, the first half of the icon referents were switched with the second half. Additionally, for each referent, the order of the 3 matching icons was randomized.

2.4 Procedure

Subjects were run in groups of 20 to 30 in hotel conference rooms. Sessions lasted approximately 90 minutes. Subjects were told that the purpose of the study was to investigate the use of icons on telephone and in computer displays. It was explained that an icon is a graphical symbol that represents an object(s) and/or action. To further clarify this definition, the experimenter referred to the "no-smoking" sign as an example of a familiar icon.

The experimenter explained that the session tasks would require subjects to select and evaluate several different icons. Subjects were told that, during the recognition task, they would read an icon referent description, look at a list of 23 icons, and then select the most appropriate icons for that referent. Subjects were also told that they were required to select both a first and second choice and to provide a certainty rating for each of their choices. Specifically, they were to answer the question, "to what degree are you certain that your choice is correct?" The 7 point rating scale that subjects were to use for this task was then reviewed. The use of the 3 icon family lists was noted and subjects were instructed to complete all trails for one family before moving on to other family trials.

After the instructions for the recognition/subjective certainty task were given to subjects, they were told that they would also be participating in a task in which each referent would be paired with 3 matching icons. They were told that their task would be to answer the question, "to what degree does each icon represent its matching referent?" They were instructed to use the same 7 point rating scale that they would use for the recognition task. Subjects were encouraged to write down any comments that they had about specific icons.

The experimenter emphasized the importance of not skipping trials in order to return to them later. Subjects were also told that they should immediately proceed to the evaluation/preference task upon completion of the recognition/subjective certainty tasks.

3 Results

3.1 Analysis

Subjects were drawn from different geographical locations and represented different business and consumer groups in order to obtain a subject group which represented potential AT&T customers within the United States. Since response differences in each of these subject groups was not the primary focus of this research project, but rather the response of the group as a whole, responses were collapsed across subject groups.

An analysis which used only the first choice recognition data and the evaluation/preference data was conducted. It was felt that this data was enough to provide us with a comprehensive picture of the usefulness and desirability of the icons.

Recognition Data. Each subject in each group responded once to each of the icon referent trials, the response being either correct or incorrect. The responses are thus binomial. The sum of the twenty-four subjects' responses in each of the L x S categories divided by 24 and multiplied by 100 constitutes a binomial percentage. Such a percentage does not conform to the assumption of the ANOVA or t statistic and thus may lead to erroneous results. The arcsine transformation is the appropriate correction. Essentially, it transforms binomial percentages to angles, ranging from 0 to 90 degrees, which meet the assumptions of normal statistics. When percentages are calculated as described, subjects as a variable is eliminated so that the final result consists of independent variables only. A one factor (Family) ANOVA was conducted for each of the 23 referents. Post-hoc tests for significant main effects were conducted using the Games-Howell test.

Evaluation Data. The data was transcribed with values 1 through 3 representing the left side of the scale and values 5 through 7 representing the right side of the scale. A repeated measures ANOVA, with one within (FAMILY) factor, was conducted for the 23 referents. Means contrasts tests were conducted for levels of factors having significant main effects.

Table 1 depicts the 69 icons and their respective mean recognition scores and evaluation ratings. Specifically, each row is comprised of either a) the 3 icons that represent a particular referent b) the mean percent recognition scores for a specific icon and c) the mean evaluation rating for a specific icon. Columns P, A, and C are organized by Family type. For each referent, in Column 1, one asterisk indicates a statistically significant main effect for the evaluation task, while two asterisks indicate statistically significant main effects for both the recognition and evaluation tasks. For the rows "Recognition Means" and "Evaluation Means", column asterisks indicate the icons which were found to have significantly higher recognition scores and evaluation ratings, respectively.

3.2 Results Summary

Recognition Data. For each referent, the majority of icons which revealed recognition scores that were significantly higher than one or both of the other two icons that they were paired with came from the P and C families. This includes the case of a) two icons which were not significantly different from one another but which were both significantly greater than a third icon or b) one icon which was not significantly different from another icon but which was significantly greater than the third icon. Of these, those exclusively from the P family were "Speed Dial", "Help Specific", "Message", "Hold" and "Answer Ringing Call". Those exclusively from the C family were "Speakerphone", "Drop", Help System", "Achieve Dial Tone", and "Call Log". Those from both the P and C families were "Transfer", "Dialpad", "Phone Call Active", "Music on Hold", and "Ringer Select".

Icons exclusively from the A family which revealed recognition scores that were significantly higher than one or both of the other two icons (as defined above), were those of "Mute", "HFAI", and "Store". Those from both the A and C families were "Call Log", "Volume", and "Retrieve".

For each referent, icons from different families that were not significantly different from one another were those of "Switch Hook Control", "Notes", and "Conference Call".

All recognition scores that were significantly higher than one or both of the other two icons (as defined above) were tested against chance via $\underline{T}$-tests. All were significantly greater than the chance value (p<.05 for all).

Evaluation Data. The evaluation data were consistent with the recognition data: for each referent, the majority of icons which revealed mean evaluation ratings that were significantly higher than one or both of the other two icons that they were paired with came from the P and C families. This includes the cases of a) two icons which were not significantly different from one another but which were both significantly greater than a third icon or b) one icon which was not significantly different from another icon but which was significantly greater than the third icon. Of these, those exclusively from the P family were "Call Log", "Dialpad", "Speed Dial", "Help Specific", "Conference Call", and "Message". Those exclusively from the C family were "Phone Call Active", "Switch Hook Control", "Notes", "Speakerphone", "Hold", "Ringer Select", "Retrieve", "Achieve Dial Tone", and "Drop". Those from both the P and C family were "Transfer", "Answer Ringing Call", "Music on Hold", and "Help System".

Icons exclusively from the A family which revealed recognition scores that were significantly higher than one or both of the other two icons (as defined above), were those of "Volume", "Store", and "HFAI". The only icon from both the A and C families was "Mute" and there were no icons from both the A and P families.

Combined Results. Taking both the recognition data and the evaluation data into account, the following conclusions can be generated from the data: Family P icons were best for the referents "Dialpad", "Speed Dial", "Help Specific", "Conference Call", "Answer Ringing Call", and "Message". Family C icons were best for the referents "Phone Call Active", "Switch Hook Control", "Notes", "Speakerphone", "Ringer Select", "Help System", "Retrieve", "Achieve Dial Tone", and "Drop". Both Family P and Family C icons were best for the referents "Transfer" and "Music on Hold". Family A icons were best for the referents "Volume", "Store", "Mute", "HFAI". The results for the referents "Call Log" and "Hold" were unusual as recognition data were not at all consistent with evaluation data. For "Call Log", Family C and A icons revealed the highest mean recognition scores, whereas the Family P icon revealed the highest mean evaluation rating. For "Hold", the Family P icon revealed the highest mean recognition score, whereas the Family C icon revealed the highest mean evaluation rating.

When the 7 original CIAJ icons were tested, recognition scores and evaluation ratings varied. Of these, the Family P icons that received both recognition scores and evaluation ratings that were significantly lower than their Family A and/or C counterparts were those of "Mute", "Volume", "Speakerphone", "Store", and "Achieve Dial Tone'. The Family P icon that received a recognition score that was significantly higher than it's Family A and C counterparts, but which was significantly lower in it's evaluation rating than it's C counterpart, was that of "Hold". Finally, both the recognition score and evaluation rating of the Family P icon "Music on Hold" did not significantly vary from the score and rating of it's Family C counterpart.

Standardization Consideration. Despite the finding that several icons which represented a specific referent received significantly higher recognition scores than did others, some of these relatively high recognition scores were quite low. "Best of Class" icons with recognition scores that fell at or below 30 percent were those of "Achieve Dial Tone", "Retrieve", "Switch Hook Control", "Help System", and "Phone Call Active". Even though all but the "Help System" icon received mean evaluation/preference ratings which were higher than a neutral rating of "4", the fact that recognition scores were low is cause for concern and indicates that these icons cannot confidently be considered for standardization. "Best of Class" icons which revealed mean recognition scores between 30 and 60 percent were those of "Call Log", (Families A and C), "Message", "HFAI", "Hold", "Store", "Speed Dial", and "Answer Ringing Call". All but the "Call Log - Family C" icon had mean evaluation/preference scores that were higher than a neutral rating of "4". These icons should be considered for standardization only if further testing and perhaps some design modifications take place. "Best of Class" icons which revealed mean recognition scores between 60 and 100 percent were those of "Drop", "Notes", "Ringer Select", "Volume", "Dialpad", "Help Specific", "Transfer", "Music on Hold", "Mute", "Speakerphone", and "Conference". These icons also had mean evaluation/preference scores that were higher than a neutral rating of "4". These icons might be considered for standardization, due to their relatively high recognition scores.

4 Discussion

The data clearly show that icons which were designed to mimic their physical referents usually received more favorable recognition scores and evaluation ratings than those which were more symbolic in nature. There were, however, exceptions to this rule. For example, the Family P icon for the referent "Help Specific" received the most favorable score and rating. However, this could be because this icon is already well known by many users of both personal and business machines. The Family A icon for the referent "Retrieve" also received a relatively favorable recognition score. Perhaps this is because the arrow is a universally well understood symbol and the 3-sided box it originates from may be perceived by most subjects as a container.

Still, if subjects are more prone to respond favorably to icons which are designed to look like what they represent, why did the icons from Family P receive such favorable scores and ratings? As was previously mentioned, many of the Family P icons were rather "concrete", although the primary motivation behind their design was to keep them stylistically consistent with the icons proposed by the CIAJ.

Therefore, subjects may have been responding to the concrete aspects of Family P icons which were favored. Alternately, it may also be that some of the Family C icons did not actually look like their physical analogs, despite design attempts. For example, the Family C icon for "Message" was designed to look like a bottle with a message inside of it. However, it is possible that subjects may have perceived a bottle containing a long, thin, rectangular bar instead of a letter or message. As for the Family C icon for the referent "Answer Ringing Call", it is possible that subjects perceived the icon as a descending, as opposed to an ascending, receiver. These are the types of issues that make icon design and testing so difficult. It is never completely clear whether the metaphor or design concept being used is inadequate or if the design itself does not adequately represent the metaphor or concept.

Aside from determining which icons in each "referent family" received the most favorable scores and ratings, it is also important to look at the highest scores and ratings in isolation. The notion of what constitutes a "respectable" score must be considered. For example, even though the "best of class" icon for the referent "Answer Ringing Call" was determined to be from Family P, is a recognition score of 31% considered to be impressive in light of the fact that a chance response is a mere 4%? Should the design and standards community accept nothing less than a "substantial" recognition score and, if so, what might this score be?

Finally, an issue which must be raised is that these icons were designed by a team of professional graphic designers and telecommunications "experts". Prospective users of the products that the icons were developed for were excluded from the design process. Research has shown that it is often quite risky to allow non-users to allow themselves to imagine what the users' needs are. Ideally, prospective users should be included in the icon design process, just as they often are in user-centered design sessions for software products.

5 References

Bocker, M. (1992, May). Report about the results of an evaluation study of pictograms for point-to-point videotelephony. *European Telecommunications Standards Institute,* Work Item No: DTR/HF-1010.

Communication Industry of Japan (CIAJ). (1991, June). Supplementary information on new pictograms and symbols for telephones. *CCITT,* Delayed Contribution D265, Geneva, Switzerland.

Whitten, W. (1992, April). Procedures for designing, selecting, and evaluating symbols, pictograms, and icons. *CCITT,* Draft Recommendation F.910, Geneva, Switzerland.

Exploring Graphical Feedback in a Demonstrational Visual Shell

Francesmary Modugno and Brad A. Myers

School of Computer Science, Carnegie Mellon University, Pittsburgh, PA 15213 USA

Abstract. We present a visual language that serves as a novel form of feedback in a Programming by Demonstration (PBD) interface. The language explicitly represents data, such as files, with unique icons and implicitly represents operations by changes to data icons, so that operations reflect the changes seen in the interface when executed. In addition, the language is used to provide feedback to the user by indicating loops and inferred sets, specifying parameters, etc., and is integrated into other parts of the PBD system, such as the editor. This forms a close union between the interface, the PBD system and the program representation and helps bridge the gap between the user's mental model of the programming process and the actual programming task.

1 Introduction

In his classic 1983 article, Ben Shneiderman introduced the concept of a "direct manipulation" interface, in which objects on the screen can be pointed to and manipulated using the mouse and keyboard[25]. The Apple Macintosh, introduced in 1984, quickly popularized this interface style and today direct manipulation interfaces are widely used. Unfortunately, these interfaces have some well recognized limitations. For example, in textual interfaces such as the Unix shell, it is common for users to construct parameterized procedures (called "shell scripts") that automate repetitive tasks. This is often difficult to do in the Macintosh Finder or other "visual shells". Direct manipulation interfaces also do not provide convenient mechanisms for expressing abstraction or generalizations, such as "all .tex files edited on August 19, 1993." As a result, while direct manipulation interfaces are often easier to learn and use than their textual counterparts, users often find that complex, high-level, repetitive tasks are more difficult to perform in this domain.

Programming by Demonstration (PBD) systems[5] can potentially solve this problem. In a PBD system, users execute actions on concrete examples and the system constructs a general program[23]. Such systems enable users to create general procedures without having special programming skills. They are easy to use because users operate by manipulating data the way they normally do in the interface. Unfortunately, they have limitations: they can infer incorrectly; most contain no static representation of the inferred program; feedback is often obscure or missing; and few provide editing facilities. This makes it difficult for users to know if the system has inferred correctly, to correct any errors, and to revise or change a program.

In order to address these problems, the Pursuit[19] demonstrational visual shell is exploring the use of a *graphical* representation of the program *while it is being written*. Programs are represented in a visual language in which data objects, such as files and folders, are represented as icons and operations are represented by the changes they cause to data icons. In addition to representing the program code, the graphical representations are used throughout the programming process in order to communicate with users. By addressing some of the limitations of PBD systems, this approach should make PBD techniques more effective in helping users manipulate and customize their systems.

2   Related Work

There have been several approaches to adding end-user programming to visual shells. Some visual shells contain a macro recorder (*e.g.*, SmallStar[9]; QuicKeys2, MacroMaker and Tempo II for the Macintosh; and HP NewWave) that makes a transcript of user actions that can be replayed later. Although effective in automating simple, repetitive tasks, macro recorders are limited because they record exactly what users do – only the object that is pointed to can be a parameter and the transcript consists of a straight-line sequence of commands. To generalize transcripts, some macro recorders produce a representation of the transcript in a textual programming language for users to edit. However, this requires users to understand a programming language that is significantly different from the desktop and does not take advantage of the visual aspects of the interface.

Some visual shells have invented a special graphical programming language (*e.g.*, [2, 8, 10, 12]) to enable users to write programs. Most of these languages are based on the data flow model, in which icons represent utilities and lines connecting them represent data paths. Unfortunately, most contain no way to depict abstractions or control structures. The types of programs users can write are quite limited. In addition, these languages require users to learn a special programming language whose syntax differs significantly from what they see in the interface. Finally, constructing programs by wiring together objects is quite different from the way users ordinarily interact with the system.

3   Motivation for the Pursuit Approach

Visual shells are easy to use because of the constantly visible, concrete, familiar representations of data objects and the illusion of concrete manipulation of these data objects[25]. Unfortunately, this "conceptual simplicity" is often lost when programming is introduced: users interact with the system visually, but usually program it off-line in a textual programming language. Users must develop two very different bodies of knowledge: one for interacting with the system and one for programming it. Pursuit attempts to bridge this gap. By allowing programs to be specified by demonstration and by representing programs in a visual programming language that reflects the desktop, users can apply knowledge of the interface and its objects to the visual language and its objects when constructing, viewing and editing a program.

3.1 Benefits of Representing the Program

There are several reasons to have a static representation of the program. First, it allows users to review the program's code and confirm that it does what they intended. It also gives them the opportunity to alter the code in order to correct errors, or to generalize the program further.

Furthermore, providing a representation of the program and its components *during* the demonstration gives users *feedback*. Feedback informs users of the system's inferences. Users can verify these inferences and suggest important features of the example to generalize.

Pursuit can detect loops over sets of data, branches on exit code conditions, and common substring patterns (see [19] for details). A good representation of the program *during* the demonstration informs users of the system's inferences as they are made. Furthermore, Pursuit's visual language not only represents the program code, but also indicates which operations to collapse into a loop, which data objects to execute the loop over, which data objects to use as parameters, etc.

There are other forms of feedback we could have chosen: dialog boxes[9]; questions and answers[17, 22]; textual representation of the code[14]; changing the appearance of actual interface objects (e.g. anticipation highlighting[4]); animation[7]; and sound[16]. Our approach has several benefits over these other forms. Unlike dialog boxes and the question-and-answer style, it is not always disruptive, since users can ignore the program representation until they are finished demonstrating it. Unlike programs represented in a textual language, it does not require that users learn a language that is very different from the interface. Finally, unlike anticipation highlighting, animation, and sound, there is a static representation for users to examine and edit.

4 The Representation Language

The Pursuit visual language[20] is based on the comic strip metaphor[13]. Familiar icons are used to represent data objects, such as files and folders. Sets of data objects are represented by overlaying two icons of the same type (Figure 1). For *abstract* sets of objects, graphical constructs called *attributes* are attached to set icons. Attributes constrain the properties of set objects and indicate the underlying PBD system's inferences. For example, the attribute in Figure 1 constrains the set to files smaller than 1000 bytes.

Each data icon contains a set of graphical properties, such as its location, icon appearance, name, etc. These graphical properties represent properties of the real data object in the interface. Operations are represented by changes in the graphical properties of data icons. Two panels are used to represent an operation. The *prologue* shows the data icons before the operation and the *epilogue* shows

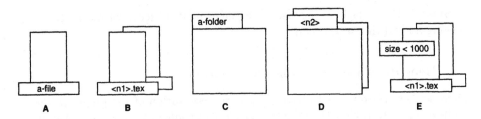

Fig. 1. The basic data types in the Pursuit visual language: (A) a file; (B) a set of files; (C) a folder; (D) a set of folders. Attributes attached to set icons constrain the objects in the set to have particular properties. They are also used to depict system inferences. For example, the first set of files (B) contains all those files whose name ends in .tex. The other set (E) contains all .tex files smaller than 1000 bytes.

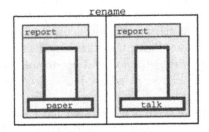

Fig. 2. The representation of the operation rename paper talk. The first panel shows the icon representing the file paper located in the report folder before it is renamed. The second panel shows the same file after the rename operation. The change in the icon's name represents the rename operation.

the icons after the operation (Figure 2). An operation's representation, therefore, resembles changes users see in the real interface when executing the operation[1].

A program is a series of operation panels concatenated together, along with representations of loops, conditionals, variables and parameters. However, using two panels per operations can produce space-inefficient scripts. To make programs more concise, Pursuit contains heuristics that combine knowledge of the domain with information about operations. The following examples illustrate these heuristics and other features of Pursuit.

4.1 A Simple Visual Program

This example illustrates how to write a program to backup all the .tex files in the **papers** folder. To backup the files, the user copies them to the **backups** folder

---

[1] Pursuit's visual representations are similar to those of Chimera[13] and Mondrian[15]. However, there are many differences. The most notable is that Pursuit contains explicit representations of variables, loops and conditionals and that Pursuit's layout is two-dimensional. See [19] for further comparisons.

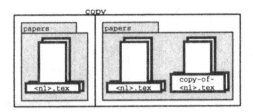

Fig. 3. The copy operation. The name on the file sets indicate the inferences the system made: all copied files have a name ending in .tex.

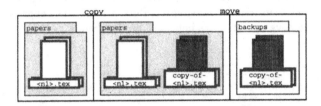

Fig. 4. After the user drags (moves) the copies to the backups folder, the third panel appears. Notice that in the script the set of copies icon has moved from the papers folder to the backups folder, reflecting the changes seen in the actual interface when the real copies were moved.

and then compresses the copies. To automate this task, the user demonstrates its actions on a particular set of files. During the demonstration, the PBD system tries to create a program.

Figures 3-5 show the developing script during the demonstration. The first two panels (Figure 3) appear after the user opens the papers folder, selects the files to be copied and copies them. After the user moves the copies to the backups folder, the new panel in figure 4 appears depicting the move. Only one panel is added because Pursuit notices that *the epilogue of the* copy *contains the prologue of the* move *operation.*

Finally, the user selects all the copies and compresses them. Figure 5 shows the completed program. Another heuristic determines when several operations can be represented in a single panel. The shadow beneath the third panel indicates that it contains both the move and compress operations. By clicking on it, users can see the individual panels for the two operations.

4.2 More Complex Visual Programs

Next we illustrate Pursuit's representations of loops, conditionals and abstraction. Assume a user wishes to write a program to copy all the .tex files that were edited today. This could be done by demonstrating the script as in the previous example. However, suppose the papers folder contains a file named

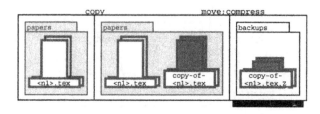

Fig. 5. The completed script. The `compress` operation is represented by the difference in the height and the name of the icon for the copies between the second and third panels. This difference is similar to the change in appearance of the icons for the real files on the desktop, where the `compress` operation replaces a file's icon with a shorter one and appends ".Z" to its name. To save space, Pursuit added the `compress` operation to the panel for the `move` operation, as indicated by the shadow.

Fig. 6. The two examples used to demonstrate the copy program. The first two panels show a successful execution of the `copy` operation. The remainder of the script shows the unsuccessful execution and corrective actions. The black box on the prolog of the second `copy` operation (panel 3) indicates that the operation failed. The predicate following explains why – the existence of a file with the name `copy-of-biblio.tex`. The dialog box icon indicates that the operation popped up a dialog box. Clicking on the icon pops up the dialog box displayed when the operation failed. To correct the operation, the user deletes the error causing file (panels 4 and 5) and re-executes the copy operation (panels 6 and 7).

`copy-of-paper.tex`. If `copy` is executed on any set containing the `paper` file, it will fail because `copy` must produce an output file called `copy-of-paper.tex`. Therefore, the user must demonstrate this program on *two* examples – one in which the `copy` operation succeeds, and one in which it fails. In the latter case, the user must demonstrate what the program should do: delete the error causing file and re-execute the copy operation. Figure 6 shows the visual script after the second example is demonstrated.

After Pursuit confirms and executes the loop, it updates the visual script. The updated script (Figure 7) is an example of an explicit loop containing an explicit conditional. The panel in the upper left corner is a *declaration* and states that the loop iterates over the set of all `.tex` files in the `papers` folder that were edited today. The loop body is surrounded by the large outer rectangle. The black square on the right edge of the prologue of the first `copy` operation indicates that the program branches at this point. The first branch (containing the string "no errors") is taken when `copy` executes successfully. The lower branch is taken when `copy` fails because a file with the output filename already exists.

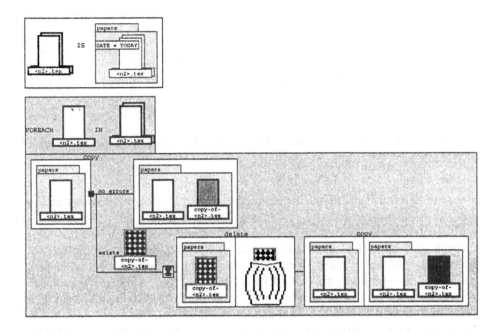

Fig. 7. The Pursuit script that copies each ***.tex** file in the **papers** folder that was edited today. If the **copy** operation fails because of the existence of a file with the output filename, the program deletes that old output file, and re-executes the **copy** operation. The upper panel is a declaration. It defines the loop set and depicts the inferences made by the PBD system.

5 Feedback Beyond Program Representation

The main purpose of Pursuit's visual language is to represent demonstrated programs. In addition, Pursuit integrates the visual language into other parts of the PBD system. This helps improve feedback and forms a closer union between the PBD system and the program representation.

5.1 Inferring Iterations

Pursuit uses the visual script to indicate that it has inferred a loop. For example, suppose the user wishes to extend the program of Figure 5 so that the "copy-of-"prefix is removed from the compressed copies' names. To do so, the user removes the prefix from one of the copies and then another. Once Pursuit detects a loop, it highlights the panels containing the loop's operations (Figure 8). In this way,

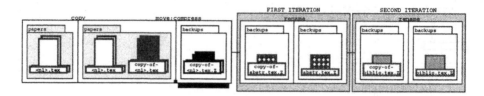

Fig. 8. When Pursuit detects a loop, it highlights the operations in the visual program so that users can confirm the inference.

users can determine if Pursuit has correctly inferred the loop by looking at the highlighted operations.

Predictive methods (*e.g.*, Eager[4] and Metamouse[18]) force users to step through each operation of the iteration to verify the PBD system's inference. For a loop containing many operations, this could be tedious. To avoid this tedium, users can blindly trust the PBD system and have it complete the loop. They then can examine the interface to see if the PBD system was right. For loops that make many changes throughout the interface, this could be difficult and is very prone to error. By allowing users to confirm the loop's operations *before* it is executed, Pursuit reduces users' work and worry.

5.2   Inferring Sets and Subsets

When Pursuit identifies a set to loop over, it displays a dialog box containing the set's graphical representation (Figure 9). Users can confirm whether or not Pursuit has chosen the correct set by identifying the set's icon. This could be quicker and less error prone than displaying a dialog box listing all the set members.

Set icons are also used in a unique way in the visual script – to indicate the subset relationship. When Pursuit identifies one set as a subset of another, it defines the subset using the icon for the original set (Figure 10). In this way, the subset relationship is graphically depicted.

5.3   Editing Programs

Any PBD system will sometimes infer incorrectly or incompletely. Sometimes users might not think of all possible conditions that their program must work for. Hence the PBD system must provide a way for users to edit a script. Pursuit uses a program's visual representation to assist in the editing process. For example, when the user has forgotten to demonstrate a program path and the program is executed in a state that causes it to go down that path, Pursuit pops up the visual representation of the program and highlights the path that the program has taken, indicating where the program is incomplete. The user can then continue

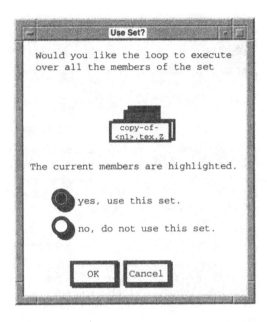

Fig. 9. A Pursuit dialog box asking the user to confirm the set to loop over. The icon for the set of files is the same icon found in the third panel of Figure 8. The dialog box appears when the user executes the **rename** operation on two members of the set representing the copied files.

demonstrating what the program should do and Pursuit automatically updates the script.

Data icons are also used by the editor. Sometimes users wishes to select a data object based on some criteria that cannot be expressed using attributes. For example, users might wish to check for the existence of an object or compare a property of one data object with a property of another data object. In this case users must construct an explicit branch with user defined predicates. To do so, the editor provides a menu of predicate templates describing all possible forms that a predicate can take. Each template contains a list of menus for users to choose from in order to construct the predicate. To describe the data objects that users can select, each menu presents a list of the data objects using their visual representations (Figure 11). Users can select the desired data object by selecting its icon from the menu.

Other ways that data icons are used by the editor include indicating program parameters when saving a script, binding actual parameters to formal parameters when executing a script, and indicating the loop iteration set when wrapping a sequence of operations in an explicit loop.

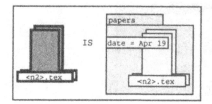 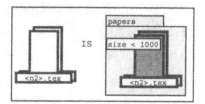

Fig. 10. Two Pursuit declarations. The first declaration defines the red set of files icon to represent all the `.tex` files in the `papers` folder that were edited on April 19. The second declaration defines the purple set of files icon to represent those files with size less than 1000 bytes in the red file set. Using the red file set icon in the second declaration concisely depicts the subset relationship.

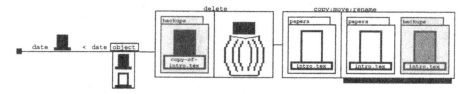

Fig. 11. The user is adding a branch before the demonstrated operations. To construct the predicate, the user selected a predicate template and directly edits it using the pull down menus in the template. The menus for objects in the template contain miniature representations of the objects' data icons.

6   Additional Benefits of Pursuit's Representations

The visual language representation provides a familiar and concrete representation of the program as well as immediate and easy to recognize feedback. It has several advantages.

6.1   Reducing the Use of Variables

Figure 5 illustrates an advantage of having icons represent data: the icons reduce the use of explicit variables, and remove a level of indirection that variables introduce. To identify an icon in a script, Pursuit assigns it a unique color. Although an icon's appearance may change throughout the script, its color remains the same. For example, in the second panel the set icon representing the output of the **copy** operation has the name "copy-of-<n1>.tex" and is in the **papers** folder. In the third panel, the same icon has the name "copy-of-<n1>.tex.Z" and is in the **backups** folder. Users can tell that two icons represent the same set because they have the same color. Color serves the same purpose as a variable name in textual programming languages.

6.2 Reducing the Use of Control Constructs

By concretely representing abstractions, attributes and sets, Pursuit reduces the need to explicitly represent loops and conditionals, constructs that are difficult for users to understand[6]. For example, in order to define the loop set in figure 7 in a traditional programming language, one would have to write code to loop through all the files in the **papers** folder and test to see which ones had names ending in .**tex** and were modified today. Attributes and sets make this looping and testing implicit.

6.3 Unifying the Interface, the Program and the Process

In general, programming forces users to navigate in two distinct work spaces[1]: the *physical* reality of the data, computer and programming language and the *psychological* reality of their mental model. The larger the gap between these work spaces, the more difficult the programming process[11], because users are forced to make paradigm shifts between the two spaces[3]. By integrating familiar visual representations within three different parts of the PBD system – the program representation, the communication of inferences, and the editor – Pursuit's visual language attempts to reduce these paradigm shifts. This saves time, decreases working memory load and reduces the chance for errors.

7 Status and Future Work

A prototype of Pursuit[21] has been implemented using Garnet[24]. We have been doing informal user studies to improve the system. For example, Pursuit initially contained a heuristic that often eliminated the prologue of the first operation of a program. Since several people had difficulty understanding scripts in which this heuristic was applied, it was eliminated. Further studies should help refine Pursuit's heuristics both in generating panels and generating attributes on sets.

In addition, we recognize that Pursuit programs can be space-inefficient and are exploring ways to remedy this, such as enabling users to select a sequence of panels to collapse into a single panel or automatically collapsing explicit loops into a single small panel.

Currently, Pursuit contains an editor to enable users to change set attributes; copy, cut and paste operations; add loops and user-defined branches; and demonstrate unfinished paths. We are expanding the editor to help insure that users do not create meaningless programs. For example, if the user deletes a **copy** operation then all subsequent operations that use the output copies could be deleted.

We are also exploring other ways of using visual representations as feedback, such as with animation. For example, consider the dialog box in Figure 9. Instead of suddenly appearing in the middle of the screen, a representation of the file set could emerge from the script, move to the center of the screen, and expand into the dialog box. Similarly, rather than disappearing instantly, the dialog box could shrink back into the set icon. Adding this animation would more closely link dialog boxes to the relevant section of the visual script.

Finally, formal user studies are planned to evaluate the system and determine how easy it is to use, how easy the visual language is to recall, and how well the system supports automating tasks.

8 Conclusion

We have presented a visual language that serves as both the main form of feedback and program representation for a demonstrational visual shell. By integrating visual feedback *throughout* the PBD system, Pursuit helps bridge the gap between users' mental model and the difficult task of programming. This should make the PBD system more effective.

9 Acknowledgments

The authors thank the participants at the Apple Computer 1992 Programming by Demonstration Workshop, especially Allan Cypher, David Kosbie, David Kurlander and David Maulsby, for helpful and continued feedback on this work. We also thank James Landay for his comments on this paper. This research was supported by NSF grant number IRI-9020089 and by grants from the Hertz Foundation and AAUW.

References

1. D. Ackermann and J. Stelovsky. The Role of Mental Models in Programming: From Experiments to Requirements for an Interactive System. In P. Gorny and M.J. Tauber, editors, *Visualization in Programming*, pages 53–69. Springer-Verlag, 1986.
2. Kjell Borg. IShell: A Visual UNIX Shell. In *Proceedings of CHI '90*, pages 201–207, Seattle, Washington, April 1990.
3. Wayne Citrin. Visualization-Based Visual Programming. Technical Report CU-CS-535-91, Unversity of Colorado, July 1991.
4. Allen Cypher. EAGER: Programming Repetitive Tasks by Example. In *Proceedings of CHI '91*, pages 33–40, New Orleans, LA, April 1991.
5. Allen Cypher. *Watch What I Do: Programming by Demonstration*. The MIT Press, Cambridge, MA, 1993.
6. Stephanie M. Doane, James W. Pellegrino, and Roberta L. Klatzky. Expertise in a Computer Operation System: Conceptualization and Performance. *Human-Computer Interaction*, 5:267–304, 1990.
7. William Finzer and Laura Gould. Programming by Rehearsal. *Byte Magazine*, 9(6):187–210, June 1984.
8. P.E. Haeberli. ConMan: A Visual Programming Language for Interactive Graphics. In *ACM SIGGRAPH*, pages 103–111, Atlanta, Ga, 1988.
9. Daniel C. Halbert. *Programming by Example*. PhD thesis, Computer Science Division, University of California, Berkeley, CA, 1984.

10. Tyson R. Henry and Scott E. Hudson. Squish: A Graphical Shell for UNIX. In *Graphics Interface*, pages 43–49, 1988.

11. Edwin L. Hutchins, James D. Hollan, and Donald A. Norman. Direct Manipulation Interfaces. In Donald A. Norman and Stephen W. Draper, editors, *User Centered System Design*, chapter 5, pages 87–124. Lawrence Erlbaum Associates, Hillsdale, New Jersey, 1986.

12. Branka Jovanovic and James D. Foley. A Simple Graphics Interface to UNIX. Technical Report GWU-IIST-86-23, The George Washington University, Institute for Information Science and Technology, Washington, DC 20052, 1986.

13. David Kurlander and Steven Feiner. Editable Graphical Histories. In *IEEE Workshop on Visual Languages*, pages 127–134, Pittsburgh, PA 15213, October 1988.

14. Henry Lieberman. Constructing Graphical User Interfaces By Example. In *Graphics Interface '82*, pages 295–302, Toronto, Ontario, Canada, May 1982.

15. Henry Lieberman. Capturing Design Expertise Interactively by Example. In *East-West Conference on Human-Computer Interaction*, St. Petersburg, Russia, August 1992.

16. Henry Lieberman. Mondrian: A Teachable Graphical Editor. In *Proceedings of InterCHI '93*, page 144, April 1993.

17. David L. Maulsby and Ian H. Witten. Inducing Programs in a Direct-Manipulation Environment. In *Proceedings of CHI '89*, pages 57–62, Austin, Tx, April 1989.

18. David L. Maulsby, Ian H. Witten, Kenneth A. Kittlitz, and Valerio G. Franceschin. Inferring Graphical Procedures: The Compleat Metamouse. Technical Report 91/388/12, Department of Computer Science, The University of Calgary, Calgary, Alberta, Canada, May 1990.

19. Francesmary Modugno. *Pursuit: Adding Programming to the Interface*. PhD thesis, Carnegie Mellon University, In progress.

20. Francesmary Modugno and Brad A. Myers. Graphical Representation and Feedback in a PBD System. In Allen Cypher, editor, *Watch What I Do: Programming By Demonstration*, chapter 20. MIT Press, 1993.

21. Francesmary Modugno and Brad A. Myers. Pursuit: Graphically Representing Programs in a Demonstrational Visual Shell. In *Proceedings of CHI '94*, April 1994. Video Program Presentation.

22. Brad A. Myers. *Creating User Interfaces by Demonstration*. Academic Press, Boston, Massachusetts, 1988.

23. Brad A. Myers. Demonstrational Interfaces: A Step Beyond Direct Manipulation. *IEEE Computer*, 25(8):61–73, August 1992.

24. Brad A. Myers et al. Garnet: Comprehensive Support for Graphical, Highly-Interactive User Interfaces. *IEEE Computer*, 23(11):71–85, November 1990.

25. Ben Shneiderman. Direct Manipulation: A Step Beyond Programming Languages. *Computer*, 16(8):57–69, August 1983.

ARGS: Autogenerating Documented Command Line Interfaces

Damian Conway

Victorian Centre for Image Processing and Graphics
Department of Computer Science
Monash University
Clayton, Victoria 3168
Australia
email: damian@bruce.cs.monash.edu.au

Abstract: The surprising lack of research into one of the most common forms of human-computer interaction – command line interfaces – is noted, and reasons for this deficiency suggested. The features and inadequacies of existing command line interface design systems and methodologies are discussed. A new grammar-based system for creating command-line interfaces (with integrated facilities for processing initialization files and environment variables) is described.

1 Introduction

The command line interface is widely disparaged in the HCI community as well-understood, trivial and unworthy of study, yet it still represents one of the most widely-used mediums for human-computer interaction.

References to the problems of interface design for command line systems are almost non-existent in the literature. The exception seems to be Hansen, Kraut and Farber [1] who have studied human-computer interaction via a command line interface. They found serious design flaws in many command-line driven systems and concluded that inconsistent or otherwise inadequate command line syntax design was a predominant cause of user error.

In their study, commands with poorly designed command syntaxes (such as the UNIX commands *at* and *find*) were prone to specification error rates of up to 53% Worse still, subsequent attempts to re-execute an unsuccessful command showed a *higher* probability of failure than on the original attempt. Hansen et al. concluded (rather conservatively) that the feedback users received after an error "does not often help them."

The cause of these inhibiting inconsistencies is not hard to determine. Analysis of a range of standard command line driven applications under UNIX [2] reveals a wide diversity of styles of argument specification, processing and even terminology[1] in evidence. Conventions (amounting to de

---

[1] In this paper four terms will be used throughout in describing the components of command lines. A *syntax* is a specification of the grammatical structure(s) permitted on the command line. An *argument* is a semantic place holder for a string to be supplied on the command line. A *flag* is a regular expression to be matched by a string supplied on the command line. A *subargument* is an argument which is defined only in the context of a leading flag.

facto standards) have evolved in an ad hoc fashion, and their usefulness, efficiency and consistency appears never to have been analyzed from a human factors perspective. Clearly, despite prevailing opinion, much work remains to be done on this style of computer interface.

In attempting to understand why it should be so difficult to achieve uniformity, clarity and predictability in a command line interface, it is important to consider the process of creating such interfaces. Generally, command-line processing is coded in the application language by a systems engineer. This person is typically preoccupied with the implementation of the application itself and, having no expertise in the field of interface design, constructs the command-line syntax "on-the-fly" and in a haphazard (or at best evolutionary) manner.

The systems engineer has little choice in this matter, as the HCI community has not seen fit to provide any research (let alone design tools) to assist the process of command-line interface design. Hence the software developer's own poorly-mediated interaction with computers dooms the end-user to a similar fate.

In such circumstances, the end-user has little recourse but to rely upon on-line interface documentation for assistance in coping with the poor or non-existent design of the interface. Unfortunately, as Knuth [3] observed, such documentation (when it exists at all) is one of the *least* consistent aspects of the hundreds of actual command line interfaces in common use.

Typical on-line documentation of a UNIX application consists of a terse error message, possibly summarizing the various legal syntaxes, and a somewhat more extensive *man* page, detailing the functions of the various components of those syntaxes. These resources are essential to the user but are tedious to create and time-consuming to maintain. These problems lead to incomplete, inconsistent or non-existent documentation [3].

The Argument Recognition Grammar System (*ARGS*) is an attempt to address the appalling lack of research into command-line interface design. *ARGS* provides a command line interface specification technique that is grammar-based, easy to learn, easy to use, flexible, robust, self-documenting, portable and widely applicable. *ARGS* is targeted primarily at the C and C++ programming languages but also provides an interpretive mode suitable for embedding in other languages (in particular, command shells.)

2 Existing Command Line Interface Specification Systems

The idea of providing interface building tools for command-driven software is not in itself new. There is an abundance of public-domain command line processing systems in common use. This section summarizes some of the properties of eleven separate packages [4,5,6,7,8,9,10,11] published in various Internet newsgroups over the past five years, and compares them with *ARGS*.

System	Author	Defn Lang.	Target Lang.	Flags	Args	Usage Msg.	Syntax
argproc	Steve Colwell	C	C	ESMm	P	GDSC	single explicit
cli	Darren Platt	C++	C++	ESs	P	DC	single emergent
CmdLine	Brad Appleton	C++	C++ and others	USMm	PN	GDC	single emergent
copt	Nigel Perry	C	C	USMm	PN	N	single emergent
DGetopt	David Arnstein	C++	C++	ESMs	P	GDE	multiple emergent
getlongopt	S. Manorahan	C++	C++	USMs	P	GC	single emergent
getopt	Henry Spenser	C	C	ESs	P	GES	single emergent
optgen	Panos Tsirigotis	custom	C	EMm	P	GS	single explicit
options	Brad Appleton	C++	C++	USMm	P	GEC	single emergent
parse	William R. Ward	C	C	ESs	U	N	single common
ParseArgs	Brad Appleton	C++	C++ and others	USMm	PN	GDC	single emergent
ARGS	Damian Conway	custom	C, C++, others	any regex	PN	GDCA	multiple explicit/ emergent

Key

Flags:
S = Single character flags
M = Multiple character flags
C = Can concatenate single character flags
s = Single subarguments permitted
m = Multiple subarguments permitted
E = Requires an exact match
U = Requires only a unique prefix match

Arguments: P = Are specified by position
N = May be specified by name
U = Are not supported

Usage Message:
N = Not automated in any way
G = Automatically generated
D = Automatically displayed
E = Shows error messages only
S = Shows brief syntax only
F = Shows full detail of syntax
C = Detail shown is configurable
A = Detail shown is adaptive

Fig. 1. Summary of a range of command line processing systems

The packages range from the extremely simple (*parse* and *getopt*, for example) to the quite elaborate (*CmdLine* and *getlongopts*). Eight of then are based on the specification of individual arguments, flags and subarguments (either via special functions or as C++ class objects). The syntax of the command line is then the concatenation of these components, possibly with some constraints specification. The other two packages require the user to specify the syntax of the command line explicitly.

All but two of the packages can automatically generate at least a rudimentary usage message describing the syntax of a program, but the majority of them then require the message to be explicitly issued by the program, rather than doing so automatically when a syntax error is detected.

Most systems cater to a single target language but several (including *ARGS*) provide a separate argument interpreter to handle other languages, usually command shells of various species.

Of the twelve packages, only *optgen* and *ARGS* use a preprocessing strategy and a special purpose specification language. This is surprising, since command line processing is a restricted form of input parsing, a domain in which most specifications are preprocessed [12].

3 Existing Documentation Systems

Program documentation systems are also widely available, and appear to fall into three major categories – literate programming tools, code summary generators and the usage message generators built into most command line processing systems.

Literate programming systems, such as *CWEB* [13], *NOWEB* [14], *FunnelWeb* [15] and *CLip* [16], stem from work by Knuth [17] aimed at overcoming the problems of synchronizing documentation and code. Such systems provide mechanisms whereby the programmer can intermix natural and computer languages in a single file, which can then be processed to produce formatted documentation and/or compilable source code.

Code summary generators, such as *genman* [18], *Docclass* [19] and *c2man* [20], take (annotated) source code and extract details about the interface between program modules. This information is the formatted into a standard template (often the well-known UNIX *man* page layout.) Such systems are an effective means of documenting individual components of a program (usually variables, functions and/or classes) but perform poorly when attempting to document the behaviour of the entire program.

Some systems (for example *C2Latex* [21]) straddle the gap between literate programming and code summary generation. However, except for *ARGS*, no single system of which the author is aware is capable of generating a multi-syntax command line interface, embedded usage and error messages, and textual summary pages for a program.

4 The *ARGS* system

The *ARGS* preprocessor system enables the software engineer to explicitly or implicitly specify command line syntaxes relevant to a particular program, as well as specifying the program's interaction with environment variables and initialization files.

ARGS encourages consistency in command-line interfaces in a number of ways. It supports standard argument sets, which may be shared by all programs developed with *ARGS*. It automatically generates common command line flags which provide the user with version and usage information. It supports an interpreter mode so that the interfaces to command shell scripts can be specified in the same manner as for compiled programs.

ARGS can generate type-safe argument processing code, including appropriate global variables for storing values derived from the command line, environment or initialization file. *ARGS* provides a simple means of embedding documentation within source code and can format that information in two ways, either as a range of usage messages produced by the program itself or as a textual document. *ARGS* is also aware of comments within the program source and will use these as well when documenting.

To use *ARGS*, a programmer embeds an interface specification grammar within the `main()` function of the source code of a C or C++ program. The source file is preprocessed to generate a table-driven top-down parser in which input tokens are lazily recognized using small finite state machines. The processed source code is then compiled using a standard C or C++ compiler. The implementation details of the *ARGS* system and the parsers it generates are described in [22]. This paper summarizes most of the features of the *ARGS* specification/documentation language and demonstrates two types of command line interface which may be created with them.

The specification of embedded program documentation within a source file consists of a series of information fields enclosed in a pair of delimiters: `#args` and `#endargs`. The information that may be specified using these fields and the types of documentation *ARGS* can produce is described in §4.1.

The specification of command line processing within a source file consists of up to four distinct sections, which are also enclosed in `#args`/`#endargs` delimiters[1]. These sections, which are described in §4.2 to §4.5, may be specified in any sequence. If any section is omitted entirely, the corresponding interface behaviour is disabled. The order of the four sections is significant, in that it determines the order in which the relevant interface behaviours are executed. By reordering the sections, the program designer can specify any of the sixteen possible processing sequences for various subsets of the three input channels.

---

[1]Either in the same pair of delimiters as the information fields, or in one or more separate delimiters, all of which are concatenated prior to preprocessing. The generated code replaces the first set of delimiters in the `main()` function.

The final sections of this paper illustrate the use of the *ARGS* system in documenting and creating interfaces for two programs: the UNIX file archive command *tar* (implemented in C), and a simple text processor (implemented as a *csh* shell script).

4.1 Program Documentation

The *ARGS* documentation section within a source code file is a series of free form documentation fields. Each field is introduced by a keyword, which is only reserved at the start of each line. Note that some keywords have two variants – a singular and a plural form – so that the specifications of these fields may be written so as to read naturally.

Keyword	Purpose of corresponding documentation field
`Program:`	Used in the text document. The first blank-delimited character sequence is taken as the name of the program. Any remaining text is treated as a brief statement of the program's purpose. If no information is specified, the source file name prefix is used (for example, the source file `demo.c` yields a program name "demo").
`Description:` `Author(s):`	Used in the text document and the long help flag. If the Author field is present but empty, the name of the user invoking the preprocessor is used.
`Version:` `Revision:`	Used in the text document and the version flags. If no information is specified, *ARGS* looks for an *RCS* or *SCCS* version number or, failing that, generates a version string based on the time of preprocessing.

`Support:`
`Contact(s):`
`Copyright(s):`
	Used in the text document and the long version flag. If the Support and Contact fields are empty, *ARGS* assumes the user invoking the preprocessor is responsible. If the Copyright field is specified without text, *ARGS* assigns copyright to the person named in the Author field, if it was specified.

`Algorithm(s):`
`See Also:`
`Diagnostic(s):`
`Bug(s):`
	If present, this information is included in the appropriate sections of the text document. If these fields are empty, they are ignored.

`Message:`	Appended to output produced by the long help flag.

Fig. 2. *ARGS* embedded documentation fields and their purpose.

The body of each field consists of arbitrarily formatted text (including line breaks) followed by an optional C++ comment (which may be used to specify "hidden" information). Figure 2 summarizes the purpose of each documentation field. See Figures 4 and 5 for examples of their use.

Note that in most cases, if a field is specified without any accompanying text (that is, just the keyword is given), *ARGS* attempts to generate suitable information from other on-line sources. If a field is omitted entirely (that is, the keyword itself does not appear), no information is generated for it.

ARGS will also scan the entire source code text looking for comments which commence with a documentation field keyword. For example:

```
/* Algorithm:   Loop  forever...                    */

//Diagnostic:   Exit  status  -1 if fork failed

# Bug:          Parsing  should  be  case  sensitive
```

Such comments enable documentation fields to be distributed throughout the code, which is often more appropriate than collecting such information in a single location. The information specified is treated as if it had been placed in the `#args/#endargs` block, with the ordering of the information mirroring the ordering of the comments.

ARGS uses the information provided in the documentation fields to generate a textual summary of the source file. The format of this summary is controlled by a template (which defaults to the standard UNIX *man* page format.) New templates can be created to redefine which documentation fields are included in summaries and how those fields are to be formatted (see [22] for details of this mechanism.) A global formatting template is usually specified in a `.ARGSdoc` file in the user's home directory, but may be locally overridden by a `.ARGSdoc` file in the source directory.

Flag	Description
`-v`	Prints out the version number of the program.
`-version` `-V`	Returns version information for the program, including version number, copyright information, date compiled and support contact information.
`-h`	Prints out an automatically generated synopsis of the available command line syntaxes.
`-help` `-H`	Prints out the syntax, argument and flag details and all the information produced by the `-version` flag.

Fig. 3. Automatically generated flags

In addition to generating textual summaries, *ARGS* automatically generates two flags (summarized in Figure 3.) Each flag comes in a short and long form and produces, naturally enough, a short or long information response on standard output. The automatically generated flags cannot be combined with other syntaxes and terminate the program immediately after printing out their information.

4.2 Environment Specification

The Environment section specifies environment variables which are significant to the program. It is introduced by the keyword **Environment:** (or its abbreviation, **Env:**) within the **#args/#endargs** delimiters.

Each environment variable specification consists of a (case-sensitive) identifier followed by an optional comment and up to two optional code blocks[1]. The first of these blocks is executed prior to the environment variable being retrieved, and the second, after it is loaded. If only one code block is specified, it is executed after the environment variable is retrieved. For each specification, *ARGS* generates code which searches for the named environment variable and returns its value (accessible as **$1**) to the last code block. If the variable is not found, neither code block is executed.

In addition, the environment variable may be specified with an explicit type, using a syntax similar to a C/C++ declaration. This causes *ARGS* to generate a global variable declaration with the same name as the environment variable and to assign the value of the environment variable to the global (with an explicit cast to the type declared for the variable). See §4.5 for more details.

4.3 Specification of Initialization Files

The Initialization section defines the search path for initialization files and is introduced by the keyword **Initialization:** (or its abbreviation **Init:**).

Initialization files may contain one or more arguments or flags, which must be specified as belonging to the special flag set {**INIT**} (see section §4.5). If an initialization file is found, its contents are read in and processed just as if they had appeared on the command line.

Each entry in the Initialization section must appear on a separate line and consists of a file name and an optional specification of the comment introducer character(s) for that file. The default comment introducer is "#". Each

---

[1]Note that the same "specification-then-comment-then-code-block(s)" structure is also used in the other interface definition sections of the *ARGS* specification (see §4.3-4.5.)

specification may be followed by a comment and/or code blocks (which are executed only if an initialization file is found.)

By default, all initialization files which can be located are processed in the sequence specified. In order to control the sequence of the search, one of the symbols | (OR) or & (AND) may be specified before each filename. AND has the higher precedence (as in C and C++) and is used to group sequences of initialization files between ORs. When a file is located, it is processed (as described above) and the search continues on any subsequent files ANDed to the located file, until an OR is encountered.

If the initialization section is specified but no entries are included in the path, the default search path consists of the current directory and the home directory If there is no initialization section specified or the flag set {INIT} is empty, *ARGS* does not generate initialization code.

4.4 Command Line Syntax Specification

The Syntax section specifies one or more alternative command line syntaxes for a program, and is introduced by the keyword **Syntax:**. If this section is omitted, the command line syntax is automatically constructed by concatenating individual components specified in the Arguments section (see §4.5), in a similar manner to the emergent syntax systems described in §2.

Each alternative syntax must appear on a single line and may be followed by an optional comment and/or code blocks (see Figures 4 and 5 for examples). Note that the entire line is taken as a syntactic specification, hence any comment and the code blocks must commence on or after the following line.

ARGS generates code which causes at most one of the alternative syntaxes to be chosen and its corresponding block(s) to be executed. The substrings of the command line which are matched by each component of the syntax are available within the last code block as **$1**, **$2**, etc. If no syntax can be chosen, an error message describing the allowed syntax(es) is automatically generated. If more than one syntax could match the command line, the alternative which was specified first is always selected.

In each syntax, required arguments are represented by an identifier within a pair of angle brackets. Each such argument matches the next sequence of non-blank characters appearing in the command line. Failure to find any characters to match causes the syntactic alternative currently being tried to be rejected as a candidate syntax for the current invocation of the program.

Unlike most other command line interface systems, *ARGS* does not require flags to commence with "−" or "+", nor indeed that flags be fixed literal strings at all. Instead, required flags are specified as unenclosed extended regular expressions. Each required flag must match exactly against the next sequence of non-blank characters in the command line[1]. Failure to exactly match a required flag causes its candidate syntax of which it is a part to be immediately rejected as a parser for the current invocation of the program.

It is also possible to specify a set of flags (see §4.5 below), any one of which may appear in a given position. Such flag sets are specified by enclosing the name of the set in a pair of curly brackets[2] (for example, {key} in Figure 4.) The predefined (and reserved) flag set specifier {*} represents the set of all flags belonging to any user-defined flag set except {INIT}.

Sometimes it is desirable to create a syntax in which flags may appear at any position on the command line. If a flag set is specified with colons surrounding the set name (for example, {:key:}) it is treated as a non-localized flag set. Such a specification indicates that exactly one flag belonging to the flag set must be matched at some (unspecified) position on the command line. By extension, the non-localized flag set specification {:*:} requires that exactly one flag from *any* user-defined flag set (except {INIT}) appear somewhere on the command line.

The position at which such non-localized flag sets are specified within a syntax determines the matching priority of the flag set. When attempting to match a command line string, *ARGS* will prefer to match the next available localized syntactic component if that component was specified before a given non-localized flag set, but will prefer the flag set if it was specified first. Hence, placing a non-localized flag set at the beginning of the line forces *ARGS* to match one of its components in preference to any local component, whilst placing the set at the end of a line reduces it to a "default" matching option.

A repeating argument, flag or flag set may be specified by suffixing it with an ellipsis (. . .), which acts as a "one-or-more" specifier. The substring(s) matched by the ith repeated component, i, are available within the code block of the syntax as $i(1), $i(2), etc. The number of substrings matched is available as $#i.

Syntax components (arguments, flags and flag sets) may also specified as optional, by enclosing them in a pair of round brackets[3] (including any ellipsis - which then act as "zero-or-more" specifiers). Optional components are matched from the command line exactly as their required equivalents, except that failure to match them does not invalidate a syntax.

---

[1] Note that this implies than an argument is equivalent to the flag [\t \n]+.

[2] To specify curly brackets as literal parts of a flag they should be escaped using a backslash.

[3] Flags which use surrounding round brackets to group regular expressions cannot be specified directly in a syntax. This is not a significant problem however, as the surrounding brackets are redundant in this context. Literal surrounding round brackets (with would match actual bracket characters supplied on the command line) can be specified by escaping the brackets with a backslash.

4.5 Specification Of Individual Command Line Components

The Arguments section specifies and/or documents particular properties and behaviours of the individual components (arguments and flags) of the various syntaxes. The section is introduced by the keyword **Arguments:** (or its abbreviation **Args:**).

Only those syntax components which need explicit documentation or which have some non-default behaviour need be specified in this section, although it is good practice to document all components. The order in which components are specified is not significant, unless no Syntax section is given, in which case the order defines the (single) syntax of the command line. The position of the Arguments section with respect to the other three sections is also irrelevant, unless no Syntax section is given, in which case the relative position of the section determines when argument processing is carried out.

Each argument or flag is specified on a separate single line, exactly as it appears in the Syntax section, except that flags may optionally be specified with subarguments that do not appear in the syntax. Each component may optionally be followed by an comment and up to two code blocks (see Figures 4 and 5.)

The code blocks associated with each argument or flag are executed whenever the component is matched within whichever candidate syntax is ultimately selected. Once again, the first block is executed immediately prior to retrieval of the component value and the second block immediately after retrieval. The value of the character string(s) which matched the component is available within the second code block as $1, $2, etc.

Flags may be defined as belonging to one or more flag sets by adding a curly-bracketed, comma-separated list of the set names at the end of the flag specification line. If the list is empty or no list is specified, the flag does not belong to any set (including the otherwise universal set {*}.) If the list consists of a single asterisk, the flag is defined as belonging to all available user-defined flag sets, except {INIT}.

As with environment variable specifications (§4.2 above), each argument or flag may optionally be specified with an arbitrary type (either inbuilt or user-defined). Such type declarations cause *ARGS* to generate a suitable global variable declaration just prior to the main() function. If the component matches a substring of the command line, that value (still accessed as $1) is cast to the specified type and assigned to the global variable just prior to the execution of the last code block.

ARGS understands the inbuilt C/C++ types **void, char, int, float, double** and their **long, short, signed, unsigned** and pointer variants, and will type-check and correctly convert values of these types, issuing error an message on type incompatibility. Declaring a component as **void** explicitly indicates that it is untyped and does not cause a global variable to be generated for that component.

ARGS also recognizes the user-defined type **boolean** a synonym for **int**, except that the value assigned to the corresponding global variable is always non-zero if the component is matched, and zero otherwise[1]. If the first character of the matching command line substring is a minus sign, the non-zero value assigned is negative; otherwise it is positive. This allows the program to easily distinguish between a flags starting with '-' and '+'. The C++ inbuilt type **bool** is handled in a similar manner, except that flag signs are ignored, as **bool** is an unsigned type.

Any component declared with an inbuilt type may be have that type declared within brackets (like a C/C++ typecast), in which case *ARGS* still does type checking, but does not generates a corresponding global variable. The command line substring matched by the component is still available as the character string $1 within the last code block.

Note that *ARGS* assumes that, for any flag specification consisting of a valid C/C++ identifier followed by one or more strings, the first string is a type specification and not a flag. In order to declare an untyped multi-string flag where the first string happens to be an identifier, the flag should be explicitly declared of type **void**. For example:

```
help me        // Flag "me" of type "help"

void help me // Untyped flag "help me"
```

Arguments, flags and subarguments may be marked as "prompted". Prompted components do not invalidate a syntax if omitted, even if they are required. Rather, they are assumed to be available for later input. Once a syntax has been selected, the missing components are requested via standard output and read in via standard input. To mark a component as prompted, its specification line is commenced with the keyword **prompted**. Note that the string **prompted** is only a keyword at the beginning of a specification line (that is, immediately following a newline).

Arguments may also be "named". Like ordinary arguments, named arguments may be specified positionally on the command line. However, they may alternatively be specified via an associated flag, which is automatically generated by *ARGS*. For example, the argument specification:

```
named <file>
```

automatically generates an associated flag:

```
file = <file>
```

When attempting to match any candidate syntax containing the named positional argument `<file>`, *ARGS* prescans the command line for the associated flag and "pre-matches" the named argument if that flag appears. If the argument is successfully pre-matched, it will be temporarily removed

---

[1]By comparsion, declaring a flag of type **int** causes the corresponding variable to be assigned the value zero unless the flag matched a string of digits, in which case the value assigned would be the integer represented by those digits (possibly 0!).

from the syntax (unless it is specified as a multiple argument). If pre-matching fails, the named argument must be matched positionally (that is, as if it were an unnamed argument.)

Short flags, which consist of a plus or minus sign followed by a single non-whitespace character, are treated specially when the command line is parsed. If the syntax permits, two or more of these arguments may be entered on the command line as a single substring, by omitting the leading sign characters of all but the first flag (another standard UNIX practice).

5 Specification Of Standard (Shared) Interfaces

It is often the case that a suite of related programs share common command line interface features. For example, most applications designed to run under the X windowing system provide a standard set of command line options (the "toolkit" options) which allow the user to set target display device, window geometry, window colour and text font information. The use of such standard argument sets greatly improves the uniformity, and hence the predictability, of a collection of related programs.

To accommodate this style of interface *ARGS* allows the software engineer to specify one or more standard sets of interface features which are then shared by every program processed with *ARGS*. These standard sets are specified within the file .**ARGSstd**, which may be placed in the same directory as the source files or in the home directory. Standard sets specified in the home directory are shared by all applications processed with *ARGS*. Standard sets specified in any other directory are shared by all applications processed with *ARGS* from that directory.

Any interface feature supported by *ARGS* (documentation fields, syntaxes, environment variables, initialization files, flags or arguments) may be specified as part of a standard set. The specified features are added[1] to the relevant sections of the *ARGS* specification of each source file processed.

6 An example of an *ARGS* specification – *tar*

Figure 4 presents the **main()** function from a source file containing the *ARGS* specification for an abbreviated version the standard UNIX archive utility *tar*[2]. Note that *tar* is driven by its command line arguments, so the *ARGS* specification comprises the entire **main()** function.

---

[1] By default, elements of a standard set are appended to the specification. However, *ARGS* provides a modifier keyword, **Prepended**, which causes the component(s) thus specified to be processed before those in the source file.

[2] *Tar* has a large complement of flags and an *ARGS* specification of the full version would require about 4 pages. The omitted flags similar in function to those shown in Figure 4 and would be specified in exactly the same manner.

```
main(int  argc,char  **argv)
{
#args
    Program:      tar - tape archiver

    Description:tar saves  and  restores  multiple
                files  on  a  single  file.

    Author:       Damian  Conway

    Syntax:       ({mod}...)  {key}  ({mod}...)  ({name}...)

    Arguments:
        boolean   -?r                    {key}
                  // Append  files  to  archive

        boolean   -?u                    {key}
                  // Update  files  in  archive

        boolean   -?x                    {key}
                  // Extract  files  from  archive

        boolean   -?p                    {mod}
                  // Restore  files  to  original  modes

        -?b  <block>                     {mod}
                  // Specify  blocking  size  in  kB
        unsigned  long  <block>

        -f  <file>                       {mod}
                  // Use  <file>  instead  of  /dev/tape
        char*  <file>

        <name>                           {name}
                  // Next  file/dir  to  archive
                  {  doArchive($1);  }

        -C  <dir>                        {name}
                  // Change  to  directory  <dir>
                  {  chdir($2);  }

    See  Also:    mtio(2),  tps(2)

    Bug:          There  is  no  way  to  ask  for  the  n-th
                  occurrence  of  a  file

#endargs
}
```

Fig. 4. An *ARGS* specification for the *tar* command.

The *ARGS* interface identifies the required operation by automatically setting one or more of the automatically generated global boolean variables **r**, **u**, **x** and **p**, according to the key flag and modifiers specified on the command line. The files to be archived are then processed by passing each filename to the user-defined function **doArchive()**. This function inspects the variables **r**, **u**, **x** and **p** to determined which action is to be carried out. Other autogenerated variables, such as **block** and **file** are also checked to determine blocking factors, output files, etc.

7 Command Line Processing for Other Languages

ARGS provides an interpreter mode, which attempts to match a command line string (passed on the interpreter command line) against an *ARGS* specification (passed via the standard input stream). *ARGS* interprets the command line according to the specified syntax and copies to standard output the contents of the code blocks of all matched components and syntax. A program can initiate an interprocess call to the *ARGS* interpreter, have it parse the command line and then capture the output in order to process the identified components.

Where a program is written in an interpreted language which can directly evaluate strings, the interpreter can be used almost as easily as in a C or C++ program. The commands to be executed are coded directly into the specification which is piped to the interpreter. The code block contents returned are piped into the string evaluation command for immediate execution.

Although it requires that *ARGS* be present on any system where the application is to be used, this client-server approach to command line processing has two important advantages:

- It does not require that the *ARGS* interpreter be able to parse the programming language in which the application is written. Hence this style of command line processing greatly extends the range of existing and future languages with which *ARGS* can be used.

- It may significantly reduce the collective size of executables, by eliminating the need to embed similar command line parsing code in every application. This usually also means that compilation times are commensurately reduced.

Figure 5 illustrates this approach using the *csh* command language. Note that all the features of a preprocessed *ARGS* specification (with the obvious exception of autogenerated variables) are also available in interpreter mode.

The *textproc* shell script is defined to have a single syntax consisting of two optional arguments followed by a required flag. The arguments are "named" so that they may be explicitly specified on the command line using the automatically generated flags **from=** and **to=**. The regular expressions describing the two flags are specified in such a way that they may be truncated after the first distinguishing letter.

The *csh* script calls *ARGS* in interpreter mode, passing its command line arguments via *ARGS'* command line, and its interface specification via *ARGS'* standard input. *ARGS* then evaluates the command line in terms of the specification and prints out the contents of the appropriate code blocks. In this case the instructions in each code block must end with a semi-colon as they will subsequently be concatenated into a single line by the *csh* script.

The *csh* script captures the output of *ARGS* (by surrounding the *ARGS* invocation with back-quotes) and evaluates the resulting code block contents using its inbuilt **eval** command.

```
#!  /bin/csh

set from = `tty`        # Default input from std input
set to   = `tty`        # Default output to std output

eval `ARGS -interpret $0 $argv` << 'END'
#args
    Program:    textproc - A simple text utility

    Description:textproc exists to demonstrate
                the ARGS interpreter mode

    Syntax:
        (<from>)  (<to>)  {cmd}

    Arguments:
        named <from>
            // Input file
            // $1 belongs to ARGS not csh!
            { set from = $1; }

        named <to>
            // Output file
            { set to = $1; }

        -r<ot13>                        {cmd}
            // Shroud the input text
            { tr A-Za-z N-ZA-Mn-za-m <${from} >${to}; }

        -q<uote>                        {cmd}
            // Quote the input text
            { sed 's/^/> /' <${from} >${to}; }
#endargs
'END'
```

Fig. 5. Command line processing for *csh*, using interpreter mode.

8 Conclusion and Future Work

The *ARGS* system addresses many of the deficiencies of existing command line interface development tools, providing the software engineer with a uniform and flexible method of specifying flag and argument handling. *ARGS* enables the processing of environment variables, initialization files and the command line to be sequenced and integrated. The specification grammar has a straightforward and simple syntax, and allows common interface configurations to be predefined and reused for related applications, thereby promoting greater consistency between interfaces.

The preprocessor automatically generates usage and error messages and can also produce textual documentation, even in the absence of full information. The command line parsers produced are capable of selecting between multiple command line syntaxes, whilst adhering to most UNIX conventions. The *ARGS* preprocessor produces code which may be compiled using standard C or C++ compilers, but may also be used (in interpreter mode) with any language which supports stream-based interprocess communication.

Work is currently underway on porting *ARGS* to other command line oriented operating systems , in particular VMS and DOS. In addition, preprocessor mode support for other programming languages, including Pascal, Eiffel and Fortran is currently being examined.

Another interesting possibility currently under investigation is the use of *ARGS* specifications to generate forms-based graphical interfaces to programs. For example, instead of printing an error message in response to an incorrect command line, an application might display a window containing fields and buttons corresponding to the arguments and flags of each of the permissible syntaxes for the program. The interface could ensure command line correctness by sequentially deactivating parts of the interface which are incompatible with previous choices. Such a system might successfully address the problem of repeated errors discussed by Hanson et al. [1], by replacing a recall task with a (much simpler) recognition task after the first failed attempt.

References

[1] Hanson, S.J., Kraut, R.E. & Farber, J.M., *Interface Design and Multivariate Analysis of UNIX Command Use*, ACM Transactions on Office Information Systems, vol.2, no.1, pp. 42-57, March 1984.

[2] Sobell, M., *A Practical Guide to the Unix System V Release 4*, Benjamin-Cummings, 1991.

[3] Brooks, F.P., *Self Documenting Programs*, in "The Mythical Man-Month, Essays on Software Engineering", pp.169-175, Addison-Wesley, 1975.

[4]   Colwell, S., *argproc*, comp.source.misc archive, wuarchive.wustl.edu, vol. 2, 1988.

[5]   Appleton, B., *CmdLine*, comp.source.misc archive, wuarchive.wustl.edu, vol. 31, 1992.

[6]   Perry, N., *copt*, comp.source.misc archive, wuarchive.wustl.edu, vol. 6, 1989.

[7]   Manorahan, S., *getlongopt*, comp.source.misc archive, wuarchive.wustl.edu, vol. 35, 1993.

[8]   Spenser, H., *getopt*, comp.source.misc archive, wuarchive.wustl.edu, vol. 2, 1988.

[9]   Appleton, B., *options*, comp.source.misc archive, wuarchive.wustl.edu, vol. 31, 1992.

[10]   Ward, W.R., *parse*, comp.source.misc archive, wuarchive.wustl.edu, vol. 16, 1991

[11]   Appleton, B., *ParseArgs*, comp.source.misc archive, wuarchive.wustl.edu, vol. 10, 1990.

[12]   Aho, A.V., Sethi, R. & Ullan, J.D., *Parser Generators*, in "Compilers – Principles, Techniques and Tools", pp.257-266, Addison-Wesley, 1986.

[13]   Levy, S. & Knuth, D.E., *CWEB*, archived at labrea.stanford.edu:/pub/cweb/

[14]   Ramsey, N., *NOWEB*, archived at bell-core.com:/pub/norman/noweb.shar.Z

[15]   Williams, R.N., *FunnelWEB*, archived at ftp.adelaide.edu.au:/pub/funnelweb/

[16]   van Amners, E.W., *CLip*, archived at sun01.info.wau.nl:/clip/

[17]   Knuth, D.E., *Literate Programming*, The Computer Journal, vol. 27, no. 2, pp. 97-111, May 1984

[18]   Mastors, B., *Genman*, comp.source.misc archive, wuarchive.wustl.edu, vol. 13, 1990.

[19]   Locke, N., *Docclass*, archived at ftp.demon.co.uk:/pub/trumphurst/docclass.zip

[20]   Stonet, G.,*c2man*, alt.sources archive, wuarchive.wustl.edu, indices 5751-5752

[21]   Ramsdell, J.D., *C2Latex*, archived at omni-gate.clarkeson.edu:/pub/tex/tex-programs/c2latex/

[22]   Conway, D.M., *The ARGS Command Line Interface Generator*, Computer Science Technical Report, Department of Computer Science, Monash University, Australia, 1994.

IDEAL: An Environment to Support Usability Engineering

Deborah Hix
H. Rex Hartson

Department of Computer Science
Virginia Tech
562 McBryde Hall
Blacksburg VA 24061 USA

internet: *lastname*@cs.vt.edu

ABSTRACT

IDEAL—the **I**nterface **D**evelopment **E**nvironment and **A**nalysis **L**attice—is an interactive tool environment that supports user-centered interface development activities. Specifically, it supports activities such as:

- task analysis, user interface design representation, and usability goal specification that occur *before* formative usability evaluation sessions with users,

- qualitative and quantitative data collection *during* formative usability evaluation sessions, and

- cost/importance and impact analyses, other data analysis techniques, and redesign that occur *after* formative usability evaluation sessions.

Users of IDEAL are HCI experts—experienced user interface developers (not necessarily programmers) who are knowledgeable in all activities of interface development. A primary goal of IDEAL is to encourage and enable user-centered development, especially focusing on formative evaluation. While other tools, such as traditional user interface management systems (UIMSs), have historically focused on improving the productivity of user interface software programmers, IDEAL supports developers of the user interaction component. This paper describes development, use, and evaluation of IDEAL.

1 INTRODUCTION

IDEAL—the **I**nterface **D**evelopment **E**nvironment and **A**nalysis **L**attice—is an interactive tool environment that supports user-centered interface development activities. Specifically, it supports activities such as:

- task analysis, user interface design representation, and usability goal specification that occur *before* formative usability evaluation sessions with users,

- qualitative and quantitative data collection *during* formative usability evaluation sessions, and

- cost/importance and impact analyses, other data analysis techniques, and redesign that occur *after* formative usability evaluation sessions.

The scope of development activities discussed in this paper will not cover all these activities, but rather is limited to discussing activities that support what has become known as *usability engineering* [Whiteside, Bennett, & Holtzblatt, 1988] — specifically, usability goal specification, data collection, and data analysis. Users of IDEAL are HCI experts—experienced user interface developers (not necessarily programmers) who are knowledgeable in all phases of interface development. IDEAL is an *Interface Development Environment* in that it provides a tool-supported framework for a broad user-centered development life cycle. *Analysis* and evaluation are essential phases of this life cycle that typically are not supported by automated tools. IDEAL can be thought of as a *lattice* because it includes hypermedia links among its different tools, helping a user interface developer to organize and manage activities and work products in the interface development process, meeting a major need that our interviews with real world developers have indicated.

A primary goal of IDEAL is to encourage and enable user-centered development, especially focusing on formative evaluation. *Formative evaluation* [Hix & Hartson, 1993] is evaluation for the purpose of improving the user interface design for a single system. It is performed early and continually throughout the development life cycle. This is in contrast to *summative evaluation* [Hix & Hartson, 1993], the purpose of which typically is a comparative evaluation of several different interfaces. While other tools, such as traditional user interface management systems (UIMSs) [Myers, 1991], have historically focused on improving the productivity of user interface software programmers, IDEAL supports developers of the interaction component. User interface development is part of a larger set of development processes for an interactive computer system. Many of these processes revolve around software engineering concepts. However, there is a distinction between developing the user interface *software* and developing the user *interaction* that is instantiated in software. Software design, even user interface software design, is properly system-centered, involving software modules, algorithms, data structures, callbacks, widgets, and so on. Interaction design should be user-centered, focusing on users' behavior as they perform tasks using the computer, and including considerations such as design guidelines, scenarios, formative usability evaluation, human factors, and so on.

2 RELATED WORK

There are few tools that support the kinds of user interface development activities that IDEAL does. Most interface tools are UIMSs, which, as mentioned above, support the constructional domain. A notable exception is the ESPRIT Project MUSIC— Metrics for Usability Standards in Computing [MUSIC, 1993]. Project MUSIC has developed both methods and support tools that have been used in commercial settings. The group of MUSIC products provides a package of usability measures and metrics, supported by proven methods and tools. Four major types of MUSIC metrics, applicable at different stages of the interface development process, are

- a *text editor* for recording design documentation, benchmark tasks, critical incidents, and so on, also transparently invokable from any window anywhere within the environment.

- *hypertext-like connections* among task descriptions, screen sketches, notes, usability specifications, benchmark tasks, and observations, with links across all windows

- connections to a tool and/or *rapid prototyper* to produce executable, interactive screens for the user interaction component of an interactive system.

3.3   Task Analysis for IDEAL

As a result of interviews and requirements definition, we performed a task analysis of activities to be supported by IDEAL. The top level of the IDEAL task structure includes support for the following major user interaction development activities:

- *perform user analysis* — producing appropriate user class descriptions

- *create/edit design representation* — developing UAN task descriptions

- *create/edit measuring instruments* — producing benchmark tasks and user questionnaires for measuring user task performance and user satisfaction

- *create/edit usability specifications* — developing quantifiable goals for user performance and satisfaction

- *perform formative evaluation* — evaluation session management, real time and post hoc data collection of both quantitative and qualitative data, and data analysis of both quantitative and qualitative data.

This IDEAL task structure incorporates the before, during, and after formative evaluation sessions activities that IDEAL supports. In particular, the first four tasks above are performed *before* formative evaluation sessions begin. *During* evaluation sessions, an interface developer (evaluator) collects real time data, both quantitative (e.g., error counts, task times, user satisfaction scores) and qualitative (e.g., critical incidents, verbal protocol). Post hoc data collection and analysis are tasks performed *after* evaluation sessions with users.

4   TOOLS IN THE IDEAL ENVIRONMENT

IDEAL is an integrated environment comprised of several different tools, each of which supports a different activity in the user interface development process. Output of each tool is appropriately accessible by that of other tools via hypermedia links— the development lattice. These links give a developer much more organization, structure, and management of the development process and access to resulting documentation than is possible with pencil and paper use of the methods supported by IDEAL's tools. This means, for example, that critical incidents (see Section 4.3) observed during a user session or unmet usability specifications (see Section 4.2) can be easily traced to the appropriate UAN task descriptions (see Section 4.1). Specific benchmark tasks can be traced to their corresponding generic UAN task description. IDEAL supports videotaping of user sessions, coupling videotape capture and replay with real time data collection, as well as with post hoc data collection and analysis.

The IDEAL hardware configuration, shown in Figure 1, consists of a DECstation 5000/133 capable of showing real time video in a window. A Sony video monitor can also show this real time video or be used for playback. Videotape deck control is through MacroMind Media Maker on a Macintosh Quadra 800. Shown here is the experimental setup we are using as we develop IDEAL; a real production setup would not have the Quadra, so video deck control would be done with the DECstation.

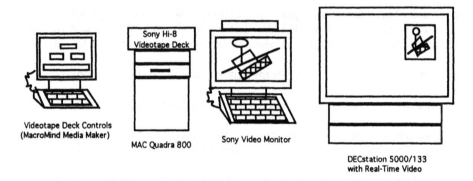

FIGURE 1. IDEAL Hardware Configuration

We will use examples from an application called SLIK (Simulated Logic Instruction Kit), for designing simple integrated circuits, to explain use of various tools in IDEAL. That is, we will explain IDEAL as it might used to perform various activities in the development of the SLIK user interface. Figure 2 shows a sample screen from the SLIK user interface.

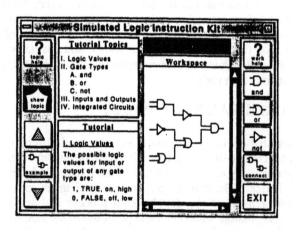

FIGURE 2. SLIK User Interface

Due to space limitations, we assume that readers are at least somewhat familiar with the general kinds of interface development activities supported by IDEAL, and we will give only a brief summary of each activity as we discuss the specific IDEAL tool that supports it. Further details of the interface development process can be found in [Hix & Hartson, 1993].

4.1 UAN Tool (QUANTUM)

To support development of interaction designs, IDEAL has as its foundation the *User Action Notation*, or *UAN* [Hix & hartson, 1993], a behavioral, user-centered design representation technique. The UAN originated in our research group more than five years ago, and has been used experimentally by more than 100 sites around the world. However, UAN has always been created and edited manually (i.e., with pencil and paper), with no automated support. IDEAL incorporates QUANTUM—the Quick User Action Notation Tool for User interface Management—to support automated writing of UAN task descriptions. The user task name for a UAN task description is the linking mechanism across all tools of IDEAL. A library of UAN descriptions and macros (e.g., for select, delete, move) is available to a developer. QUANTUM can access a graphical editor, for creating screen sketches to accompany UAN task descriptions. Using QUANTUM, a developer creates UAN task descriptions for tasks a user can perform with a particular interface (in our example, SLIK). Outputs of subsequent activities in the development process are linked to these task descriptions as development progresses.

4.2 Usability Specifications Tool

The usability specifications tool in IDEAL is used by a developer to create benchmark tasks that a user performs during a formative evaluation session. *Benchmark tasks* are specific instantiations of the more generic UAN task descriptions. For example, in SLIK, for a generic "build circuit" task, a specific benchmark task might be "place one AND gate and one OR gate in the workspace, then connect them". As part of the development process, a developer creates *usability specifications* [Whiteside, Bennett, & Holtzblatt, 1988] for each benchmark task that users perform. Usability specifications are quantifiable usability metrics that show an evolving interface is converging toward specific usability goals. An example of a usability specifications tool window is shown in Figure 3.

An example of what a row in this usability specification table might contain, for SLIK, could be the following: A usability attribute of "first use" (i.e., the first time a user ever tries to use SLIK for a particular task) might have as its measuring instrument "build circuit task", with a value to be measured of "time to perform the build circuit task". Perhaps, from observations, we determine that the current level for this task is 5 minutes, so we use this as our worst acceptable level. Planned target level might be a substantial improvement, to 1.5 minutes for a user to perform the "build circuit task", and best possible level might be 0.5 minutes to perform the task.

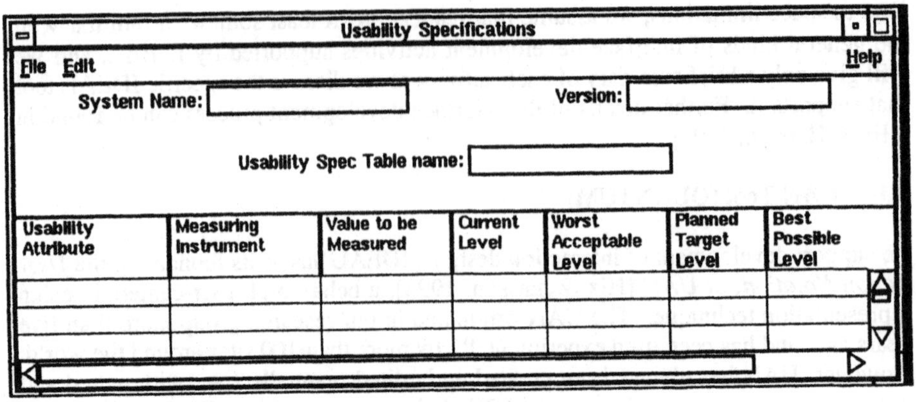

FIGURE 3. Usability Specifications Tool Window

Columns in Figure 3 are as follows:

Usability Attribute is the usability characteristic to be measured

Measuring Instrument is a description of what task will be measured, the vehicle for providing a value (e.g., benchmark task or questionnaire)

Value to be Measured is the metric for which values are taken as data (e.g., what will be measured by a benchmark task, such as time to perform task or error rate, or by a questionnaire, such as average numeric score over all questions)

Current Level is the present level of the usability attribute (when available)

Worst Acceptable Level is the lowest acceptable level for the attribute, the border of failure for usability

Planned Target Level is the target indicating usability success for the current version

Best Possible Level is a realistic state-of-the-art upper limit

Observed Results (not shown, but accessible by scrolling) is actual user performance (usually a mean of performance across all users for a task) during an evaluation session

This usability specification table is easily linked to the UAN task description for "build circuit" and to the specific benchmark task, as well as to other IDEAL tools.

4.3   Data Collection Tool

UAN task descriptions and usability specifications are developed *before* formative evaluation sessions with users. However, data are collected during and even after those sessions. In order to obtain observed results for the usability specification table, an evaluator observes a user performing benchmark tasks and records results using the data collection tool. These *quantitative data* are captured using the counters and timers in this tool, shown in Figure 4.

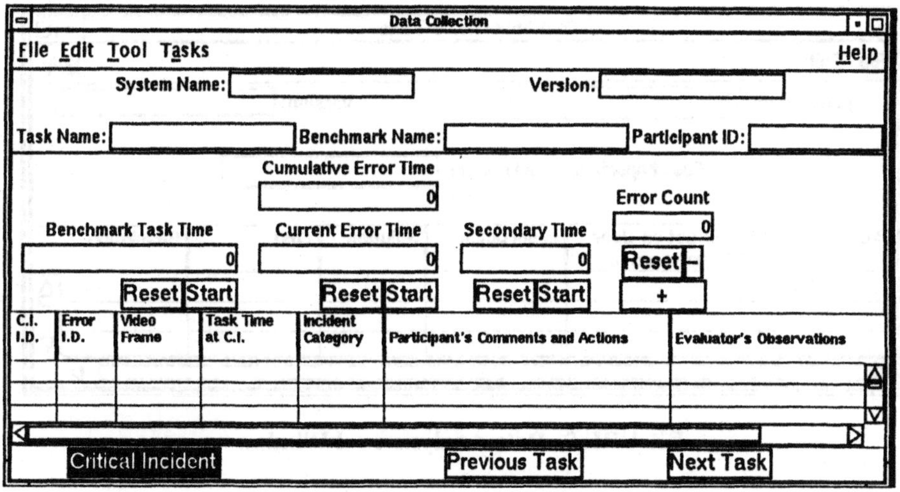

FIGURE 4. Data Collection Tool Showing Timers, Counters, and Other Kinds of Data Collected

Qualitative data, in the form of critical incidents (indicated as C.I. in Figure 4) and verbal protocol taking, are also collected by an evaluator observing a participant during a session. A critical incident is something that happens while a participant is performing a task that has significant effect, either positive or negative, on task performance or user satisfaction, and thus on usability of the interface. An example of a critical incident of a user using SLIK might be that user having difficulty determining how logic gates are duplicated. Many critical incidents can be captured in real time, but an evaluator can return to this tool after a session, and can review problematic areas of the videotape in order to further study specific events. For example, several critical incidents may have occurred so close together that the evaluator simply could not capture comments about them all during the session. In fact, any data that an evaluator can capture in real time must be editable (for corrections, augmentation) after evaluation sessions are complete.

IDEAL makes it easy, via an automated time stamp feature, for an evaluator to return to marked sections of the videotape and review them. When an evaluator identifies a critical incident, IDEAL automatically marks it with the current video time stamp. In post hoc analysis, an evaluator can request and automatically return to marked events on the tape for further review and analysis.

4.4 Data Analysis Tool

Finally, after user sessions and post hoc data capture, a developer (evaluator) must analyze the data from those sessions. Again, IDEAL provides automated support for this activity, in particular cost/importance analysis and impact analysis. Critical incidents from the data collection tool typically become problems recorded in the data analysis tool. A data analysis tool window is shown in Figure 5.

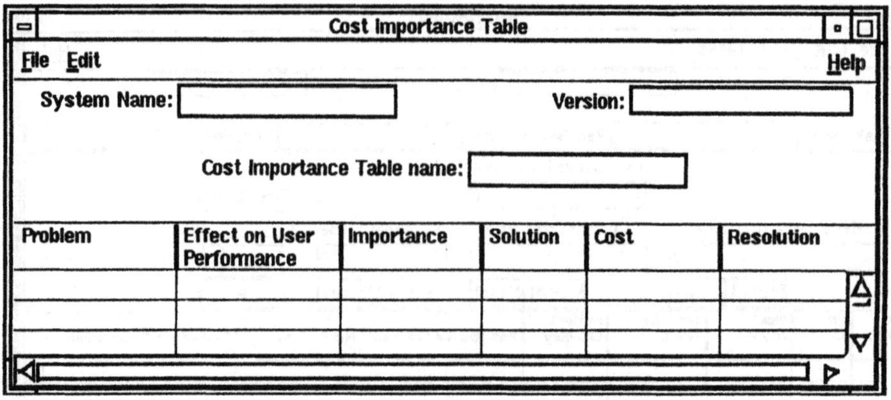

```
┌─┬─────────────────────────────────────────────────────────────────────┬───────┐
│ ▭ │                        Cost Importance Table                      │ ▪  ▢  │
├───────────────────────────────────────────────────────────────────────────────┤
│ File  Edit                                                              Help    │
│                                                                                 │
│    System Name: [                    ]          Version: [              ]       │
│                                                                                 │
│              Cost Importance Table name: [                    ]                 │
│                                                                                 │
│  ┌──────────┬──────────────┬────────────┬──────────┬────────┬────────────┐     │
│  │ Problem  │ Effect on User│ Importance │ Solution │ Cost   │ Resolution │     │
│  │          │ Performance   │            │          │        │            │     │
│  ├──────────┼──────────────┼────────────┼──────────┼────────┼────────────┤   △ │
│  │          │              │            │          │        │            │   ▯ │
│  │          │              │            │          │        │            │   ▽ │
│  └──────────┴──────────────┴────────────┴──────────┴────────┴────────────┘     │
│  ◀ ▮▮▮▮▮▮▮▮▮▮▮▮▮▮▮▮▮▮▮▮▮▮▮▮▮▮▮▮▮▮▮▮▮▮▮▮▮▮▮▮▮▮▮▮▮▮▮▮▮▮▮▮▮▮▮▮▮▮  ▷           │
└─────────────────────────────────────────────────────────────────────────────────┘
```

FIGURE 5. Data Analysis Tool Window

Columns in Figure 5 are as follows:

Problem is an interface problem observed as users interact with the system during evaluation

Effect on User Performance is data about the amount of time spent by the user dealing with a specific problem

Importance is an indication of a problem's overall effect on user performance (e.g., high, medium, low)

Solution is one or more proposed changes to solve a problem

Cost is the resources (e.g., time, money) needed for each proposed solution

Resolution is the final decision made to address each problem

From these data, a developer can, through impact analysis [Good, Spine, Whiteside, & George, 1986], determine which interface design problems have the biggest effect on usability, and then, through cost/importance analysis, systematically determine which problems to fix and in what order. These kinds of decisions are key to effective utilization of ever-limited resources (time and personnel) during subsequent redesign and iterative refinement cycles of interface development.

5 FORMATIVE EVALUATION OF IDEAL

5.1 Protocol for Formative Evaluation

Design of the IDEAL tools as presented in Section 4 has evolved from two phases of formative evaluation that we have done of IDEAL itself. Participants in the evaluation sessions were professional user interface design consultants and computer science graduate students trained in human-computer interaction. All participants had extensive experience with the techniques that IDEAL supports.

The first evaluation phase for IDEAL consisted of six sessions, each with a group of two participants to encourage discussion. Each group used IDEAL to evaluate a prototype of SLIK. We wanted to determine how well IDEAL supported the formative evaluation process. To provide a starting point, the IDEAL prototype included the following (for SLIK): some UAN task descriptions, benchmark task descriptions, and a usability specification table. During evaluation sessions, we collected verbal protocol and critical incidents for qualitative analysis of IDEAL.

While the first phase of evaluation had each group using IDEAL and SLIK displayed on one 19 inch monitor, the second phase of evaluation provided a more realistic set-up. During each of three evaluation sessions, one participant (a user interface developer/evaluator) used IDEAL on one computer, while another participant (a typical interface user) used SLIK on another computer in the same room. The participant using IDEAL evaluated IDEAL by instructing the participant using SLIK to perform various benchmark tasks. We again collected primarily qualitative data on use of IDEAL.

5.2   Results of Formative Evaluation and Discussion

The first phase of IDEAL evaluation yielded considerable feedback on coordination among tools and windows in IDEAL. Since IDEAL supports and organizes the activities of user-centered development into separate windows, most participants remarked that the number of windows could become unmanageable. Multiple, resizable, scrollable, editable windows were a clear benefit over current manual (pencil and paper) approaches to formative evaluation, but coordination among that same multitude of windows was also confusing at times. As a result, window manipulation was modified for the second version of IDEAL. Specifically, window manipulation was revised from its original design based on various activities in the development process to support development based more on user tasks. Further, window coordination was centralized in the main IDEAL window, except for user-developed hypermedia links, which remain at the IDEAL user's discretion and are accessible from any window.

Participants noted that use of UAN supported by IDEAL was effective for comparison of interface design representations (in UAN) and the implemented design. Participants also asked for additional automated data capture capabilities in IDEAL's data collection windows. As a result, such features as automated timers, stop watches, and error counters, as well as automatically generated critical incident and error identifiers, were added. Overall, all participants found IDEAL to be useful in managing the activities of formative evaluation and user-centered development.

The second phase of IDEAL evaluation yielded data on how participants would use IDEAL in a real evaluation session. Some IDEAL users initially had difficulty using IDEAL while concurrently observing SLIK users performing benchmark tasks. However, IDEAL users became facile with IDEAL with practice (about 30 minutes on average) and were able to use it effectively to evaluate SLIK. Participants had much less difficulty with window coordination after the revisions to simplify creating and moving among windows. Further suggestions for IDEAL included voice input, to facilitate easier data input while observing a user; and videotaping user sessions to allow later review, post hoc analysis, and editing in a new IDEAL window. As a result of these suggestions, we have incorporated videotaping into the current version of IDEAL, as previously described. Other suggestions from this phase of formative evaluation of IDEAL included a user-definable set of controls for noting types of critical incidents. On-line questionnaires and increased use of hypermedia links were also requested, and will be incorporated into later versions.

Participants stated that, even with an interactive set of tools such as IDEAL to manage the activities of interface development in an integrated environment, the process remains complex. However, all participants felt that IDEAL helps manage this process by coordinating and linking related activities, providing automated facilities for such tasks as formative evaluation, data collection, and data analysis. All participants felt that IDEAL shows promise as a unique environment for supporting user-centered development.

6 FUTURE WORK

We have many yet-unincorporated ideas for extending IDEAL. These include exporting appropriate data to statistical packages for further analysis, such as trend analysis. Further support for task and user analysis, as well as project management, are also needed. Improved traceability of observed problems and further hypermedia links will help pull together all relevant parts of a usability problem. Categorization of critical incidents and errors, more control of videotaped sessions, and perhaps voice input are being considered. Sound- and/or video-clips, especially those attached to critical incidents and proposed solutions to usability problems, can be used to produce "morning rushes" (as is done in movie production), providing extremely rapid reporting of results of evaluation sessions to developers. Digitization of video-clips will allow a developer to attach them via hypermedia links as annotation to various products of the development process (e.g., UAN task representation, evaluation reports, and so on).

And finally, we will continue formative evaluation of IDEAL itself. We have at least three real world user interface development organizations anxious to put IDEAL to the test in their development environments in the near future. Our goal is that IDEAL does, indeed, provide a user interface developer with an integrated environment for usability engineering.

ACKNOWLEDGMENTS

We wish to thank Stacey Ashlund for prototyping and evaluating the first version of IDEAL. Craig Struble, Matt Jackson, Brian Amento, and Arcel Castillo implemented the second version, described in this paper. Human-Computer Interaction research at Virginia Tech is funded by the National Science Foundation, Dr. Oscar Garcia and Dr. John Cherniavsky, monitors.

REFERENCES

M. Good, T. Spine, J. Whiteside, & P. George. 1986. User Derived Impact Analysis as a Tool for Usability Engineering. *Proceedings of CHI Conference on Human Factors in Computing Systems*, New York: ACM.

D. Hix & H. R. Hartson. 1993. *Developing User Interfaces: Ensuring Usability through Product & Process*. John Wiley & Sons, Inc.

MUSIC. 1993. Supplement to *Proceedings of INTERCHI Conference on Human Factors in Computing Systems*, New York: ACM.

B. Myers. 1991. State of the Art in User Interface Software Tools. *IEEE Software* (January).

J. Whiteside, J. Bennett, & K. Holtzblatt. 1988. Usability Engineering: Our Experience and Evolution. In M. Helander (ed.), *Handbook of Human-Computer Interaction* . Amsterdam: Elsevier North-Holland.

Specification and Generation of User Interfaces with the BOSS–System

Siegfried Schreiber

Institute of Computer Science, Munich University of Technology,
Arcisstr. 21, 80290 Munich, Germany
email: schreibs@informatik.tu-muenchen.de

Abstract. The paper describes the BOSS–System belonging to the class of model based user interface construction tools, which generate an executable user interface out of a declarative description (model) of an interactive application. BOSS gains a rather high level of usability due to a couple of reasons: BOSS employs an encompassing specification model (HIT, Hierarchic Interaction graph Templates) which allows the declarative description of all parts of the model of an interactive application (application interface, user interaction task space, presentation design rules) in a natural, designer oriented way. BOSS offers an integrated development environment in which user interface designers can elaborate specifications in a graphical, visual-programming–like manner. Through a refinement component, specifications can be refined according to high–level design goals. From a refined specification BOSS generates automatically working user interfaces using modified techniques from compiler construction.

1 Introduction

Due to well known limitations [5, 11] of direct manipulation User Interface Management Systems, model based user interface tools or user interface generators [8, 18, 11, 4, 1] gain rising research interest. This category of tools follows the notion of generating an executable user interface out of a declarative descripiton (model) of an interactive application (application interface, user interaction task space, presentation design rules). Adopting the principle of separating logical from layout structure, also known from related research domains like document architecture [7, 17], user interface designers are freed from the burden of making presentation design commitments (e.g. designing menus or dialogue boxes) at early stages of the design process, thus being able to design user interfaces centered around the concepts of users and tasks.

However, current model based tools are rarely used by interface designers, as they "often use cryptic languages for the model specification" [9]. Moreover, interface designers often have to learn different specification techniques for setting up different parts of the model. The BOSS–system [1] described in this paper tries

---

[1] BOSS is the acronym of "Bedienoberflächenspezifikationssystem", the german translation of "user interface specification system"

to increase the level of usability reached by current model based approaches. Important properties of BOSS are:

- BOSS supports the systematic development of user interfaces from early activities (e.g. task analysis) to presentation design and implementation. As BOSS allows the derivation of working user interfaces out of task–level descriptions, user interfaces can be tested and evaluated at early stages in the development process.
- Unlike other model based systems, BOSS uses an encompassing specification model (HIT, Hierarchic Interaction graph Templates) to cover all parts (see above) of the model of an interactive application. HIT is well–suited for supporting different roles of persons in user interface design: Application analysts specify the structure of the task space, which the interactive application offers to its users. Human factors experts describe presentation design rules, which capture software ergonomic guidelines. HIT combines properties of well–known methods in software construction (attribute grammars, data flow diagrams) and allows user interface designers setting up the model in a rather natural, designer–oriented way.
- BOSS is not tailored to any specific application domain (e.g. business oriented systems [11, 1]), but can handle also interfaces with e.g. animated, interactive graphics and application specific objects.
- Based on the same specification the specification refinement component of BOSS generates automatically different kinds of user interfaces according to high level design goals like "build an interface for users with little experience". The refinement component supports transformations, which change the behaviour and presentation of an user interface in a global way.
- BOSS offers an integrated development environment, in which specifications are elaborated graphically in a visual–programming–like fashion.

In the following, we will describe first the steps in model based interface design. An example illustrates how the specification model HIT of BOSS contributes to this design process.

2 Model Based User Interface Design with BOSS

Like every model based interface tool BOSS is based on an user interface design model, which structures the space of properties of interactive applications into design dimensions corresponding to different roles of persons in user interface design [14, 2]:

- Description of the Application Interface, i.e. specifying application data structures and functions relevant for the user interface (role of application analyst).
- Description of the space of interaction tasks users can perform within the application interface. This User Interaction Task Space (UITS) is a structured, high–level description of "what an user can do with an application", which does not consider presentation aspects (role of application analyst).

– Description of the mapping of user interaction tasks to interaction techniques and objects, (presentation design, role of human factors expert).

While the first two dimensions are specific for each application, the last can be regarded as specification of a reusable user interface style guide of which many (but not all) parts are application independent.

In 2.1 we will introduce an encompassing specification model used to describe the dimensions listed above. The sections 2.2, 2.3 and 2.4 describe by an example, how these dimensions are represented within this specification model.

2.1 The HIT Specification Model: An Overview

The HIT specification model combines properties of object–oriented and rule–based specification techniques. A HIT–specification consists of a set of basic data type and function definitions and a set of templates called HITs (Hierarchic Interaction Graph Template). Within a specification, HITs are used mainly for two purposes:

– HITs may serve as prototypes for creating objects (HIT–instances) maintaining their own state, reacting in response to external messages and being connected with other objects in an object structure (object–oriented view). In the context of user interface design, these object–oriented properties are employed e.g. for describing objects representing instances of those user interaction tasks, which are part of the user interaction task space UITS.
– HITs may be used for specifying rules describing the transformation of input data into output data (rule–based view). The rule–based properties of the HIT specification model are important in the context of presentation design, where rules capturing software–ergonomic guidelines e.g. for the presentation of application data have to be defined.

The HIT specification model shares properties with extended data flow diagrams used for the specification of information systems [16] and techniques known from compiler construction like dynamic and higher order attribute grammars [10, 6]. A definition of a HIT consists of a structural (syntactical) and a semantic part. The structural definition describes how a HIT h is constructed from "simpler" HITs $h_1, ..., h_n$ using operators like construction of records (i.e. "parallel" composition, $h = rec(h_1, ..., h_n)$), alternatives ($h = alt(h_1, ..., h_n)$) or sequences ($h = seq(h_1, ..., h_n)$). As in attribute grammars the structural description is enriched by semantic information. Associated with a HIT, there are various kinds of data flow constraints between the following entities:

– slots (in the context of attribute grammars named attributes) representing the state of an HIT instance. Through its input–, input/output– and output–parameter slots a HIT instance shares information with its neighbours in an object structure. Input slots may be modified by an external entity (e.g. a human user), the values of output slots are relevant to the environment.

- message ports for receiving events from external entities and for the distribution of messages across a structure of HIT–instances.
- rules defining either a directed equation in a "spreadsheet–like" manner (i.e. one–way constraints which should hold at every time) or a transaction caused by an external entity (e.g. an application function called by an user). A rule invokes either an external function or an instance of a HIT. A rule may have a precondition which is normally the precondition of the called function.

A HIT containing input slots, message ports or component–HITs with input slots or message ports is said to be interactive. Interactive HITs and input slots are called interactions. Interactions in a HIT instance can be enabled (allowing users to interact) or disabled. Together with the output slots, the interactions define the observable state of a HIT instance. The lifetime of a particular HIT – instance i is determined by the structural context of i (i.e. whether i is part of e.g. a sequential or alternative HIT instance) and by an applicability condition depending on the values of the input parameter slots and a termination condition depending on the so called termination slots, which are usually a subset of the output parameter slots. With these mechanisms a set of HITs describes an object space changing dynamically to satisfy the context conditions given by applicability and termination conditions. E.g. when a HIT $h = alt(h_1, ..., h_n)$ consisting of the alternatives $h_1, ..., h_n$ is instantiated, only one of those alternatives with satisfied applicability condition is instantiated too. This results in a dynamically growing and shrinking tree of HIT–instances (and therefore in a dynamically growing and shrinking data flow graph, too). A tree of HIT–instances is called consistent when (among other criteria), at each node, the applicability condition is satisfied and the termination condition is not satisfied.

From a rather abstract point of view, an user interacts with an user interface described by a set of HITs in the following way:

- The user instantiates a HIT (normally the HIT encapsulating the top–level task decomposition of the interactive application, see 2.3) by indicating its current input parameter values. Starting with this toplevel HIT instance, BOSS constructs a consistent tree of HIT instances, which is called Current UITS. Current UITS represents the task–level state of the interactive application capturing knowledge about the tasks the user has completed, is currently working on and has to complete to achieve a certain goal.
- From Current UITS a presentation consisting of interaction objects like buttons or menus has to be constructed. As a HIT instance like Current UITS is treated as a normal data instance within the HIT specification model, the process of constructing the presentation can be specified within HIT itsself.
- The user interacts with Current UITS by changing (via the presentation) the values of input slots or by sending messages to message ports of a HIT instance in Current UITS. If Current UITS becomes inconsistent through this interactions BOSS constructs a new consistent Current UITS. If, e.g., in an instance $i = seq(i_1)$ of the sequential HIT $h = seq(h_1, h_2)$ the instance i_1 of h_1 has terminated, an instance i_2 of h_2 is created as child of i.

The HIT–specification model incorporates a few extensions by which the behaviour of an user interface can be specified in a "fine grained" way: e.g. rules
can demand their input parameters in a particular order, the behaviour of rules
wrt. violated preconditions can be tailored, "generic" user interface features like
UNDO/REDO are supported.

From each specified HIT a corresponding C++ – class with appropriate construc-
tors, destructors, members and member functions is generated using modified
techniques from compiler construction like incremental attribute evaluation [19]
or pre–generation of evaluation strategies.

To illustrate the use of the HIT–specification model at the various levels of user
interface design, we outline the specification of an example: a simple Order Management System (OMS), in which customers, products and orders are handled.

2.2 Setting up the Model of the Application Interface

The application interface is described by modeling conceptual application data
structures and functions from the user's point of view.

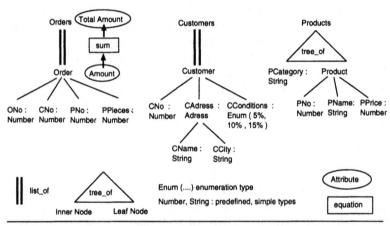

fig. 1 : semantic data model of the OMS

Fig. 1 shows the semantic data model of the OMS in a graphical, grammar–like
notation. Based on predefined, simple data types (here: *Number, Enum(...),
String*), complex data structures are built using operators for constructing
records, alternatives, lists, trees, tables, graphs or sets. Data structures may be
assigned additional semantic information via attributes and attribute evaluation
rules (usually directed equations). In our example the attribute *TotalAmount* of
Orders holds the *sum* of the values of all orders in the order–list *Orders*. Every
time, when an instance of *Orders* is modified (e.g. by the insertion of a new
order), *TotalAmount* is kept automatically up to date.

The functional part of the application interface consists of the functions which
the OMS exports to the user (see fig. 2):

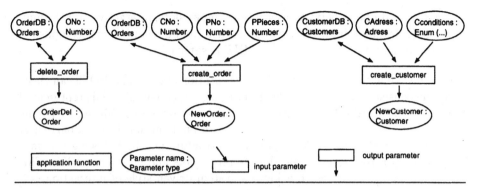

fig. 2 : application functions in the OMS

A function is described by indicating its formal input, input/output and output parameters and a precondition on the values of its input parameters. In our example *create_order* creates a new order and *delete_order* is used for removing existing orders. New customers are created with *create_customer*. *create_order* and *delete_order* modify their input/output parameter *OrderDB*, which is denoted by the double–headed arrow. Preconditions describe constraints on the input parameter values of a function. For the function *delete_order*, e.g., we demand that the parameter *ONo* (the number of the order to be deleted) denotes an existing order in the parameter *OrderDB*. In contrast to other model based systems like UIDE [8] preconditions are not used to describe sequencing constraints of functions in a task, but describe only "intrinsic" properties of functions.

2.3 Using HITs for the Representation of the User Interaction Task Space

Identifying potential classes of end users and the tasks they want to accomplish with an interactive application is a main step in user centered interface design [12]. Within the HIT specification model application analysts describe the User Interaction Task Space (UITS) in a two step process closely related to phsychologically motivated modelling approaches in HCI (e.g. [15]):

- First, the structure of the UITS is described. Complex user interaction tasks (e.g. interaction with the entire OMS) are decomposed into simpler tasks until the level of application functions is reached. Within HIT such a task hierarchy is modeled in a grammar–like, structured manner as a set of HITs. Each task corresponds to a HIT. The task structure is represented by the structure of the HIT, i.e. the composition (e.g. sequential or parallel) of "simpler" HITs it consists of.
- In the second step the structural description of the UITS is enriched by semantic information. This involves identifying the data (provided by or delivered to the environment, local data) the task is working on, determining the conditions in which a task may be started or in which it is regarded as accomplished and defining the interactions by which a user transforms input into output data. Within HIT, user interaction in a task is described by

defining data flows between user inputs (input slots, interactive HITs), functions (rules) and data stores (slots). A task can be regarded as accomplished if the termination condition of the HIT is satisfied.

Due to the explicite, declarative HIT representation of the UITS BOSS can check easily the consistency of the specification. If, e.g., a sequential task is represented by the sequential HIT $h = seq(h_1, h_2)$ and h_1 needs data produced by h_2 the specification is not consistent. Moreover, it can be determined how a particular task is accomplished by analyzing the task structure and by following the data flows backward from termination slots to input slots and interactive HITs. This knowledge can be used e.g. to achieve a system driven style of interaction (see 2.5).

Fig. 3 shows the HIT representation of the OMS toplevel task decomposition, which an application analyst would draw comfortably within the integrated development environment of BOSS. If not stated otherwise the applicability and termination conditions of a specified HIT are *true* and *false* per default.

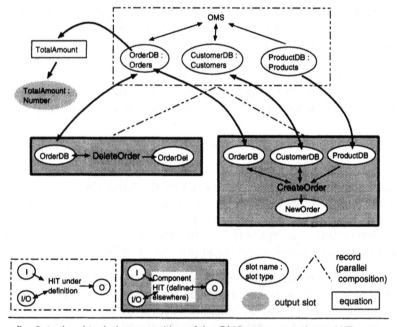

fig. 3: toplevel task decomposition of the OMS represented as a HIT

The environment of the OMS is given by the "data bases" *OrderDB*, *CustomerDB* and *ProductDB*, which are input*(ProductDB)* and input/output*(OrderDB, CustomerDB)* parameters of the HIT *OMS*. The OMS supports the independent subtasks *CreateOrder* and *DeleteOrder* working on the same data bases as the *OMS* (indicated by the data flows in fig. 3). As the user should be permanently informed about the amount of all orders in *OrderDB*, we introduce an output slot *TotalAmount*, whose value is computed by an equation rule (see 2.1) accessing the value of the attribute *TotalAmount(OrderDB)* of

OrderDB. Every time when the attribute *TotalAmount(OrderDB)* changes (e.g. when a new order is created), the value of the slot *TotalAmount* is recomputed automatically via incremental attribute evaluation.

The component HITs *CreateOrder* and *DeleteOrder* of the HIT *OMS* represent mutually independent subtasks in the order management system. When the HIT *OMS* is instantiated and becomes part of Current UITS, instances of *CreateOrder* and *DeleteOrder* become part of Current UITS too, as *OMS* is structured in a record–like manner.

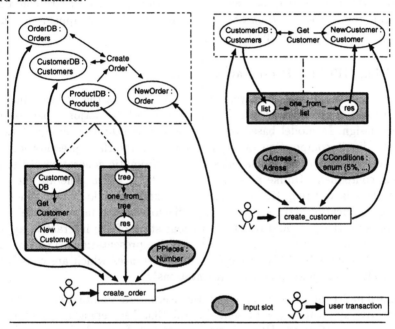

fig.4 : HIT representation of CreateOrder and GetCustomer

In the task *CreateOrder* (see fig. 4) new orders are added to the system by invoking the application function *create_order* represented by a transaction rule. While an equation–rule (see above) is evaluated automatically to satisfy constraints which should hold at every time, a transaction has to be triggered explicitly by an user. For the input parameter *PNo* of *create_order* users should be allowed to enter only products from the product data base *ProductDB*. This is accomplished by introducing an *one-from_tree*–HIT ensuring that users can enter only values from a given tree (here: *ProductDB*, which is organized hierarchically as a tree of products, see fig. 4). The input parameter *CNo* can be entered through a *one-from_list* selection from the customer data base *CustomerDB*. If a "new" customer has not been found in *CustomerDB* users should be able to create a new customer account becoming automatically the required parameter for *create_order*. This behaviour is encapsulated in the HIT *GetCustomer* shown also in fig. 4, where the output parameter slot *NewCustomer* is connected to an *one-from_list* HIT and to the result of the *create_customer* transaction.

Representing the user interaction task space UITS within the HIT specification model is a designer–friendly and problem–oriented way to describe the task–level dynamics of an interactive application, as application analysts are not concerned with the details of a rather low–level interaction model. Of course, in practice, the UITS has a much richer structure than in our OMS. This complexity is handled by application analysts by composing the UITS in a graphical, visual–programming–like manner out of reusable, simple structured building blocks like e.g. *GetCustomer*. When modeling the UITS, application analysts do not have to start from scratch, but can rely on a standard task library containing interaction tasks like *one_from_list* or *one_from_tree*, which appear in almost every user interaction task space.

2.4 Using HITs for Presentation Design

Together with the refinement layer outlined in 2.5, it is the design dimension presentation design, where human factors principles have major impact on user interface design. In model based interface design presentation design does not mean the direct composition of a particular user interface presentation, but consists of setting up executable rules for the automatic generation of the presentation component. Unlike most model based tools which generate the static user interface layout (e.g. [13, 1, 4, 11]) out of knowledge known at generation time (e.g. application data structures), BOSS follows the more flexible notion of determining the presentation of the current state of the interactive application, thus being able to support context sensitive presentations [18] depending on data available only at run–time (e.g. data instances which are constructed interactively by the user, adaptive presentations).

As outlined in 2.1 the current state (wrt. the user interaction task space UITS) of an interactive application is represented in the BOSS system as a consistent tree of HIT instances (Current UITS, logical structure), from which a presentation consisting of so called Abstract Interaction Objects [4] has to be constructed (layout structure), which allows the user to interact with the logical structure (e.g. by changing the values of input slots). This involves the specification

- of application specific interaction objects, if required
- of the selection of appropriate predefined or application specific interaction objects by which e.g. a user triggers transactions, modifies the values of input slots or by which the values of output slots are displayed.
- of the composition of those selected interaction objects into a presentation which visually reinforces the logical structure. E.g. for an input slot storing a "complex" data instance, the interaction objects building up the presentation generated to allow users to edit that instance should be arranged according to the logical data structure.

As HIT instances are treated as normal data instances within the HIT specification model, the presentation of a HIT instance being part of Current UITS can be specified within the HIT specification model. With BOSS, human factors experts identify common user interaction tasks like browsing through large object structures (e.g. *one_from_list, one_from_tree*) or editing data instances. Software–ergonomic guidelines determining the presentation of these tasks are represented in a constructive, formal and unambigous manner as a set of HITs in the BOSS system. This can be regarded as the formal representation of an reusable user interface style guide. Compared with the WYSIWYG–like direct composition of the user interface presentation, this approach has a couple of advantages.

- Similar interaction tasks are mapped to similar interaction techniques and objects (consistency across user interface presentation). Deriving presentations from task–level specifications like in fig. 3 and 4 and style–guide compliance of user interfaces come almost for free (assuming a given style guide).
- Keeping the presentation of the user interface consistent with the interactive application's state, a major effort using a conventional user interface tool, is handeled automatically by the system (runtime consistency between application and user interface state).

Let us regard an example: The presentation of an HIT instance being part of Current UITS (e.g. an instance of the HIT *OMS* from fig. 3) may be specified through a HIT *PresentTaskInstance*, which requests as input parameter the HIT instance to be presented and produces a presentation built from interaction objects like buttons or menus. In each HIT instance which is part of Current UITS an enabled input slot stands for the elementary interaction task "edit a possibly complex structured object". The HIT *EditObj* (see fig. 5), which is part of the definition of *PresentTaskInstance*, defines generic presentations for editing arbitrary objects. *EditObj* consists of a couple of alternative HITs arranged in a decision–tree–like structure according to the structure of the object to be edited.

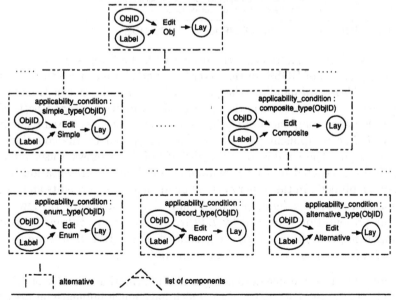

fig. 5 : HIT representation of EditObj

The HIT *EditObj* requests as input parameters the object instance to be edited *(ObjID)* and a optional label *Label* and produces a presentation *Lay*, by which an user can edit *ObjID*.

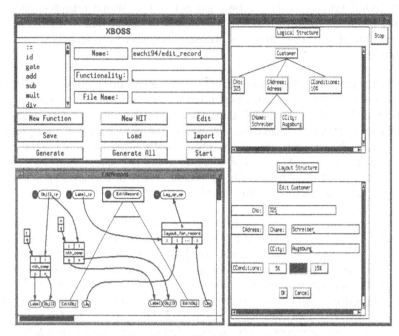

nth-comp :   function yielding the name of the n-th component and the n-th component of an object

layout_for_record :   function calculating an appropriate screen layout for records here : horizontal arrangement between label and the vertical arrangement of the record components

fig. 6 : HIT representation of EditRecord , BOSS - IDE

Fig. 6 shows a human factors expert working with the Integrated Development Environment (IDE) of BOSS. In the lower left window we can see the definition of the HIT *EditRecord* handling the presentation of an object constructed in a record–like manner (expressed in the applicability–condition *record_type(ObjID)*, see fig. 5). For each component of *ObjID* a presentation is constructed recursively by *EditObj*. The component presentations are composed by the equation–rule *layout_for_record*. The window on the right side of fig. 6 shows a user interface automatically generated by BOSS containing two different presentations of the task "edit an object". In the upper part, a human factors expert edits an instance of the data structure *Customer* (see fig. 1) in its logical structure, the lower part shows the presentation produced by *EditRecord*. The *radio buttons* for editing the component *CConditions*, e.g., are generated by the HIT *EditEnum* (see fig. 5), as *CConditions* is an instance of an enumeration type.

Please note that the example does not consider information like user preferences or spatial constraints (e.g. screen size), which have much influence on presentation design [4]. As there are often many possibilities for determining presentations, the HIT specification model allows to find the "best" solution employing techniques from dynamic programming. A noninteractive, alternative HIT is assigned a cost function to choose the branch yielding the lowest costs among all applicable branches.

It is important to note, that transferring an user interface style guide into the HIT specification model is a major effort, which requires both skills in human factors principles and in software construction methods. This effort, however, has to be carried out once.

2.5   Specification Refinement Trough High–Level Transformations

It is well recognized that different kinds of users (e.g. concerning the knowledge about the application domain, semantic knowledge [3]) should be supported by different kinds of user interfaces. To support this requirement, the BOSS system offers an refinement component, which is able to refine an "underspecified" user interface description (i.e. a specification making no design commitments concerning e.g. low level dialogue sequencing) according to high level design goals like "build an interface for an user with little knowledge about the application domain". To be able to do so, BOSS organizes possible properties of user interfaces into a design space, where each property corresponds to a particular transformation in the underlying HIT user interface specification.

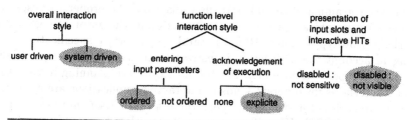

fig. 7 : design space for determining user interface properties
at different levels of abstraction

Let us watch the property "overall interaction style" from fig. 7. A specification as depicted in fig. 3 and 4 allows users to enter values into input slots and triggering transactions in arbitrary order (user driven interaction style), which means in our OMS example the interleaving execution of *CreateOrder* and *DeleteOrder*. For less experienced users it would be more appropriate if the system informs the user about the available tasks, let the user choose one of these tasks first, and then demands step by step all information from the user, which is needed to accomplish the task (system driven interaction style). The refinement component of BOSS contains a set of transformation rules, which describe how a given model has to be transformed to achieve certain user interface properties. The transformations performed by BOSS to achieve system driven behaviour include transformations on the structure of the user interaction task space UITS. E.g. a record–like, parallel HIT like OMS is transformed into a sequential HIT made up of a *one_from_list* selection (users have to choose the task first) and an alternative HIT containing the former record components (in our example *DeleteOrder* and *CreateOrder*) as branches. Each branch is guarded with an additional applicability condition ensuring to be the selected task. Additional interactions and termination conditions are generated to allow users to terminate the branch.

Assuming a given set of such refinement rules, user interface designers can derive easily, based on the same model, a broad range of user interfaces, which differ in those user interface properties given in the designspace from fig. 7. E.g. the properties emphasized in fig. 7 denote an user interface, which would be suited for an user with little semantic knowledge.

3 Experience and further research

To show whether HIT is in practice a step into our vision of a "designer friendly" user interface specification model, we built a first protoype of BOSS (about 85000 lines of C++ code) running under UNIX/X11R5. Corresponding to the roles in interface design supported by BOSS, we represented parts of a user interface style guide within HIT (role of human factors expert). Based on this style guide interfaces for different application classes were built (role of application analyst), e.g. graphical domain specific editors (e.g. for constructing arithmetic formulae, SQL – queries), business–oriented applications. We believe that the combination between grammar–like and data–flow–diagram–like properties (especially together with graphical specification techniques and the automatic generation of working prototypes) makes HIT a natural user interface specification model (taking in account the high level of abstraction in user interface specification employed by model based tools). For the future we are planning a case study, in which interfaces for different kinds of interactive applications are built using different categories of user interface construction tools (User Interface Management Systems, BOSS). We will examine criteria related to the user interface design process (e.g. degree of end user participation, time for building the first and alternative interfaces) and the quality of the resulting interface.

4 Acknowledgements

This work has been supported by Siemens Corporate Research and Development, Department of System Ergonomics and Interaction (ZFE ST SN 51). I would like to thank Werner Schreiber, Bernhard Bauer and Frank Lonczewski for their useful comments and suggestions on draft versions of this paper.

References

1. H. Balzert. Der JANUS–Dialogexperte: Vom Fachkonzept zur Dialogstruktur. *Softwaretechnik 93*, 13(3), 11 1993.

2. L. Bass, C. Cockton, and C. Unger. IFIP Working group 2.7 User Interface Engeneering: A Reference Model for Interactive System Construction. In J. Larson and C. Unger, editors, *Engeneering for Human-Computer Interaction*. North Holland, 1992.

3. L. Bass and J. Coutaz. *Developing Software for the User Interface* . Addison-Wesley, 1991.

4. F. Bodard, A.M. Hennebert, J.M. Leheureux, I. Sacre, and J. Vanderdonckt. Architecture Elements for Highly-Interactive Business-Oriented Applications . In L. Bass, J. Gornostaev, and C. Unger, editors, *Human-Computer Interaction: EWHCI 93 Proceedings* . Springer LNCS 753 , 8 1993.

5. D.J.M.J. de Baar and J. Foley. Coupling Application Design and User Interface Design . In *ACM CHI 92 Proceedings*. ACM, 1992.

6. P. Deransart, M. Jourdan, and B. Lorho. *Attribute Grammars: Definitions, Systems and Bibliography* . Springer, 1988.

7. J. Eickel. Logical and layout structures of documents. *Computer Physics Communication*, 61:201-208, 1990.

8. J. Foley, W. C. Kim, S. Kovacevic, and K. Murray. UIDE – An Intelligent User Interface Design Enironment . In *Intelligent User Interfaces*. Addison-Wesley, 1991.

9. M. Frank and J. Foley. Model-Based Interface Design By Example and By Interview . In *Proceedings of the UIST 93, ACM Symposium on User Interface Software and Technology* . ACM , 11 1993.

10. H. Ganzinger. *Optimierende Erzeugung von Übersetzerteilen aus implementierungsorientierten Sprachbeschreibungen*. PhD thesis, Technische Universität München, 1978.

11. C. Janssen, A. Weisbecker, and J. Ziegler. Generating User Interfaces from Data Models and Dialogue Net Specifications . In *ACM Interchi 93 Proceedings* . ACM, 1993.

12. P. Johnsen, S. Wilson, C. Kelly, and P. Markopoulos. Beyond hacking: a model based approach to user interface design . In *BCS HCI 93 Conference*. Cambrigde University Press , 1993.

13. W.C. Kim and J.D. Foley. Providing High-level Control and Expert Assistance in the User Interface Presentation Design . In *ACM INTERCHI'93 Proceedings* . ACM, 1993.

14. J.A. Larson. *Interactive Software: Tools for building interactive user interfaces*. Prentice Hall, 1992.

15. S.J. Payne and T.R.G. Greene. Task-Action Grammars: A Model of the Mental Representation of Task Languages . *Human-Computer Interaction* , 2, 1986.

16. S. Peretz. ADISSA: Architectural Design of Information Systems based on structured analysis. *Information systems*, 13(2):193-210, 1988.

17. W. Schreiber. Prosaische Logik für Dichter und Denker – Textverarbeitung maßgeschneidert . *Forschung für Bayern*, (6), 1993.

18. P. Szekely, P. Luo, and R. Neches. Faciliating the Exploration of Design Alternatives: The HUMANOID Model of User Interface Design . In *ACM CHI 92 Proceedings*. ACM, 1992.

19. T. Weiske. SICK: Inkrementelle Auswertung von Attributgrammatiken . In G. Snelting, editor, *Sprachspezifische Programmierumgebungen: Workshop der Fachgruppe Implementierung von Programmiersprachen, T.H. Darmstadt 6.4 - 8.4.88* , 4 1988.

An Architecture for Object Oriented User Interfaces

M. V. Donskoy

Donskoy Interactive Software Company
81, Vavilov str, #97 117335, Moscow, Russia
donskoy@kaissa.msk.su

Abstract. An object oriented architecture for building user interfaces is presented. It is based on a finite state machine with a stack for translating system input events into application dependent events and on a "best fit" method of looking for an object to process an event. As a result, the user can more easily understand the implemented interface environment and the programmer can more simply code it.

1 Introduction

The problem of constructing a neat and comprehensive description of a complex user interface environment is critical to both implementing and using such an environment. The contradiction between ease of use and ease of implementation can be solved by building an environment that addresses both issues. In some sense, much of the history of programming environment technology has been concerned with this problem.

When a program has extensive functionality and/or a complex set of user interface behaviors (i.e., many different interface modes and rules), it is very difficult both to design and to understand it. Object-oriented design requires that too many design decisions be made locally; therefore, the global behavior of the program is very difficult to understand. Part of this problem is due to inconsistent program behavior. Different objects that are very similar to the user interact in different ways because they are derived from different object classes.

This paper proposes a way to solve this problem, and therefore, to make program behavior more consistent and understandable, without making the program designer's life too complex. The approach presented here uses a novel program structure for organizing the program's user interface as a set of interface objects reacting to events, both user-generated and system-generated.

In the first section the general description of the architecture is given, outlining the event processing.

The two main parts of this architecture are described independently, with the primary emphasis on the distinction between this architecture and other well-known approaches.

As an example, a drag-and-drop routine in an implemented system for image editing in documents is described.

2 General Description

The proposed architecture works in an event-based operating environment, such as MS-Windows, Macintosh System 7, X-Windows, etc. [1,2,3,4]. The environment sends the program a sequence of events and the program has to react to them. The essential part of the architecture is the object world of the program - the set of all interface objects accessible to the user. In traditional window systems, such entities as windows, dialog boxes, scroll bars, icons, and menus are examples of interface objects.

Object-oriented design techniques are used to implement interface object descriptions, including class hierarchies with behavior inheritance, object behaviors deduced from the object appearance on the screen, and so on.

The most difficult problem for this kind of architecture is how to determine which object should react to an input event. The traditional solution [5,6,7] can be called "hit at" method. Namely, the event is shown to every object (in some order, usually starting with the focus object) and the first object that can be considered as the target of the event processes it. For mouse events, the target is usually the object that the mouse cursor is pointed at, hence the term "hit at."

The proposed alternative is the "best fit" method. The event is shown to every object, and each object replies with a "distance" from the event. Then, the object with the shortest distance from the event processes it. The details of this method are described in the section "Event processing."

A difficult interface architecture problem involves implementing programs with a variety of modes. In such programs, the same input event may have different meanings in different situations. For example, a "Mouse button up" event while dragging an object means "drop the object," while the same event while drawing a line means "end of the line."

Accordingly, any object involved in making a decision about whether it can process an event or not must take the program mode into consideration. This requirement usually makes the program code really ugly. To solve this problem, an event translation schema is proposed that translates each system event into an application dependent event before showing it to the interface objects. Examples of application dependent events include the "drop an object" event and the "end of Line" event. The details of this part of the architecture are described in the section "Event Translation."

Another problem involves what should happen when an object has finished procesing an event. As a result of the way in which a program works, the program may change modes after an event is processed. There should be a clear method in the architecture for dealing with such mode changes. This problem of event postprocessing is discussed in the section "After an event was processed."

3 Event Translation

To overcome the difficulties in implementing and understanding programs with a variety of modes, each system event is translated into anapplication dependent event (ADE) that reflects the interpretation of the event given the current mode of the program. To accomplish this translation, different program states must be explicitly described. Each state description consists of an event translation list and four procedure names.

Each event translation on the event translation list contains a system event identifier, an ADE identifier, and a foreground/background flag that will be described later. For example, for the "dragging an object" state one event translation would include a "Left mouse button up" system event identifier, a "Drop the object" ADE identifier, and a foreground flag.

The four procedures that must be described for each state are the procedures for creating, destroying, opening, and closing the state.

Unlike the traditional finite state machines that are frequently used for user interface descriptions [8], in this architecture there is a stack of states roughly reflecting the program execution history. For example, if the user asks for help while drawing a line, the two upper states on the stack will be the "Help" and "Drawing a line" states. Thus, this state stack defines the program interface context.

When a system event is sent to the program, the event translation list for the top state on the stack is searched to find the event. If it is found, then the ADE from the appropriate event translation is sent to the object world.

If the system event is not found in the top state description, the other state descriptions on the stack are searched from the top to the bottom. This stack mechanism provides one of the crucial difference between this architecture and other approaches. In other approaches, if the system event is not defined in the current program state it is usually ignored.

Assume that the event to be found is in the event translation list for some program state description S that is on the stack, but not at the top. If the value of the flag for the desired event translation is "background," then the corresponding ADE is sent to the object world. This is a convenient and efficient mechanism for implementing hot key translation, such as the "F1 key up" system event that is usually translated into a "Call Help" ADE.

If the flag value for the desired event translation is "foreground," then all of the state descriptions above the state description S (from the top of the stack to the one above S) are first destroyed and then removed from the stack. To destroy a state means to call the "Destroy" procedure defined in the state description, and this procedure may be quite complex. For example, destroying an "Edit" state may involve asking the user whether to save the edited file or not. Destroying the "Help" state closes the Help window. After all of these states are destroyed, the statedescription S is opened, that is, the "Open" procedure for the state description S is called. This procedure may be quite complex as well.

Thus, any input events may change the program state stack, and the effect of some events is to only change the program state stack. In other words, it is quite possible to have zero ADE's in an event translation (for example, the "Escape key down").

After an event is processed by the object world, the processing object returns a value. This value is then used for "postmortem" stack changes. If a menu object has processed an event and decided to change the program state then it can be done in three different ways. The first way is to add a new state description to the stack. In this case, the current state description is closed (i.e., the "Close" procedure is called), the new state description is created, and this new state description is pushed onto the stack.

The second way is to replace the top state description on the stack with a new one. The previous state description is destroyed (i.e., the "Destroy" procedure is called) and removed from the stack, and the new state description is created and pushed onto the stack.

The third way is to pop the top state description from the stack making the second state description on the stack the new current state. The top state description is destroyed and removed from the stack, and the new top state description on the stack is opened (i.e., the "Open" procedure is called).

This mechanism simplifies the definition of program state description classes. All of the default program behaviors are described in the bottom state description, which is never destroyed or removed from stack. For example, a program's hot keys are described in this bottom state description as background events and are always available without having to be described in any other states. Thus, it is possible to define a re-usable "Drawing a line" state description class, instances of which react to all hot keys of any program from the user's point of view, without requireing the programmer to painstakingly enumerate all of the hot keys for every use. As a result, a programmer must describe only the essential behaviors for every state.

4 The Object World

All user interactions with a program begin with interface objects. The interface objects usually have visual representations on the screen, and their appearance gives a hint to their usage. In any given application, the interface objects form some kind of structure (it maybe a list or a hierarchy, for example, depending on the particular application) which is used for event processing. For this event processing it is required that the structure allows some sort of iteration over all objects. Usually a tree structure is most convenient. In such a structure, all objects are tied to tree nodes and have natural parents and children. Unlike the standard window hierarchies, in this object world children do not have to be geometrically inside the parent.

Really there are two different hierarchies involved that must be clearly distinguished. The first is an object class hierarchy (for example, the dialog box class is a child of the general window class), and the second is the actual object hierarchy in the object world (for example, an icon is a child of the toolbar). The first one is static, and the latter is dynamic.

5 Event Processing

Once the system event is translated into an ADE, the ADE is shown to every object in the object world. Each object returns a formal "distance" integer value - how far the event is from that object. An infinite distance means that the object does not react to that event. Next, the object with the smallest distance from the event receives the ADE for processing.

The distance can depend on many factors. The general idea is that every object has a set of "valencies" - potential event places. For example, in the Math Formula Editor (an application that is implemented using this schema), a dragged expression can be dropped as a subscript to an identifier object. Of course, the user cannot be exact in dropping the expression, but assume that the expression is dropped somewhere that can be reasonable understood as either in line with the object or as a subscript of it. Not every object can have subscript, so these objects do not have "right down" valency. In the Formula Editor there are seven potential valencies defined - "inside," "right," "left," "above," "below," "right up" and "right down." Different object classes have different valencies allowed.

When the program is attempting to interpret the user's intention in dropping an expression, the program decides how far the expression was dropped from the point that is ideal for each valency and multiplies this distance by the weight of that valency. This may make, for example, the "right" valency preferable to the "left" one. The smallest distance of all of the valencies is returned as the distance of this object from the drop event.

Two important points should be mentioned about this schema. First, almost any action of the user can somehow be understood. From psychological point of view, an incorrect but reasonable reaction to an unclear user action is much more appropriate than a simple refusal to react (usually accompanied by a penalizing beep).

Second, if the object world contains many small objects, it is very difficult for the user to be precise in hitting the object he or she wants. The "best fit" approach makes such interactions more comfortable, because, there are usually not that many objects that can reply to a particular ADE (i.e. have a finite distance from it). Furthermore, the user need not precisely hit an object on the screen but can miss it by a little bit. This is especially useful if the user wants to interact with an object that is very small on the screen. This flexibility allows the designer to use smaller screen objects, thereby giving more usable screen space.

Once the best fit object is found, the ADE is sent to it. The object processes it according to the object functionality description.

6 After an Event is Processed

After the best fit object has processed the ADE, the value returned by this object points to a structure that contains several important features. The first denotes any important changes in the object world that may cause visible changes on the screen. If there are, then the object world view is rebuilt from scratch. For example, in the case of a hierarchical object world, this rebuilding is done in two tree traversals. The first calculates each objects' size and position relative to its parents, and the second calculates absolute screen coordinates for each object.

This view rebuilding handles the possibility of major view changes caused by very slight changes in the object world. In real applications using the "best fit" strategy, it is almost never the case that a dragged object is positioned at exactly the point where it was dropped. From the user's point of view it looks like the program is making nice corrections to his or her imprecise actions.

The second part of the return structure is a message to the state description stack. If the object finds it necessary to change the program mode by changing the state of the stack it has to put a description of the necessary changes in the return structure.

7 An Example

As an example of this architecture at work, let us look more carefully at how a drag-and-drop operation is handled.

The "Drag an object" state is described. Its event translation list includes the "Mouse move" and "Mouse button up" system events. These system events are mapped to the "Dragging the object" and "Drop the object" ADE's respectively. The creation procedure of the state description has a reference to the dragged object as a parameter and builds a dragging environment, including a background image. The destroy procedure releases the environment.

Dragging starts when the user clicks the mouse button while pointing near an object. The "best fit" strategy finds the object, and if the distance is not larger than a given threshold, the object is selected. This is done in the "Normal state" of the application.

When the user moves the mouse while holding the mouse button down, the "mouse move with pressed button" system event is translated into the "Start drag" ADE described in the "Normal state" event translation. The "Start drag" event is then sent to the selected object. This object cannot drag itself, so it notifies its parent that dragging is about to be started.

When the parent processes the event, the "Drag an object" state description is created. During the creation of this state description, the dragging environment is built. Finally, the event return structure specifies that the "Drag an object" state should be pushed onto the stack. Part of this state description is the dragged object.

When the user moves the mouse with the button pressed, this event is translated into the "Dragging an object" ADE pointing to the dragged object. This ADE is sent to the object world to provide the user with the visual feedback about what would happen if the mouse button were released at that point. Every object in the object world replies to the "Dragging an object" ADE by estimating the distance between it and the dragged object. This estimate takes into account the semantic relations between objects. For example, some objects cannot be tied with another even if it is dropped nearby. A part of the estimation function for every object distinguishes between different dragged objects.

Usually, feedback is provided either by changing a cursor shape or by rescaling the dragging object. For example if the nearest object to the moving point is the "Trash" object (e.g., trash can on the Macintosh desktop), its reply to the "Dragging an object" event may be to change the cursor shape to a "Cross out."

When the mouse button is released, the "Drop an object" ADE is shown to the object world, and again, all objects reply with a calculated distance. Next, the ADE is sent to the best fit object. Usually, this causes a change of the object world because the dropped object is removed from one place in the world (that is, both a place on the screen and a place in the object world structure) and put into another. As the last step of dragging, the "Drag an object" state description is destroyed, releasing the dragging environment, and removed from the state stack.

8 Conclusions

There are several advantages in the proposed architecture. First, the "best fit" approach provides the capability for interacting with very small interface objects on the screen,and even some invisible ones. That gives the user interface designer more screen space and better view. This is an especially striking contrast to the large caption bars windows in the MS-Windows environment. Second, the architecture gives a consistent solution for multimodal applications development. A programmer can have a state description class library for reusing typical states such as "Drag an object" or "Drawing a line" in a number of applications. Finally, the architecture provides a consistent mechanism for handling default application behaviors, such as the "Help" hot key, in a cleanly coded manner.

Our experience showsthat this architecture is also well suited for building animated user interfaces because it accommodates the dynamic changes in the object world both in object structures and in object positions.

The usage of ADE's provides the capability for handling the same events in application terms for different goals, for example, this can greatly simplify event macro recording.

The author wishes to thank A.Dubec, V.Kokin and I.Shabalin for their help in building the architecture and solving many technical problems while implementing it. Brad Blumenthal's help in improving English was tremendous.

References

1. Macintosh Human Interface Guidelines. Addison-Wesley, 1992.
2. The Windows Interface: An Application Design Guide. Microsoft Corp., 1992.
3. Open Look: Graphical User Interface Functional Specifications. Addison-Wesley, 1989.
4. OSF/Motif Style Guide. Prentice Hall, 1991.
5. Michael Chen: A Framework for Describing Interactions with Graphical Widgets Using State-Transition Diagrams. In INTERCHI'93 Adjunct Proceedings, Amsterdam, Holland, 1993.
6. Andy Holyer: Top-Down Object-Based User Interface Definition and Design Paradigms. In Proc. of EWHCI'92 St. Petersburg, Russia, 1992.
7. Brad A. Myers: User Interface Tools: Introduction and Survey. IEEE Software, January 1989.
8. James Rumbaugh, State Trees as Structured Finite State Machines for User Interface. In Proc. of ACM SIGGRAPH Symposium on User Interface Software. Banff, Alberta, Canada, 1988.

Extending Programming by Demonstration with Hierarchical Event Histories

David S. Kosbie and Brad A. Myers

School of Computer Science, Carnegie Mellon University, Pittsburgh, PA 15213 USA

Abstract. Programming by Demonstration, or PBD, is an exciting and developing branch of HCI research. With PBD techniques, end-users can add functionality to their environments without programming in the conventional sense. Virtually all research into PBD, however, presumes that the event history is a linear sequence of user actions. This paper challenges that notion by introducing *Hierarchical Event Histories*, a new approach which represents some of the end-user's task structure directly in the event history. PBD systems can then take advantage of this structure to operate more correctly and in more situations. To assist programmers in generating structured histories, we also present *Hieractors*, a new model that provides a simple and clear syntax for describing arbitrary, high-level application behaviors.

1 Introduction

In the early days of computers, there was little distinction between the *programmer* and the *end-user*. Programs were designed to solve a particular task, and to be used exclusively by programmers. Today, this could hardly be less true. Programs such as word processors, spreadsheets, and databases are designed to be very general and apply to a large class of problems. Contemporary end-users, meanwhile, have little or no experience or even interest in programming.

These two trends have created a problem: generic software packages must be *customized* to suit end-users' specific needs, but many end-users have no means available to them to do such customization. This often results in end-users performing tedious, repetitive tasks that computers *could* have performed for them. For example, consider the simple task of using a word processor to insert a line number before each line in a large document. We posed this problem to a small sample of our colleagues, and they all came to the same conclusion: programming. Some considered Emacs macros, or Hypertalk scripts, or even Unix scripts. However, not one respondent knew how to perform this task *without programming*. In fact, in virtually all word processors, there is no other alternative. Thus, most end-users would have no choice but to painstakingly enter all the line numbers manually. Sadly, a large amount of human-computer interaction is exactly this sort of tedium.

1.1 Programming by Demonstration

These issues prompted research into *Programming by Demonstration*, or PBD, an exciting and developing branch of HCI. The basic goal of PBD is to allow end-users to customize their software by *demonstrating* the desired behavior. In the line numbering example, the user might type "1" on line 1, and "2" on line 2. From this, the PBD system should *infer* the line numbering task, and perhaps automatically complete the task for the user. Indeed, research systems like Eager [3] can already do this. Other systems have applied PBD to such domains as widget creation [18], graphical editing [15], and general-purpose programming [16].

The key advantage of PBD is that it allows end-users to specify programs *in the user interface*. They do not have to learn any special syntax or programming constructs. In essence, they do not have to program in the conventional sense, yet they are able to customize their software to suit their particular needs.

1.2 Challenges to PBD

PBD is a technology of great promise. However, there are numerous problems yet to be solved before PBD will realize its full potential. These include:

- **User Intent**
  The primary concern of PBD is determining the *user's intent* in performing some actions. This requires *generalizing* the user's actions into a script which runs correctly under different circumstances. For example, say we have a word processor which has a **Style** menu and one of this menu's choices is **Bold**. Selecting **Bold** toggles the boldness of the selected text. We next demonstrate a script where we only select **Bold** from the **Style** menu. What should happen when we replay the script? This is unclear. We *might* have intended to record *setting* the text to bold. However, we also might have intended to record *toggling* the boldness of the text. Moreover, the difficulty of determining user intent grows quickly as the complexity of scripts increases.

- **Context**
  PBD systems often require access to the *context* in which a demonstration occurs. For example, if the user's intention was to set the text to bold, the inferred script should resemble the following:

```
unless <the-selected-text-is-bold>
    select "Bold" from the "Style" menu
```

The **unless** is necessary to prevent toggling when the selected text is already bold. To create this script, the PBD system must know whether the selected text was bold during the demonstration (*i.e.*, it must have accessed some context of the word processor). This poses several unsolved problems; specifically, how should the PBD system

  - determine the available context from an application?
  - access the context?
  - reason over the context?

- **Script Matching**

  Many behaviors are too complex to infer from a single demonstration. In this case, users must give *multiple demonstrations*, showing how the script runs in different situations. Conditionals are the most common case: as users can demonstrate only one branch at a time, conditionals require multiple demonstrations. This presents a problem: given two demonstrations of the same script, the PBD system must *match* the scripts, determining which steps are the same and which differ (and, ultimately, *why* they differ). Matching can be complicated because there can be several ways of accomplishing the same task, and users may be inconsistent across examples. For example, a desktop interface might support file deletion either by dragging the file icon to the trash icon, or first selecting the file icon and then selecting **Delete** from the **File** menu. While both methods satisfy the same high-level goal, few existing PBD systems could match them. This may generate a useless rule for selecting which method to use, which then may require more examples than are strictly necessary to learn the behavior.

- **Anticipation Feedback**

  Script mismatches can be reduced with *Anticipation Feedback*, as demonstrated in Eager [3]. Here, the PBD system encourages consistency across examples by indicating what event the PBD system anticipates will next occur. For example, if the PBD system anticipates that the user will select a certain button, it may highlight the button in green. The user can then perform the action, or tell the PBD system to do it. In any case, if selecting the button is a reasonable alternative, the user is more likely to do so.

  Developers wishing to include Anticipation Feedback in their applications must address the *reverse-mapping* problem: if the PBD system records events at a high level (as most do), these high-level events must be mapped back into widget-level events for anticipation. To do this, the PBD system must first be aware of the possible mappings. Second, it must *choose* one, probably the same one the user last chose. Indeed, Eager includes special code to do this. The challenge is to provide this to PBD systems in a general manner.

- **Invocation**

  In [14], we propose that PBD systems should allow users to demonstrate both programs as well as *when to invoke* those programs. Furthermore, they should not restrict the kinds of events which invoke programs. Most PBD systems only support a small, fixed selection of invoking events, such as clicking on certain icons or choosing certain menu items. This limits the utility of the PBD system, however. For example, say that a user wishes to copy all files to a backup directory before they are deleted. The script which performs the copying is easy to demonstrate, but most systems could not invoke the script before each **Delete-File** event. Thus, expanding the invocation techniques extends PBD to solve problems it otherwise could not.

This is by no means an exhaustive list. Other issues include how to represent the inferred script, allow the user to edit the script, and recover from errors while running the script. A more complete discussion of these issues is in [5].

1.3 High-Level Event Histories

A major factor in the quality of a PBD system is the level at which events are recorded. PBD systems based on *device-level events* (*i.e.*, mouse and keyboard events) are very unreliable. For example, if a **Mouse-Down** event selected some object, replaying the same event would select the same object only if the object is uncovered, in the same location, and not selected. Indeed, the same **Mouse-Down** event might invoke other, possibly destructive behavior.

In response to these concerns, various notions of *high-level events* were developed. High-level events vary by system, but generally equate to user actions such as **Delete-File**, **Make-Bold**, and **Quit-Application**. In these systems, an application processes low-level events in the normal manner until it determines that a high-level event should be performed. This event is then passed to the PBD system, *where it is recorded*, then back to the application, where it is finally executed. Thus, PBD systems can ignore device-level events, and reason over high-level event histories. This produces scripts which are more correct, more efficient, and more understandable.

2 Hierarchical Event Histories

The same arguments that favor high-level events over device-level events, however, also favor even *higher*-level events. Moreover, there is an occasional need for low-level events, too. For example, consider the user of a word processor saving the current file under the name "foo". To do this, she first selects **Save** from the **File** menu. This generates a dialog box for specifying the filename. There is a default value—the current filename—so she enters **control-u** to delete the text. She then enters the new name. Finally, she clicks on the "OK" button. How should the event history depict this sequence?

One possibility is a single high-level event, namely **Save-File("foo")**. This has the virtues listed in the previous section on high-level events. Unfortunately, it is also limiting. The most compelling argument is based on *correctness*— occasionally, only device-level events accurately portray the user's intent. Say the user demonstrates making a backup copy by appending ".bak" to the current filename. If the current filename is "foo", the macro should save the backup as "foo.bak". To demonstrate this, the user brings up the dialog box from the previous example, but does not delete the filename. Instead, she appends to it by typing ".bak". Then she clicks on the "OK" button. How should this sequence appear in the history?

The corresponding high-level event is **Save-File("foo.bak")**. Replaying this when the current filename is "bar", however, would produce a file called "foo.bak", not "bar.bak". An advanced PBD system might fix this with *context* and *inferencing*, generalizing the event to:

Save-File(append *current-filename* ".bak")

However, the PBD system might require vast time and space resources to make this inference. Even worse, it might fail to infer this at all. Notice, however, that the net effect of the device-level events is equivalent to the generalized **Save-File** event. Thus, if device-level events are in the event history, they can be replayed directly, and *no inferencing is necessary!*

Including low-level events in the history has additional benefits for PBD and other areas as well. In the file-saving example, events such as **Open-Dialog**, **Set-String**, and **Close-Dialog** can be applied to:

- **Invocation:** A third-party vendor might provide a *macro-based help facility* for the word processor. This might include a window with some text on how to specify the filename when saving a file. The help facility would include a macro which displays this window upon the **Open-Dialog** event, and another macro which hides the window upon the **Close-Dialog** event. Similarly, another vendor might supply an *automatic spell-checker* which is invoked by the **Set-String** event.
- **Undo:** Suppose the user errantly typed **control-u** and deleted the current filename. In most systems, she must then retype the entire filename or abort the save operation. Including low-level events in the event stream, however, allows her to Undo the errant **Key-Press**.
- **Anticipation feedback:** Say that the PBD system correctly anticipates that the user will next issue a **Save-File** event. How should this be conveyed to the user? This is the reverse-mapping problem mentioned above. If the widget-level events are in the event history, the PBD system can iteratively anticipate those.

Thus, many different levels of events should be included in the history. However, it is semantically incorrect to include multiple event levels in a *linear* event stream. That is, the history cannot be flat, as in Figure 1.

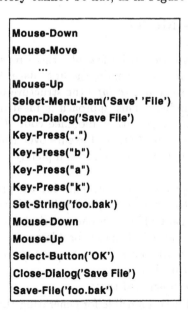

Fig. 1. A flat history comprised of multiple levels of events.

If this sequence were played back, the device-level events would generate extra instances of each high-level event. This would result in *three* `Close-Dialog` events, for example. Thus, if multiple event levels are in the event stream, the event stream itself cannot be linear—it must reflect the actual hierarchy of events. In this example, it must be structured as in Figure 2.

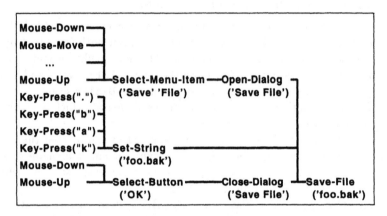

Fig. 2. The same history as in Figure 1, but here we show the hierarchical structure.

This argument is the basis for *Hierarchical Event Histories*. We propose that applications should be structured so that they generate histories such as the one above. This will allow PBD systems, Undo facilities, and other history mechanisms to operate more correctly and in more situations.

3 The Hieractors Model

For hierarchical event histories to be feasible, there must be a simple way for application designers to *generate* them in the first place. We attacked this problem in three ways. First, we hoped to *infer* the structure based on the read-write patterns of the event handlers. This approach is ideal from the programmer's perspective, since it would work with unmodified code. Unfortunately, while we could infer the *partial sequential order* of events over time, read-write patterns alone do not provide enough information to completely determine the hierarchical structure.

We then tried the opposite approach, requiring the programmer to *explicitly construct* the hierarchy. To that end, we provided functions such as `Create-Event`, `Add-Child`, and `Set-Parent`. This approach worked fine for simple cases, but did not scale well. As we attacked harder problems, we had to repeatedly add new history-manipulation functions. These became so unwieldy that it was impractical to continue in this direction.

From these efforts we concluded that:

– programmers should be responsible for generating the event hierarchy; and
– there should be some architectural support to simplify this process.

We satisfied these criteria by developing *Hieractors*, a new model for expressing high-level behaviors. Hieractors (from *Hierarchical Interactors*) are inspired by the Interactors model [19]. Interactors are effective in describing widget-level interface behaviors. Hieractors generalize this model to provide a simple and clear syntax for describing arbitrary, high-level application behaviors.

The basic idea behind hieractors is that most application behaviors are naturally defined in terms of the events which start, run, stop, and abort them. For example, consider the behavior of selecting a button in a graphical interface. The hieractor providing this behavior would start on a **Mouse-Down** in the button, run on **Mouse-Moves**, and stop on a **Mouse-Up** in the button (aborting on other **Mouse-Ups**). This behavior is supplied by the following code fragment:

```
(create-instance 'Button-Behavior *hieractor*
  (:result-type  'Select-Button)
  (:start-when   'Mouse-Down)
  (:running-when 'Mouse-Move)
  (:stop-when    '(Mouse-Up :where in-original-button?))
  (:abort-when   '(Mouse-Up :where outside-original-button?))
  ...)
```

When a hieractor completes, it issues a higher-level event (in this example, a **Select-Button** event). The children of this event are precisely the events which triggered the start, running, and stop actions. This leads to the simple, but hierarchical, history seen in Figure 3.

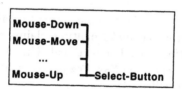

Fig. 3. A simple hierarchical history for selecting a button.

High-level events can also start, run, stop, or abort even *higher*-level behaviors. This leads to more complex hierarchical histories, such as the history depicted in the file saving example above. To illustrate, the **Save-File** event from that example could have been generated by the following:

```
(create-instance 'File-Saver *hieractor*
  (:result-type  'Save-File)
  (:start-when   '(Open-Dialog :where save-file-dialog?))
  (:running-when 'Set-String)
  (:stop-when    '(Close-Dialog :where save-file-dialog?))
  (:abort-when   '(Abort-Dialog :where save-file-dialog?))
  ...)
```

Expressing the common high-level application behaviors required some extensions to this model, the most important being:

- **Event Combinations**

Some behaviors make a transition (*i.e.*, start, run, stop, or abort) after a *sequence* of events. For example, in a calculator, the **Add-Numbers** behavior starts on an **Enter-Number** followed by a **Select-Button** where the selected button's label is "+". Similarly, transitions can occur after *either* of two (or more) events.

- **Scoping**

When a hieractor, such as the "file-saver" above, is defined, it is attached to an object called its *scope*. The hieractor can only observe events which pass through this scope. For widgets, the scope usually corresponds to the graphical objects making up the widget. Thus, mouse clicks over a scrollbar are not needlessly processed by, say, the menubar in the same window. Sometimes behaviors must observe events from multiple widgets, or events that are not even associated with widgets. These behaviors can have a scope of any window, any application, or the entire system (where they observe every event).

Behaviors sometimes start in one scope, but run in another. For example, consider moving an object in a graphical editor. When idle, this behavior should wait for a **Mouse-Down** event *inside an object*. Once running, however, it must observe **Mouse-Move** events *anywhere in the window*. For this reason, behaviors can specify a separate *running scope*. For convenience, this can be specified relative to the initial scope. In the example, the running scope is :window, meaning whatever window the object is in.

- **Priorities**

It is possible (and common) for two hieractors to claim the same event. In fact, the *same* hieractor can make multiple claims on a single event. For example, consider editing a one-line text field. This starts on any **Key-Press** event, but it also runs over other **Key-Press** events, and stops when the user hits **Return**. This is specified as:

```
(create-instance 'Simple-Text-Editor *hieractor*
  (:start-when   'Key-Press)
  (:running-when 'Key-Press)
  (:stop-when    '(Key-Press :where return-key?))
  ...)
```

Say the user types "H", then "i", then **Return**. The "H" unambiguously starts the hieractor. The "i", however, can either be a running event or *another start event*. Which transition should be favored by the event dispatcher? One solution is to disallow hieractors from starting while running. This is unnecessary and restrictive, however. Instead, transitions have integer *priorities*, where the larger priority is favored (and ties are decided randomly). Also, priorities can be *absolute*, or *relative* to the start priority. By default, abort events have the highest priority, followed by stop events, running events, and finally start events. Thus, for example, the text editor would process the "i" as a running event.

A more complete discussion of Hieractors is given in [13]. Note, however, that we have satisfied the design criteria for Hieractors. First, the programmer, not the PBD system, defines the structure of the application. Second, Hieractors provide significant architectural support to assist in this task. Our experiences indicate that programming with Hieractors requires about the same effort as conventional programming. However, Hieractors provide hierarchical event histories, with all their advantages.

4   Advantages of Hierarchical Event Histories

The key advantage to our model is that it represents some of the end-user's task structure directly in the event history. PBD systems can then take advantage of this structure to operate more correctly and in more situations. Referring back to the various challenges facing PBD systems, hierarchical event histories address many of these issues:

- **User Intent**
  Hierarchical event histories can aid in determining user intent because they expose more levels of user actions to the PBD system. Each level of the event hierarchy is typically a *specialization* of the level below it, corresponding to the effect the lower level events have *in the current context*. For example, consider when the user selects **Bold** from the **Style** menu. This would produce a **Toggle-Bold** event, which then produces a **Set-Bold** event in some contexts and a **Clear-Bold** event in others. Thus, the history contains *both* the toggle and setting (or clearing) behaviors, enabling the PBD system to offer both options to the end-user *without making any inferences!*
- **Context**
  While our approach does not address the context problem directly, it does reduce the situations in which context is even necessary. Or, to rephrase this, hierarchical event histories extend the coverage of PBD systems which do not have access to application context. This is because high-level events *implicitly* include some context, as just described. Note that this is only a partial solution, however, as the user's intent may depend on context that is not implicit in the hierarchy. Even in these cases, however, the PBD system can select from the various levels to choose which should be generalized.
- **Script Matching**
  One cause of mismatched events in multiple scripts is when there are multiple ways to perform some action, as in the file deletion example from above. Hierarchical event histories can reduce script mismatches in many of these cases, as the mismatched low-level events may be children of easily matchable high-level events. For example, say the user first demonstrates deleting a file by dragging it to the trash, and later demonstrates the same step by selecting the file and selecting **Delete** from the **File** menu. While the low-level events are completely different, both actions will produce *the same high-level event*, namely **Delete-File**, thus making the matching a trivial task. While this

does not solve the generalization problem (*i.e.*, what the *arguments* to the `Delete-File` should be), at least it advances the PBD system to that step.

- **Anticipation Feedback**

  Hierarchical event histories provide exactly the low-level support needed to solve the reverse-mapping problem for Anticipation Feedback. This is because the recorded script *contains the widget-level events*. This enables the PBD system to anticipate an event above the widget level by iteratively anticipating the low-level events it comprises.

- **Invocation**

  PBD systems that allow arbitrary events to invoke user-defined programs can further benefit from hierarchical event histories. Including high-level events such as `Delete-File` in the event history allows programs to be invoked when these events occur. Moreover, including low-level events such as `Key-Press` and `Select-Button` in the event history supports the invocation techniques currently available to users. By exposing more levels of a user's task structure, our approach gives users more control over how and when their programs are invoked.

There are additional benefits to hierarchical event histories. For example, by allowing recorded scripts to be replayed at the highest semantically correct level, they can be *more efficient* than linear events. Also, while outside the scope of this paper, hierarchical event histories benefit other parts of HCI, such as Undo, Help, and Task Analysis.

5 Related Work

For people interested in learning more about Programming by Demonstration, [4] presents a thorough overview and history of the field and describes the current state-of-the-art. The crucial problem of determining user intent was first described in [8]. While many systems have made inroads on this problem, perhaps the most promising is Cima [17], a learning architecture being developed specifically for PBD systems. We are currently pursuing ways to integrate our work with the Cima environment.

While there are many user interface specification techniques (such as [9, 11, 7]), these do not address the nature of the event history. Approaches such as TAG [21] and GOMS [2] do consider the hierarchical task structure, but not how to *generate* such a history (*i.e.*, they are *analytical*, not *constructive*). A more hybrid approach is taken in Task-Oriented Parsing [10], which is somewhat constructive and hierarchical. It is based on context-free grammars, however, which are less powerful than event-based models, and cannot describe some important user interface behaviors [7]. Moreover, their approach is not truly constructive because they provide "normal feedback" only for "meaningful tasks", and not "all [user] input actions."

The simpler high-level event model is supported by numerous systems. In particular, most model-based UIMS's, including MIKE [12], UIDE [6], Humanoid [22], and others. We extended Garnet [20] because of our expertise with that model, and because the resulting Hieractors model is clear, concise, and efficient. It seems reasonable that other model-based UIMS's could be adapted to generate hierarchical event histories as well. Also, Apple Events [1] are a high-level event paradigm now employed by a large and growing vendor population. Because of this, we are considering converting Hieractors to operate over Apple Events.

6 Status and Future Work

The ideas presented here serve as the basis for Katie [13], an application environment which includes a Hieractors interpreter for the basic model with the extensions listed in this paper. Katie also includes two widget sets (a basic set and a more complicated Motif look-and-feel set), several small applications, and a larger database-type application. At this point, we have proven the viability of the Hieractors model for generating hierarchical event histories. The next phase of this research will focus on the graphical presentation and manipulation of the structured history, and the many applications of hierarchical event histories.

7 Acknowledgments

We would like to thank Allen Cypher, Francesmary Modugno, and James Landay for their help with this paper.

This research was sponsored by the Avionics Lab, Wright Research and Development Center, Aeronautical Systems Division (AFSC), U. S. Air Force, Wright-Patterson AFB, OH 45433-6543 under Contract F33615-90-C-1465, Arpa Order No. 7597.

The views and conclusions contained in this document are those of the authors and should not be interpreted as representing the official policies, either expressed or implied, of the U.S. Government.

References

1. Apple Computer, Inc. *Inside Macintosh Volume VI*. Addison-Wesley, Reading, MA, 1991.
2. Stuart K. Card, Thomas P. Moran, and Allen Newell. *The Psychology of Human-Computer Interaction*. Lawrence Erlbaum, Hillsdale, NJ, 1983.
3. Allen Cypher. Eager: Programming repetative tasks by example. In *Human Factors in Computing Systems*, pages 33–40, New Orleans, April 1991. ACM SIGCHI.
4. Allen Cypher, editor. *Watch What I Do: Programming by Demonstration*. MIT Press, Cambridge, MA, 1993.
5. Allen Cypher, David S. Kosbie, and David Maulsby. Characterizing PBD systems. In Allen Cypher, editor, *Watch What I Do: Programming by Demonstration*, pages 467–484. MIT Press, Cambridge, MA, 1993.
6. James Foley, Won Chul Kim, Srdjan Kovacevic, and Kevin Murray. Defining interfaces at a high level of abstraction. *IEEE Software*, 6(1):25–32, January 1989.

7. Mark Green. A survey of three dialog models. *ACM Transactions on Graphics*, 5(3):244–275, July 1986.

8. Daniel C. Halbert. SmallStar: Programming by demonstration in the desktop metaphor. In Allen Cypher, editor, *Watch What I Do: Programming by Demonstration*, pages 103–124. MIT Press, Cambridge, MA, 1993.

9. H. Rex Hartson, Antonio C. Siochi, and Deborah Hix. The UAN: A user-oriented representation for direct manipulation interface designs. *ACM Transactions on Information Systems*, 8(3):181–203, July 1990.

10. Heinz Ulrich Hoppe. A grammar-based approach to unifying task-oriented and system-oriented interface descriptions. In D. Ackermann and M.J. Tauber, editors, *Mental Models and Human-Computer Interaction 1*, pages 353–374. North-Holland, New York, 1990.

11. Robert J.K. Jacob. A specification language for direct manipulation interfaces. *ACM Transactions on Graphics*, 5(4):283–317, October 1986.

12. Dan R. Olsen Jr. Mike: The menu interaction kontrol environment. *ACM Transactions on Graphics*, 5(4):318–344, October 1986.

13. David S. Kosbie. Hierarchical event histories. PhD thesis. In preparation, 1994.

14. David S. Kosbie and Brad A. Myers. PBD invocation techniques: A review and proposal. In Allen Cypher, editor, *Watch What I Do: Programming by Demonstration*, pages 423–432. MIT Press, Cambridge, MA, 1993.

15. David Kurlander and Steven Feiner. Editable graphical histories. In *Workshop on Visual Languages*, pages 127–134, Pittsburgh, October 1988. IEEE.

16. Henry Lieberman. Tinker: A programming by demonstration system for beginning programmers. In Allen Cypher, editor, *Watch What I Do: Programming by Demonstration*, pages 49–66. MIT Press, Cambridge, MA, 1993.

17. David Maulsby. *Instructible Agents*. PhD thesis, University of Calgary, Calgary, Alberta, Canada, 1994. PhD thesis.

18. Brad A. Myers. *Creating User Interfaces by Demonstration*. Academic Press, Boston, 1988.

19. Brad A. Myers. A new model for handling input. *ACM Transactions on Information Systems*, 8(3):289–320, July 1990.

20. Brad A. Myers et al. Garnet: Comprehensive support for graphical, highly-interactive user interfaces. *IEEE Computer*, 23(11):71–85, November 1990.

21. Franz Sciele and Thomas Green. HCI formalisms and cognitive psychology: The case of task-action grammar. In Michael Harrison and Harold Thimbleby, editors, *Formal Methods in Human-Computer Interaction*, pages 9–62. Cambridge University Press, Cambridge, 1990.

22. Pedro Szekely, Ping Luo, and Robert Neches. Facilitating the exploration of interface design alternatives: The Humanoid model of interface design. In *Human Factors in Computing Systems*, pages 507–515, Monterrey, CA, May 1992. ACM SIGCHI.

Hierarchical Design of User Interfaces

Mark Sh. Levin

Independent Consultant/Researcher,
Sumskoy Proezd, 5-1-103, Moscow, 113208, Russia
mark@levin.msk.su

Abstract. This paper describes a method for designing a user interface from a variety of presentation elements (e.g., icon, menu, flowchart, bar chart, etc.). The interface is composed hierarchically, and at each step the most appropriate design alternatives (hereafter denoted by "As") are selected, based on "hierarchical morphological multicriteria design" (HMMD). We will present a detailed example for data processing in a decision support system (DSS) for multicriteria ranking.

1 Introduction

Recently, there has been considerable interest in User Interface Development Environments (UIDE) and User Interface Management Systems (UIMS) [1, 2, 9, 10, 12, etc.]. Hix investigated four generations of UIMSs [9]. Usually functional / task analysis and models of human computer interaction (HCI) are used as the main approaches to user interface design [10, 18, etc.]. The list of basic HCI models includes the following [10, 18]: (1) Command Language Grammar (CLG); (2) Task Action Language (TAL); (3) Task Analysis for Knowledge Description (TAKD); (4) GOMS approach (Goals, Operators, Methods and Selection Models); (5) Task Mapping Model (TMM); etc.

Traditional approaches to interface design are oriented to the analysis, evaluation and selection of design choices [1, 10, 12, etc.]. Mainly, comparison and selection of various versions of interface component (e.g., icon, text, direct manipulation, menu, etc.) is based on the following techniques:

(a) experimental investigation [3];
(b) rules [1, 4, 12, etc.];
(c) Analytic Hierarchical Process (AHP) [19].

In recent years object oriented development techniques are used for user interface design also [5, 20, etc.]. Fisher reviews some investigations in the optimal design of human interfaces, including combinatorial optimization problems [8]. The use of object-oriented development, TMM, and optimal design approach point out that there is a movement towards synthesizing techniques for implementation in human interface design.

This paper describes a process for hierarchically composing a user interface from presentation elements. HMMD is proposed [17] as a basis for composing from various "As" (i.e. Alternatives). We investigate a hypothetical example, based on the interface of DSS COMBI for multicriteria ranking [14, 15]. Our example may be considered as a posteriori analysis of this interface.

2 HMMD

HMMD is similar to some discipline-independent approaches based on decision making, creation and knowledge-based technology, e.g., Morphological Analysis [25], AHP [21], Structured Design [24, etc.], Object Oriented Development [5], Design Methodology of Carnegie Mellon University [7], etc. HMMD is described in details in [17].

The following assumptions are taken into account:

1. Tree-like structure of the designed system.
2. System effectiveness is represented as an aggregation of two parts: subsystem effectiveness, and effectiveness of compatibility among subsystems.
3. Monotonic criteria (Cr) for system components are used.
4. Effectiveness of subsystem interconnections (Is) is equal to an aggregation of all pairwise compatibilities between subsystems. Here we use an ordinal scale of pairwise compatibility (0...5; '5' is the best one, '0' corresponds to impossible Is).
5. For As, multicriteria descriptions (without compatibility) are transformed into effectiveness that is evaluated on an ordinal scale r=1...k, ('1' corresponds to the best group, here k=4).
6. All scales of component assessment are coordinated.

HMMD consists of information elements (a tree-like model of the designed system and the design module), procedures, and user(s). The design module corresponds to a node in the hierarchical model and includes the following: Cr; As and their estimates on Cr; estimates of Is between As of different components (morphoclasses); constraints (for composition nodes); result information (ranking of As, etc.).

The generalized scheme of HMMD is:

Phase 1. Top-Down design of system model (the design of a tree-like model; design of Cr; specification of constraints for composed As.

Phase 2. Generation of As for leaf nodes of the model.

Phase 3. Bottom-Up hierarchical selection and composition (iterative): evaluation of As on Cr; multicriteria comparison of As; specification of Is among As; composition of As for higher hierarchical level.

HMMD includes two main problems: multicriteria selection of As, and composition of As. The techniques for solving the first problem are well-known [6, etc.]. DSS COMBI is used for multicriteria ranking in our example. However, the results for other techniques will be similar. Let us consider the composition problem [16]: Find a composition (S=S1*...*Si*...*Sm, where Si is the ith component) of As (one representative from each morphoclass) with non-zero Is. Similar problems (e.g., problem on compatible representatives, clique) have been considered by a number of authors [11, 23, 25, etc.]. Here the following quality vector for solution S is used: N(S)=(w(S);n(S)), where w(S) is the minimum of pairwise compatibilities in S, n(S)=(n(1),...,n(r),...,n(k)), where n(r) is the number of components of the rth quality in S. Thus, we search for solutions which are nondominated by N(S).

The composition scheme is based on the following two stages:
  (1) construction of admissible morphoschemes [11, 23, 25];
  (2) selection of Pareto-effective solutions by N.

For analysis of composed solutions we use the following types of elements (As, Is) with respect to a solution S: S-improving, S-neutral, and S-aggravating ones by vector N, where elements of the latter type are considered as 'bottlenecks'. Finally, it is reasonable to introduce a series of solution sets, which form an ordinal scale of system perfection:
  (1) ideal solution (from the best components);
  (2) Pareto-points by N;
  (3) quasi-solutions (a solution from this set may be transformed by only one improving step into Pareto-point).

3 Fragment of User Interface

We study only one basic flow of data in DSS COMBI, where the element of information is a preference relation or matrix, and the problem solving process is represented as a series transformation of the data $\{D^v\}$ [15]:
  (1) aernatives, criteria, multicriteria estimates of alternatives upon criteria (D^0);
  (2) preference relation of alternatives (D^1);
  (3) termediate linear ordering of alternatives (D^2);
  (4) intermediate group ordering of alternatives (D^3);
  (5) result data (ranking of alternatives, e.g., result group ordering, fuzzy group ordering) (D^4).

The list of functional operations realizes a processing of the following kind: $D^v \rightarrow D^j$, when $v=0,...,3$; $j=1,...,4$; $j>v$. Data editing operations are: (a) input, (b) correction, (c) presentation, (d) output, and (e) import/export. COMBI involves the following main modes: (a) choice or creation of the application problem; (b) problem solving (multicriteria ranking) on the basis of various techniques; (c) result analysis; (d) help (learning, training); (e) data import / export; (f) quit.
  Thus, we consider the following components of a user interface fragment: (1) system mode management; (2) planning / management of the solution process; (3) data processing operations; and (4) data editing and presentation.

4 Composing a User Interface Fragment

Let us consider the steps of user interface design and analysis based on HMMD. Here we do not use constraints.
  A model of a user interface fragment is depicted in Fig. 1 (phase 1 of HMMD). The notations on leaf nodes are the following: Y is a presentation of main modes (solving, help, quit, etc.); Z is a basic colour composition for the presentation of main modes (screen background, presentation element background, text, frame); J is a presentation of a functional scheme for data processing; L is a presentation of

functional operations for data processing ($D^v \rightarrow D^j$); H is a presentation of connections among functional operations; K is an acoustic effect (sound) for an operational part; X is a colour composition for the presentation of an operational part (background, text, frame); E is a scheme for presenting data; R is a presentation of data (numbers, table, flowchart, etc.); Q is a presentation of data editing operations (input, correction, etc.); B is a sound for a factual part; C is a colour composition for the presentation of a factual part (background, text, frame).

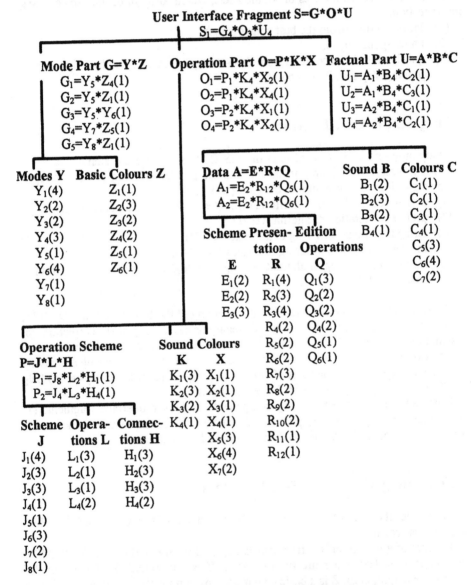

Fig. 1. Hierarchical scheme of a user interface fragment
(effectiveness of As is shown in brackets)

Usually the following main Cr for interface evaluation are considered: acceptability; usability; learnability; efficiency; easy of use [10, 20, etc.]. We use a similar set of Cr (Table 1).

The results of As generation for leaf nodes are shown in Tables 2, 3, 4 (phase 2 of HMMD). These tables contain estimates of As on Cr. Results of multicriteria ranking (effectiveness of As) are shown in Fig. 1 (in brackets). Table 5 contains compatibility of As.

Table 1 Criteria and their weights for components

Cr	W e i g h t s										
	Y	J	L	H	E	R	Q	Z	X	C	K	B
1. Tradition (habits)	5	3	5	5	5	3	2	-	-	-	-	-
2. Volume of information	1	6	4	2	4	-	4	-	-	-	-	-
3. Complexity of development (negative)	3	3	3	4	4	2	3	-	-	-	2	2
4. Usability	6	6	6	5	5	5	6	5	6	6	6	-	-
5. Ease of use	6	6	6	5	5	5	6	5	-	-	-	-
6. Possibility for extension	4	2	2	3	5	5	3	-	-	-	-	-
7. Learnability	2	6	6	4	6	6	4	-	-	-	3	3
8. Acceptability	-	-	-	-	-	-	-	5	5	5	5	5
9. Efficiency	-	-	-	-	-	-	-	-	-	-	3	3

Table 2 *As* of basic presentation elements

Desig-nation	As	C r						
		1	2	3	4	5	6	7
Y_1	Command language	4	6	5	2	2	5	2
Y_2	Vertical menu	4	6	2	4	4	3	4
Y_3	Horizontal menu	4	6	2	4	4	3	4
Y_4	Flowchart	2	3	4	6	5	2	6
Y_5	Icon	3	4	3	5	6	3	6
Y_6	Matrix menu	1	5	3	4	4	2	4
Y_7	Pop-Up menu	4	6	5	5	4	5	3
Y_8	Catalogue menu	3	6	4	5	4	5	4
J_1	Command language	4	6	5	2	2	5	2
J_2	Vertical menu	4	4	2	4	4	3	4
J_3	Horizontal menu	4	4	2	4	4	3	4
J_4	Flowchart	3	4	3	5	6	2	6
J_5	Icon	3	4	3	5	6	3	6
J_6	Matrix menu	1	5	3	4	4	2	4
J_7	Pop-Up menu	3	6	5	5	4	5	3
J_8	Catalogue menu	3	6	4	5	4	5	4

Table 2. *As* of basic presentation elements (continued)

Desig-nation	As	C r						
		1	2	3	4	5	6	7
L_1	Command language	4	6	5	2	2	5	2
L_2	Icon	3	3	3	5	6	3	6
L_3	Elements of flowchart	2	3	3	5	6	2	6
L_4	Elements of menu	3	6	5	5	4	3	3
H_1	Table (matrix)	4	5	4	3	2	4	3
H_2	Element (pair)	3	6	2	2	3	5	2
H_3	List of elements	2	6	3	3	3	5	2
H_4	Graph	3	3	5	5	4	3	6
E_1	Table of connections	4	3	3	2	2	2	2
E_2	Flowchart	3	3	4	5	5	2	6
E_3	Catalogue	3	6	5	5	4	5	3
R_1	Numbers	3	-	1	1	3	1	4
R_2	Table (matrix)	3	-	2	3	3	2	4
R_3	Preference graph	2	-	5	4	2	3	3
R_4	Vertical bar chart	3	-	3	3	4	3	4
R_5	Horizontal bar chart	3	-	3	3	4	3	4
R_6	Pie chart	3	-	3	3	4	3	4
R_7	Star chart	2	-	3	4	4	2	5
R_8	Graphical presentation of layers (e.g., Pareto effective points)	2	-	4	5	4	4	5
R_9	Animation	2	-	6	5	3	3	6
R_{10}	Table & bar chart	3	-	4	5	4	3	4
R_{11}	Table & bar chart & pie chart	3	-	5	6	4	3	4
R_{12}	All versions	3	-	8	8	5	4	2
Q_1	Command language	4	6	5	2	2	5	2
Q_2	Vertical menu	4	5	2	4	4	3	4
Q_3	Horizontal menu	4	5	2	4	4	3	4
Q_4	Matrix menu	2	6	3	4	4	3	5
Q_5	List of icons	3	4	3	5	6	3	6
Q_6	Pop-Up menu	3	6	4	5	4	5	3

Table 3. *As* of colour compositions

Designation	As	C	r
		4	8
Z_1	black-blue-white-white	6	5
Z_2	white-blue-yellow-black	5	2
Z_3	cyan-blue-white-black	3	6
Z_4	cyan-blue-cyan-black	4	4
Z_5	cyan-white-blue-black	5	5
Z_6	blue-white-black-black	6	4
$X_1(C_1)$	green-black-black	5	4
$X_2(C_2)$	blue-yellow-black	5	4
$X_3(C_3)$	blue-white-black	6	4
$X_4(C_4)$	blue-cyan-black	6	4
$X_5(C_5)$	blue-cyan-white	4	3
$X_6(C_6)$	white-blue-black	3	2
$X_7(C_7)$	grey-black-black	4	4

Table 4. *As* of sound

Designation	As	C	.	r	
		3	7	8	9
K1	None	0	0	3	0
K2	Start	1	1	1	2
K3	End	1	2	1	2
K4	Process	3	2	2	1
B1	None	0	0	3	0
B2	Start	1	1	1	1
B3	End	1	2	1	1
B4	Process	3	2	2	1

Table 5. Compatibility between *As*

	Y_1	Y_2	Y_3	Y_4	Y_5	Y_6	Y_7	Y_8
Z_1	3	1	1	3	4	3	3	4
Z_2	2	1	1	2	4	3	2	2
Z_3	2	4	4	4	4	4	4	3
Z_4	2	4	4	4	5	3	3	3
Z_5	2	4	4	4	3	4	3	3
Z_6	3	2	2	3	4	3	3	3

	L_1	L_2	L_3	L_4	H_1	H_2	H_3	H_4
J_1	5	0	0	0	1	2	2	1
J_2	0	0	0	5	1	2	2	1
J_3	0	0	0	5	1	2	2	1
J_4	1	1	5	1	3	2	2	4
J_5	0	5	0	0	3	2	2	3
J_6	1	2	0	4	4	2	2	2
J_7	1	2	0	5	0	1	1	3
J_8	2	5	0	4	5	2	2	2
L_1					4	3	3	2
L_2					5	3	3	4
L_3					3	2	2	5
L_4					4	3	3	3

	Q_1	Q_2	Q_3	Q_4	Q_5	Q_6	E_1	E_2	E_3
R_1	3	3	3	4	4	4	0	0	2
R_2	3	3	3	5	4	4	3	5	1
R_3	3	3	3	4	4	4	2	5	2
R_4	3	4	2	4	3	2	4	4	4
R_5	3	2	4	4	3	2	4	4	4
R_6	3	3	4	4	4	3	4	4	4
R_7	3	3	4	4	4	3	4	4	4
R_8	3	3	4	4	4	3	4	4	4
R_9	3	3	4	3	4	4	4	4	4
R_{10}	3	4	4	5	4	4	4	5	4
R_{11}	3	4	4	5	4	4	4	5	4
R_{12}	5	5	5	5	5	5	5	5	5
Q_1							3	4	3
Q_2							4	3	5
Q_3							4	4	5
Q_4							3	5	3
Q_5							4	5	3
Q_6							4	5	3

	K_1	K_2	K_3	K_4	P_1	P_2
X_1	5	5	5	5	4	5
X_2	5	5	5	5	5	5
X_3	5	5	5	5	4	4
X_4	5	5	5	5	5	4
X_5	5	5	5	5	4	4
X_6	5	5	5	5	4	4
X_7	5	5	5	5	4	4
K_1					5	5
....					....	....
K_4					5	5

	B_1	B_2	B_3	B_4	A_1	A_2
C_1	5	5	5	5	4	5
C_2	5	5	5	5	5	5
C_3	5	5	5	5	5	4
C_4	5	5	5	5	4	4
....					....	....
C_7	5	5	5	5	4	4
B_1					5	5
....					....	....
B_4					5	5

	O_1	O_2	O_3	O_4	U_1	U_2	U_3	U_4
G_1	1	3	5	1	1	3	5	1
G_2	2	3	5	2	2	2	5	2
G_3	2	4	5	2	2	2	5	2
G_4	5	3	5	5	5	3	5	5
G_5	2	4	5	2	2	2	5	2
O_1					0	2	5	0
O_2					2	0	5	2
O_3					5	5	0	5
O_4					0	2	5	0

Composed As are presented in Table 6. Table 7 contains bottlenecks and improving activities.

Table 6. Composed solutions

As	N
$G_1=Y_5*Z_4$	5;1,1,0,0
$G_2=Y_5*Z_1$	4;2,0,0,0
$G_3=Y_5*Z_6$	4;2,0,0,0
$G_4=Y_7*Z_5$	4;2,0,0,0
$G_5=Y_8*Z_1$	4;2,0,0,0
$P_1=J_8*L_2*H_1$	5;2,0,1,0
$P_2=J_4*L_3*H_4$	4;2,1,0,0
$O_1=P_1*K_4*X_2$	5;3,0,0,0
$O_2=P_1*K_4*X_4$	5;3,0,0,0
$O_3=P_2*K_4*X_1$	5;3,0,0,0
$O_4=P_2*K_4*X_2$	5;3,0,0,0

As	N
$A_1=E_2*R_{12}*Q_5$	5;2,1,0,0
$A_2=E_2*R_{12}*Q_6$	5;2,1,0,0
$U_1=A_1*B_4*C_2$	5;3,0,0,0
$U_2=A_1*B_4*C_3$	5;3,0,0,0
$U_3=A_2*B_4*C_1$	5;3,0,0,0
$U_4=A_2*B_4*C_2$	5;3,0,0,0
$S_1=G_4*O_3*U_4$	5;3,0,0,0

Table7. Bottlenecks and improving activities

#	Composed solution	Bottleneck Component	Interconnection	Improvement activity w/r	Type
1	$G_1=Y_5*Z_4$	Z_4		2 -> 1	1
2	$G_2=Y_5*Z_1$		(Y_5,Z_1)	4 -> 5	1
3	$G_3=Y_5*Z_6$		(Y_5,Z_6)	4 -> 5	1
4	$G_4=Y_7*Z_5$		(Y_7,Z_5)	4 -> 5	1
5	$G_5=Y_8*Z_1$		(Y_8,Z_1)	4 -> 5	1
6	Y_2*Z_5	Y_2		2 -> 1	3
7	Y_3*Z_5	Y_3		2 -> 1	3
8	Y_5*Z_3	Z_3		2 -> 1	3
9	Y_7*Z_3	Z_3		2 -> 1	3
10	$P_1=J_8*L_2*H_1$	H_1		3 -> 1	1
11	$P_2=J_4*L_3*H_4$	H_4		2 -> 1	2
12	$P_2=J_4*L_3*H_4$		(J_4,H_4)	4 -> 5	2
13	$A_1=E_2*R_{12}*Q_5$	E_2		2 -> 1	1
14	$A_2=E_2*R_{12}*Q_6$	E_3		2 -> 1	1

Designation of improvement activity types are as follows:
1 corresponds to a generation of an ideal point; 2 corresponds to an improvement of a Pareto-point; 3 corresponds to an extension of a Pareto-point set.

5 Discussion

This example of human interface design corresponds to real stages of DSS COMBI development and implementation (Table 8).

The development of the first package was oriented to constructing DSS consisting of various techniques for multicriteria ranking. At the second stage, a flowchart of the solution process as a functional graph menu, including both operations and data, was realized [15]. This effort was based on an attempt to improve the interface by a diagram with direct manipulation of operations and data [13, 22]. However, experience using the package showed that the complete morphological solution scheme, presented on the screen, was difficult for many users to understand. In the third package, the operational part was implemented at an easier level and various bar & pie charts were added for data presentation.

Table 8. User interface elements of DSS COMBI versions

#	Version	Modes	Operations	Data presen-tation	data edition
1	Version for minicomputer (1987)	Command language (Y_1)	Command language $(J_1 * L_1 * H_3)$	Numbers $(E_1 * R_1)$	Command language (Q_1)
2	1st version for IBM PC/AT (1989)	Menu & catalogue $(Y_2 \& Y_8)$	Flowchart of solving scheme $(J_4 * L_3 * H_4)$	Table $(E_2 * R_2)$	Matrix menu (Q_4)
3	2nd version for IBM PC/AT (1991)	Pop-Up menu (Y_7)	Pop-Up menu $(J_7 * L_4 * H_4)$	Table & bar, pie charts $(E_2 * R_{11})$	Pop-Up menu (Q_6)

6 Conclusion

It is important to emphasize that these results are preliminary and are presented here primarily to illustrate the possibility of using hierarchical composition to design a user interface.

The author is indebted to a reviewer for helpful comments.

References

1. Bass, J. Coutaz: Developing Software for the User Interface. Series in Software Engineering. Reading, Addison Wesley (1991)
2. Bass, J. Coutaz, C. Unger: A Reference Model for Interactive System Construction. In: Proc. of International Conference on Human-Computer Interaction EWHCI'92, ICSTI, Moscow, Part 1, 23-30 (1992)
3. Benbasat and P. Todd: An Experimental Investigation of Interface Design Alternatives: Icon vs. Text and Direct Manipulation vs. Menus. Int. J. Man-Machine Studies, Vol. 38, 369-402 (1993)
4. Bodart, A.-M. Hennebert, J.M. Leheureux, I. Sacre, J. Vanderdonckt: Architecture Elements for Highly-Interactive Business-Oriented Applications. In: L.E. Bass, J. Gornostaev, and C. Unger (Eds.) Human-Computer Interaction. Proc., Lecture Notes in Computer Science, Vol. 753, Springer-Verlag, Berlin, 83-104 (1993)
5. Booch: Object Oriented Development. The Benjamin/Cummings Publishing Company, Inc., Redwood City, California (1991)
6. Buede: Software Review. Overview of MCDA Software Market, J. of Multi-Criteria Decision Analysis, No. 1, Vol. 1, 5 9-61 (1992)
7. Demes, S.J. Fenves, I.E. Grossmann, C.T. Hendrickson, T.M. Mitchell, F.B. Prinz, D.P. Siewiorek, E. Subrahmanian, S. Talukdar, and A.W. Westerberg: The Engineering Design Research Center of Carnegie Mellon University, Proc. of the IEEE, Vol. 81, No. 1, 10-23 (1993)
8. Fisher: Optimal Performance Engineering: Good, Better, Best. Human Factors, Vol. 35, No. 1, 115-139 (1993)
9. Hix: Generations of User-Interface Management Systems. IEEE Computer, Vol. 5, No. 5, 77-87 (1990)
10. Johnson: Human Computer Interaction. Psychology, Task Analysis and Software Engineering. McGraw-Hill, London (1992)
11. Knuth, and A. Raghunathan: The Problem of Compatible Representatives. SIAM Disc. Math., Vol. 5, No. 3, 422-427 (1992)
12. Larson: Interactive Software - Tools for Building Interactive User Interfaces. Yourdon Press Computing Series. Englewood Cliffs, Prentice Hall (1992)
13. Larkin and H. Simon: Why a diagram is (sometimes) worth 10,000 words. Cognitive Science, 11, 65-99 (1987)
14. M.Sh. Levin, and A.A. Michailov: Fragments of objects set stratification technology. Moscow, Institute for Systems Studies (in Russian) (1988)
15. M.Sh. Levin: Hierarchical Components of Human-Computer Systems. In: L.E. Bass, J. Gornostaev, and C. Unger (Eds.) Human-Computer Interaction. Proc., Lecture Notes in Computer Science, Vol. 753, Springer-Verlag, Berlin, 37-52 (1993)
16. M.Sh. Levin: Design and Analysis of Morphological Clique Problem. In: Abstracts of the 8th Conference on Combinatorial Optimization CO94, Amsterdam (1994)

17. M.Sh. Levin: Hierarchical Morphological Multicriteria Design. (in preparation) (1994)

18. Mayo, and H.R. Hartson: Synthesis-Oriented Situational Analysis in User Interface Design. In: L.E. Bass, J. Gornostaev, and C. Unger (Eds.) Human-Computer Interaction. Proc., Lecture Notes in Computer Science, Vol. 753, Springer-Verlag, Berlin, 53-67 (1993)

19. Mitta: An Application of the Analytic Hierarchy Process: A Rank-Ordering of Computer Interfaces, Human Factors, Vol. 35, No. 1, 141-157 (1993)

20. Nielsen: Usability Engineering. Academic Press. (1993)

21. Saaty: The Analytic Hierarchy Process. McGraw Hill, NY. (1988)

22. Shneiderman: Designing User Interface. Strategies for Effective Human-Computer Interaction. Addison-Wesley (1987)

23. Singhal, and J.L. Katz: A Branch-And-Fathom Algorithm for the Longe Range Process Design Problem, Management Science, Vol. 36, No. 4, 513-516 (1990)

24. Yourdon: Techniques of Program Structure and Design. Prentice-Hall, Inc., Englewood Cliffs, NJ. (1975)

25. Zwicky: Discovery Invention, Research Through the Morphological Approach. New York: McMillan & Co. (1969)

Conflict Resolution
in Computer-Supported Cooperative Design

Igor V. Kotenko

Telecommunication Academy
Tihorezky 3, K - 64, St.-Petersburg, 194064, RUSSIA
Ph. (812)556-94-97

Abstract. In this paper the problems of cooperative group design and its intelligent multi-agent computer-supported realization are considered. The subject of this paper is conflict resolution in multi-agent systems, where the agents might be human or computer. The principal roles of design conflict and conflict resolution are emphasized, and computational models of design conflict and conflict resolution are described. We propose a cooperative design system (CDS) architecture, as well as possible strategies for design, mechanisms for conflict detection, strategies for conflict resolution, and a heuristic scheme for choosing the most effective conflict resolution strategy. We also describe an object-oriented implementation of CDS using Smalltalk/V 286.

1 Introduction

One of the most appropriate application domains for research results in the area of cooperative work is design. As a rule, the design of complex artifacts is a problem-solving process between a set of cooperating specialists, or agents, where each agent (human or computer) has different goals, knowledge, constraints, resources and evaluation criteria.

Each design agent has insufficient local knowledge to solve the common problem, so the agents have to cooperate. The diversity of agents' knowledge, constraints etc. results in inconsistent proposals (solutions) and conflicts that have to be resolved. It is very difficult to resolve these conflicts, because the agents don't possess the same mental design model and don't use the same language and knowledge. When there is no strong global model of optimality (the global evaluation criterion is absent, or is too expensive to compute, or is a combination of agents' criteria), the problem is aggravated.

The purpose of our research was to build a computer-supported framework (and its prototype) - the cooperative design system (CDS) - to resolve the problem described.

We started our design work by studying different theoretical and practical approaches to design [1]. According to modern human activity theory [1,2], we consider computer-supported design as a cooperative multi-agent problem [3] where different human and computer agents are involved in an activity, motivated by their needs, and with corresponding goals and tasks. In addition, the computer agents in this model can be considered to be extensions of "internal planes of actions" [2].

2 The Role of Conflict Resolution

An intelligent CDS must support all aspects of conflict management [4]: conflict avoidance, detection, resolution, explanation and modification of designers' actions and also coordination of different agents' actions. These aspects of design conflict management were represented in [4].

Studies of human and computer-supported cooperative group design [4-11] show that conflicts play a principal role in the cooperative design process.

In this paper we mainly investigate the conflict resolution aspect.

3 Works on Computational Models of Conflict Resolution

The relevant directions for investigating models of conflict resolution are considered in figure 1. Almost none of these investigations (with the exception, for instance, of the LAN Designer system [5] or CEF [9]), however, constitutes a comprehensive computational model of conflict resolution for cooperative group design.

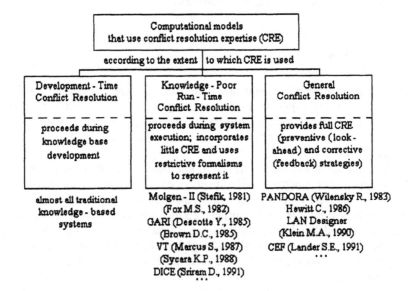

Fig. 1. Conflict resolution computational models

4 Cooperative Design Strategies

In accordance with the iterative generate-and-test process design model [4], the CDS uses a combination of refine-and-evaluate, least-commitment, constraint propagation, meta-level, case-based and qualitative reasoning (table 1).

All designed objects are represented as collections of known components with characteristic features, connected to each other via a defined set of links with known properties. Components use up or provide different kinds of resources.

Table 1. Cooperative design strategies (methods)

Strategy	Comments
Generate-and-test (refine and evaluate)	officials generate potential solutions for a given design subtask (beginning with a set of abstract specifications and finishing with a set of definitely-defined components); evaluate these solutions, identifying their negative and positive aspects (check the viability of the current design state); and modify the design to resolve the conflicts identified (generating goals to execute actions that in turn add constraints to the design, making it more specific)
Least-commitment	defer making arbitrary decisions as much as possible, until the desired data is obtained
Constraint propagation	design is a progressive refinement of an initial generic design description, through the application of successive constraints
Meta-level reasoning	reasoning about the state of the design rules and agents, as opposed to the state of the design
Skeleton (precedents) design (Case-Based Reasoning)	uses previous cases to come up with a solution to a new task. Design is provided by maintaining a knowledge base of skeleton (precedents) design, whose addressing mechanism permits the selection of the design associated with the goal "most similar" to the desired one, and then tailoring the selected design to the particular requirements of the actual design
Qualitative reasoning	uses core skills underlining designers to hypothesize, test, predict, create, optimize, diagnose and debug systems under investigation

5 Cooperative Design System Architecture

To accomplish the described strategies, we propose the CDS architecture (figure 2). It reflects a sophisticated local control approach with organizational structuring [12], elaborated in the field of artificial intelligence and based on the blackboard framework. It can also be considered as a model of human cognitive processes.

In a very real way, a sophisticated local control mechanism fully allows an agent to understand the implications of its planned design and communication actions on other agents' goals, beliefs and plans.

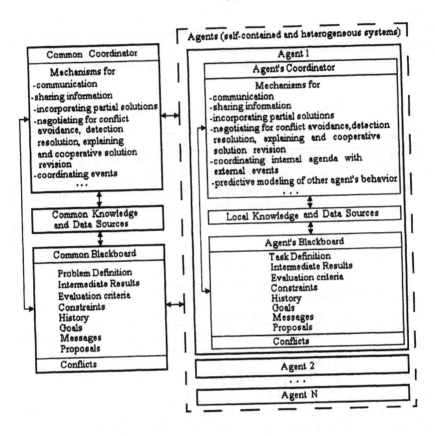

Figure 2. Cooperative design system architecture

This allows agents to decide how to coordinate and negotiate with other agents, achieve goals, exchange information to resolve conflicts, plan specific actions or interaction, combine partial decisions and so on [12]. An organizational structuring provides the design roles of agents, the authority relations between agents, the potential design paths in CDS.

CDS was planned in the generic blackboard framework. CDS Common Blackboard is used to provide agents' communication. Common Coordinator controls the processes of communication, sharing information, incorporating partial solutions, negotiating, coordinating events, etc. As in [9], CDS combines the execution of Common Knowledge and Data Sources for performing high-level tasks on Common Blackboard objects with the execution of independent agents. Each agent in CDS is also a blackboard-based task solver and possesses full functionality for forming a partial solution. CDS agents can suspend the execution of a task at any time and resume it when the situation is more suitable.

In figure 2, only computer agents are depicted. It is suggested that there is an automatic agent (interface agent) for each human one. The interface agents realize an interaction consequence and their blackboard filling.

It was decided to build a flexible coordination mechanism that allows one to change the degree of local sophistication (to increase or decrease the sphere of responsibility of the centralized controller (Common Coordinator)). The reason for this decision is the necessity of easing the adaptation of CDS to the structure and goals of different design organizations.

6 Conflict Detection

A set of conflict detection mechanisms were suggested in [5-9]. We are using and investigating two mechanisms:

a) qualitative mechanisms (figure 3) based on a hierarchy of conflict types, where conflicts are manifested as an unsatisfiable constraint set (figure 4a) (for example, as in [5]);

b) fuzzy (or quantitative) mechanisms based on using the local and global compatibility and constraint satisfaction measures of proposals (figure 5) (in this case, conflicts are manifested when the desired value of a measure is unsatisfied (figure 4b), as in [9].

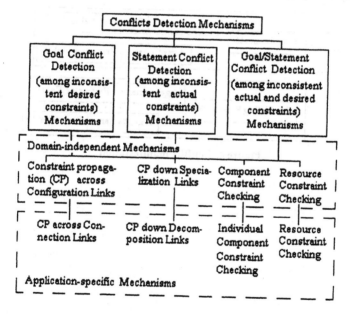

Figure 3. Conflict detection mechanisms

In the last case, each constraint must have attributes of flexibility, preference and importance (figure 5).

7 Conflict Resolution

When conflict is detected, a local or common coordinator must execute a protocol for the resolution process. To make this, a coordinator should know a set of conflict resolution strategies and a scheme (metastrategy) for choosing the most effective conflict resolution strategy. As input data, the scheme for strategy choice can use a detected type of conflict (in the case of figure 4a) or conflict symptoms which reflect the conflict situation information.

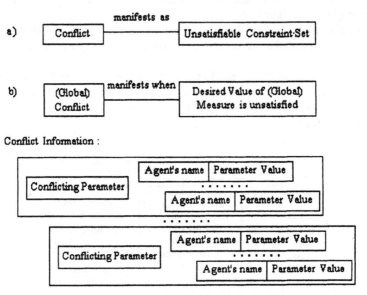

Figure 4. Conflict manifestation

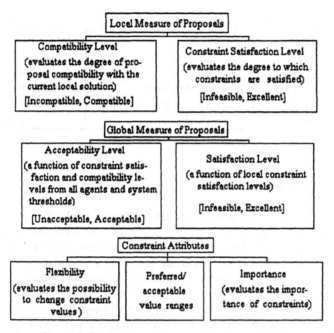

Figure 5. Evaluation of proposals and constraints

7.1 Conflict Situation Information

Basic conflict situation information (symptoms), which can be used for strategy choice, is described in table 2.

In this table, a range of subjective qualitative values is also presented. They can be applied for ordinal multiobjective decisions both about global design strategies and about conflict resolution strategies using fuzzy sets [13].

Table 2. Main characteristics of conflict situation

N	Characteristic	Range of qualitative Values
1	Restriction on amount of effort (time and other resourses) that can be expended to get a solution	low (l), middle (m), high (h)
2	Amount of effort that has already been expended in producing a solution	l, m, h
3	Estimation of the amount of processing effort required to generate a new solution or to repare the current one	l, m, h
4	Existence of other equally good proposals or of the possibility to generate them	yes (y), no (n)
5	Closeness of the proposal under consideration to being acceptable to all the agents involved	l, m, h

6	Number of conflicting parameters	l, m, h
7	Type of conflicting parameters	numeric(n), ordered (o), partially ordered (o), unordered (o)
8	Dependence of problematic constraints	unknown (u), l, m, h
9	Importance (severity) of problematic constraints	l, m, h
10	Flexibility of problematic constraints	l, m, h

7.2 Conflict Resolution Strategies

To resolve conflicts, we employ resolution strategies (table 3) suggested in [9], extended by using a set of formal rules and heuristics, which are described below.

The mapping of symptoms to strategies can be done by agents involved in a conflict, by special conflict resolution agents [4], or by a centralized coordinator. The mapping makers' choice depends on coordination mechanism fixation (turning).

The qualitative heuristic scheme for choosing the strategy is depicted in table 4. In accordance with this table, the agents choose the strategy (indicated in column 11) associated with the set of characteristic values "most similar" to the presented ones (shown in lines of the table).

Table 3. Conflict resolution strategies

N	Strategy	Comments
1	Generate Random Alternatives	If multiple solutions exist (this is typical in blackboard systems) or can be generated easily, then choose the proposals rated equally or slightly lower
2	Find Compromise (Use Constraint relaxation)	Find the solution that is within the acceptable interval using the agent's relaxation of variable values
3	Generate Constrained Alternatives	Generate new alternatives based on constraints received from an inflexible agent, or using other agent's partial solution
4	Generate Goal Alternatives	Generate proposals by looking for alternate goal enlargements. Some goals can be relaxed or relinquished
5	Find Precedent Solution (Use Case-Based Reasoning)	Find a previous solution succeeded in resolving a similar conflict situation
6	Revise and Merge Goals	Build a new mutually-defined goal structure that incorporates goals of all agents involved in the conflict and generate a solution guided by the new structure

Table 4. The mapping of symptoms to strategies

Characteristics (from table 2)										The best strategy (from tabl 3)
1	2	3	4	5	6	7	8	9	10	
h	l	l	y							1
h	m	l	n	h	l	n,o	l	l	h	2
m	m	m	n	l	l	n,o	l	h	l	3
m	m	m	n	l	h		h	h	l	4
m	m	m	n	l	h		h,u	h	l	5
l	l	h	n	l	h		h	h	l	6

Note. If the value doesn't exist the correspondening characteristic isn't very important. The most important symptoms are underlined.

When using both qualitative mechanisms of conflict detection and fuzzy mechanisms of conflict detection with conflict resolution strategies 3-5, the conflict resolution can be supported by using conflict resolution expertise. This expertise is implemented by providing the set of domain-independent and domain-specific formal rules and heuristics (figure 6), that can augmented or changed easily at any time without requiring coordinated changes in the design knowledge (since conflict resolution and design knowledge are separated).

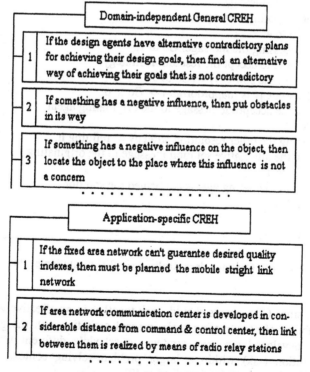

Figure 6. Conflict resolution expertise heuristics (CREH)

8 Negotiation and Conflict Resolution Coordination

All agents originating the conflict resolution or involved in the conflict must support negotiation and activity coordination.

Negotiation involves procedures for findin a compromise solution for multiple agents. It is a process in which agents iteratively exchange proposals and justification messages until an agreement is reached. Each next suggestion for resolution must draw nearer to the sphere of suitable solutions, so negotiation models must have the ability to propose suitable modifications, to evaluate narrowing the difference in the agents' proposals, and to generate arguments.

Negotiation support is a very complicated task not amenable to traditional artificial intelligence planning methods [3]. Common negotiation protocols for conflict resolution in CDS are presented in figure 7.

For the originating Agent:
1. Determination of conflict.
2. Analysis of conflict.
3. Suggesting a particular resolution strategy and possibly a
   set of resolution values.
4. Sending the solution message to the other agents involved.

For the Agents involved:
1. Waiting for message from agents.
2. Receiving the message.
3. Is it the accepting message?
   Yes -> Go to 4.
   No -> Processing the message. Go to 1.
4. Is it possible to accept the resolution strategy?
   Yes (Accept the strategy) -> Go to 5.
   No (The strategy is inappropriate) -> Go to 6.
5. Sending the accepting message to the originating agent.
   Go to 8.
6. Suggesting the other resolution strategy or refining it.
7. Sending the alternative solution message to the originating
   agent. Go to 1.
8. Have all participating agents confirmed the solution
   acceptability?
   Yes -> End.
   No -> Go to 1.

Figure 7. Common decentralized conflict resolution protocol

Furthermore, since CDS agents should work together in an effective way, they must have a possibility of coordinating their internal activities with the global problem solving. We developed our own strategy to schedule different tasks (including conflict resolution task) within a larger problem-solving context, based on the general coordination principles described in [9].

9 Summary and Status of the Project

In this paper, we have described a computer-supported framework called CDS for cooperative design and conflict resolution. According to the CDS framework, design is viewed as multi-agent problem solving involving different inevitably conflicting goals, criteria and constraints.

A prototype object-oriented version of CDS was implemented in Smalltalk/V 286. It was intended for telecommunication network design and conflict resolution between a set of designers working in different subdomains: communication centers, radio relay, troposphere, cable network, and so on. In this prototype, each agent is represented as a specialist in one of the subdomains. We have not realized a full CDS architecture because we used a centralized design approach. The common blackboard we developed is intended for communication, conflict resolution negotiation, and coordination.

We are currently implementing full agent reasoning capabilities and extending our system to support a more convenient user interface and more functionality.

References

1. Bodker S. et all. Computer Support for Cooperative Design. Conference on Computer- Supported Cooperative Work, 1988, p. 377-394.
2. Kaptelin V. Human Computer Interaction in Context: The Activity Theory Perspective. East-West International Conference on Human-Computer Interaction. EWHCI'92. Proceedings. St.-Petersburg. 1992. p.7-13.
3. Sycara K.P. Resolving Goal Conflicts via Negation. Processing of the National Conference on Artificial Intelligence. Minneapolis. Minnesota. 1988.
4. Kotenko I.V., Ryabov O.E. Computer-aided support of cooperative group design. East- West International Conference on Human-Computer Interaction. EWHCI'93. Proceedings. Moscow. V.1. 1993. p.207-218.
5. Klein M., Lu S.C.-Y. Insights into Cooperative Group Design: Experience with the LAN Designer System. Lecture Notes in Artificial Intelligence, v.549, 1991, p.354-364.
6. Descotte Y., Latombe J.C. Making Compromises Among Antagonist Constraints in a Planner. Artificial Intelligence, v.27, 1985, p.183-217.
7. Marcus S., Stout J., McDermott J. VT: An Expert Elevator Designer. Artificial Intelligence Magazine, v.8, N 4, 1987, p.39-58.
8. Stefik M.J. Planning with Constraints (Molgen: Part 1 & 2). Artificial Intelligence, v.16, N 2, 1981, p.111-170.
9. Lander S.E., Lesser V.R., Connel M.E. Knowledge-based Conflict Resolution for Cooperation among Expert Agents. Lecture Notes in Computer Science, v.492, 1991, p.253-268.
10. Talukdar S.N., Fenves S.J. Towards a Framework for Concurrent Design. Lecture Notes in Computer Science, v.492, 1991, p.140-151.

11.Sriram D., Logcher R., Wong A., Ahmed S. An Object-Oriented Framework for Collaborative Engineering Design. Lecture Notes in Computer Science, v.492, 1991, p.51-91.

12.Durfee E.H., Lesser V.R., Corkill D.D. Trends in Cooperative Distributed Problem Solving. IEEE Transactions on Knowledge and Data Engineering, v.1, N 1, 1989, p.63-83.

13.Hagman C., Unger E.A. Fuzzy Sets in Multilevel Decision Making (A LAN Small- Group DSS). Cybernetics and Systems: An International Journal, v.21, N 5, 1990, p.547-571.

Cognitive Ergonomics of Multi-Agent Systems: Observations, Principles and Research Issues *

Karel Hurts[1] and Paul de Greef[2]

[1] Leiden University, Department of Experimental Psychology,
P.O. Box 9555, 2300 RB Leiden, The Netherlands
[2] University of Amsterdam, Department of Social Science Informatics,
Roeterstraat 15, 1018 WB Amsterdam, The Netherlands

Abstract. The effectiveness of multi-agent systems — systems in which more than one human and machine agent cooperate to accomplish a common task — depends crucially on the extent to which these systems meet the psychological and social needs of the human participants. In this paper a review is provided of relevant observations, principles and theories pertaining to the cognitive ergonomics of these systems. We will focus on those ergonomics aspects that take on particular significance in multi-agent systems, including social psychological and motivational aspects. The review is organized around the distinction between technology-mediated human-human cooperation, supervisory systems, and cooperative problem solving systems. At the end of the paper an attempt will be made to summarize the implications of the review for designing multi-agent systems from a cognitive ergonomics point of view.

1 Introduction

Advances in technology cause the appearance of increasingly complicated networks of men and machines. To the extent that the human and machine agents cooperate to accomplish common goals, they may be called multi-agent systems (MAS's). In this paper we will review what is known about the cognitive ergonomics of these systems. An example of a MAS would be a system for designing a house, in which the human designer is assisted by a machine aid. This aid can monitor important constraints that have to be obeyed. In case of violations the human can be warned or perhaps be given suggestions for achieving the same objectives in another way. Another example would be an air traffic control system, consisting of several human controllers, human pilots and (software) agents who are cooperatively responsible for enabling safe and efficient air traffic. A final and perhaps more mundane example of a MAS would be a work

---

* The research reported in this paper was conducted in the context of a larger research project aimed at compiling a set of terms, models and concepts relevant to Human-Computer Cooperative Work Systems, see DeGreef et al., 1991.

flow management system in which plans for work flows are designed centrally by or with support from the computer before they are executed by human workers (e.g., a system for cooperatively writing a technical report).

An *agent* can roughly be defined as any system component (man or machine) that is capable of solving certain problems on its own, and for which it possesses some processing and memory resources. Typically, the agents who participate in a MAS need to cooperate to achieve the common goal. However, the interests of the agents may conflict and negotiation or arbitrage may be necessary to resolve the conflict. Relationships between agents that are almost completely adversary, such as those between economic or military foes, may also be considered examples of MAS's. However, because they form a rather special class of MAS, we will leave them outside the scope of this paper.

We will conduct the review in a bottom-up fashion and will first summarize observations obtained from studies of existing systems. The main purpose of this summary will be to show design pitfalls and design opportunities from the human point of view. Relevant theories and models will also be presented at this point. In the final section a summary is presented of the main contributions provided by multi-agent systems, some relevant ergonomics principles and requirements, possible ways to meet these requirements in the design of MAS's, and some issues that are still the subject of on-going research.

2 Multi-agent systems and cognitive ergonomics

2.1 Definition and restriction

Traditionally, cognitive ergonomics is concerned with man-machine interaction in a narrow sense, looking at the human being as a passive recipient of well-defined information or rather as an active controller of some mechanical device. However, in technologically more advanced environments the role of man is increasingly one of system component, being in control of some aspects of system functioning, but not in control of others. Besides, the technology increasingly acts as an adviser/expert, putting man in the role of information provider or action implementer even if he/she does not fully understand the information or actions asked for. In other words, technology increasingly acts as a semi-autonomous agent. Moreover, machines that are in different locations are increasingly connected in networks and become increasingly part of one (world-wide) large system.

These perspectives add new dimensions to cognitive ergonomics, namely those of *multi-agent systems* (MAS's), and it is these dimensions we will focus on in this paper. MAS's are systems in which at least one human and at least one machine (software) agent cooperate and where task divisions can be found between the various agents. These divisions may be based on availability (who has the time or physical proximity to do the job?) or on specialization (who has the knowledge or skills to do the job?). The exact divisions of tasks between agents often cannot be specified in advance, however, but arise dynamically during task execution.

We will use the word *cognitive* rather broadly, referring not only to such higher mental processes as perception, learning, thinking and attention, but also to (individual) human attitude, work style and communication insofar these are relevant to the understanding of human functioning in technological environments.

As one way to limit the scope of this review we have chosen not to include studies of user-centered design methods (e.g., methods of participative design), because these studies are often rather normatively (instead of empirically) oriented. Nonetheless,this review will still try to show how findings and knowledge relate to design. As the mutual adaptation between the man-machine system and the wider organizational and task context proves to be a very crucial factor in understanding the effectiveness of this system (as we will see), especially if more than one human being participates in this system, this aspect of cognitive ergonomics (also called *macro-ergonomics*, see, e.g.,[Hendrick, 1986]) takes on particular significance in this review.

The following three main modes of human functioning are often distinguished in MAS's (see, e.g., [Woods & Roth, 1988]):

- Man as participant in technology-mediated human-human interaction.
- Man as supervisor of a technical, partly automated, system.
- Man as part of a cooperative problem solving or decision making system.

Because these modes seem to provide a useful framework for organizing individual observations and conclusions, they will be used in order to structure the review of the following section.

2.2 Technology-mediated human-human interaction

Historically, the first type of MAS are systems for human-human interaction with the technology playing the role of an intermediary. Examples include telephone, fax,electronic mail, etcetera. These examples are not MAS's in the strict sense, because the machine part is not semantically integrated in the work process and is not an agent as defined above. However, more advanced systems constitute more or less "pure" forms of MAS, although they are still heavily oriented towards human-human interaction. An example of the latter category is the office procedure system in which the machine performs one or more work-related tasks such as workflow management. Another example would be a shared drawing system, which, in turn, is an example of *shared applications* ([Decouchant *et al.*, 1991]).

Collectively, these systems are called *Computer-Supported Cooperative Work Systems* (CSCW-systems), also sometimes called *groupware* systems ([Greif, 1988]). Even though many of these systems are not MAS's in the strict sense, they may all pose ergonomics problems that are representative of MAS's in general. ([Geirland, 1989]). For this reason, in the remainder of this subsection CSCW-systems are treated as one class of MAS.

Observations One of the best documented examples of a CSCW-system is the COORDINATOR ([Winograd & Flores, 1986]), which can be viewed as a form-based e-mail system. Although it has been around already for a couple of years, it can still be considered a state-of-the-art CSCW-system and shows many of the opportunities and pitfalls that are typical of multi-agent systems.

Based on speech acts, the COORDINATOR allows users to communicate by exchanging formalized messages of predefined types. The system can be used to try to delegate a task to another user. The system provides a framework for these negotiations and keeps track of these "conversations for action". Users can send messages of predefined types (e.g., request, promise). After reading a "request message" the user can press three buttons: "promise", "counter" or "cancel". The framework can be represented as a state-transition diagram (see Figure 1).

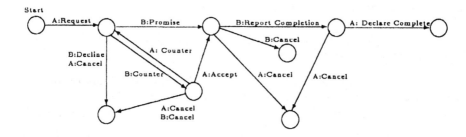

Fig. 1. Conversation for action in the COORDINATOR (after [Winograd & Flores, 1986])

The COORDINATOR knows what message classes are valid as reply upon the receipt of a certain message type and can thereby structure and support the human coordination process. Messages containing dates and commitments are automatically added to the user's personal diary, which will also alarm a user when an action should be taken or an answer from another user is due.

By providing a framework for conversations, COORDINATOR claims to improve group productivity by making communications within a group more productive and focused. Carasik and Grantham [Carasik & Grantham, 1988] have studied the effectiveness of COORDINATOR as a communication tool. This study reveals several problems with the use of the COORDINATOR. The rejection to use it is the most crucial one. This rejection is, in large part, the consequence of the effort required to learn it. In the COORDINATOR insufficient attention is paid to the affective nature of the interactions which are facilitated. Further, COORDINATOR did not fit the existing norms of interaction and was perceived as too rigid. In summary, an improved interface, better support for subtleties in human-human dialogues, and better support for user-created work procedures is needed for systems like the COORDINATOR.

A related problem is based on the fact that some tasks require more *social presence* than others, e.g., taking personnel actions as compared to distributing routine information ([Rice & Williams, 1984]; [Short *et al.*, 1976]). For the former type of tasks computer tools may not be useful. Studies of decision support systems also report the tendency of managers to make important decisions in face-to-face meetings with colleagues, while relying on a support system for more routine, computational parts of their tasks.

The form of the technology has also been found to depend on the *structure of the work group*. Flat work groups may require more complex computer support than hierarchical work groups. "Complexity", as used here, refers to the amount of integration of functions, such as data processing, (technical) design, and clerical type activities (mail, bookkeeping). [Gutek *et al.*, 1987] found that tools may not be used by flat work groups if they do not provide this integration.

We finally report some experiences with databases that are shared between work groups that are geographically separated. This separation often renders the persons or groups, that have to communicate or cooperate with each other, anonymous vis-à-vis each other. [Snellen, 1991] reports a tendency of people to be reluctant to update the portions of their databases that are public, if the sites that use these public databases are experienced as anonymous, thus resulting in "database pollution".

Implications and Theories Bannon and Schmidt [Bannon & Schmidt, 1989] state that a typical pitfall consists of groupware researchers seeing themselves as typical users, and forgetting that generalizing from one's own research setting to settings in the "real world" can be fraught with problems. More generally, Bannon and Schmidt argue that we need to achieve a true understanding of cooperative work, especially of how cooperative work differs from individual work, before we can hope to create successful CSCW-systems. Their discussion centers around three issues: support of articulation, shared information spaces and mutual or co-adaptation between organization and artifact.

Articulation work can be defined as the difference between cooperative work and individual work and is associated with researchers like Gasser ([Gasser, 1986]) who investigate how technology is actually being used by people in the workplace. The main conclusion of this work is that spontaneous articulation among people uses a lot of non-verbal, informal communication and a lot of implicit knowledge, especially in work environments with task uncertainty.

Bannon and Schmidt's ideas result in the recommendation that the design of CSCW-systems should pay attention not only to the work flow, but also to the articulation (coordination) among co-workers needed to make the flow possible. The system should support self-organization of cooperative ensembles as opposed to disrupting cooperative work by computerizing formal procedures.

By *shared information spaces* Bannon and Schmidt mean computer systems meant to support retrieval of information filed by other workers in another work context. These may pose conflicting *transparency* requirements. On the one hand, information should be completely transparent since cooperative decision making involves a continuous process of assessing the validity of the information produced by colleagues. Therefore, the shared information space should provide identity of the originator of each piece of information. In addition, the shared information space should provide the conceptual framework and contextual knowledge of the originator. On the other hand, information is not neutral and there are conflicting interests. Hence, transparency must be bounded.

The phenomenon of database pollution is related to this issue of transparency and is explained by *public choice theory* ([Müller, 1986]). In this theory, it is assumed that cooperative relations between people may take on a special form if the cooperation results in the production of so-called "public goods". These are goods of which the consumption by one individual does not reduce the amount available for consumption by others. Many services provided by the state are examples of public goods, but information that is freely accessible and reproducible (books, databases, tapes) is an example as well. Because of the definition of public goods, the individual may choose not to participate in the production of these goods (thereby avoiding the cost of participation), if he expects these goods will be produced anyway by others (who now will have to incur additional costs). This is more likely to happen if there is no social network in place that can force the individual to cooperate, as is often the case in situations of anonymity. In public choice theory this phenomenon is called the "free riding" problem. Of course, public choice theory may also explain the importance of social presence in decision making situations as mentioned in the previous subsubsection.

The final point made by Bannon and Schmidt implies that *co-adaptation* of the technology to the organization, and vice versa, is needed. A CSCW-system designer does not only design a physical artifact. What is being designed is a whole work organization. Cooperative work requires adaptation of the technology to the organization and subsequent adaptation of the organization to the artifact. Structural contingency theory ([Gutek *et al.*, 1987]) makes the same point by stressing the importance of mutually adapting work group structure and amount of function integration provided by the system.

2.3   Supervisory systems

With the increased automation of industrial processes, human tasks shifted from manual control of these processes to supervision of these processes, now being under (semi)automated (machine) control. One may say that these systems consist of at least three components: the application world (e.g., a chemical process or the domain of air traffic), the machine agent (acting directly on the world), and the human agent (supervising the machine agent). Typically, the application is controlled real-time by the machine agent. Although the human agent is not directly involved in the control loop, the real-time character may cause significant time pressures and mental load problems for the human agent, especially in situations of emergency or abnormality. In these systems the human supervisor often needs an interface not only to the machine agent (whose actions in the world are to be supervised), but to the application world as well (so that the effects of actions taken can be assessed).

Observations Supervisory systems are often designed in such a way that the lower-order machine agent cannot or can hardly be tracked or redirected by their supervisors. Human supervisors often also lack the proper knowledge and authority to exercise real supervision. Still, they are held responsible for the outcomes of the machine agent ([Roth *et al.*, 1987]).Suboptimal performance of the supervisory system as a whole and human dissatisfaction will result from responsibility without real authority or opportunity to track or redirect the machine agent's actions.

In studies of team tasks in complex systems such as military command and control systems, it was observed that under moderate work-load conditions, successful teams coordinated openly via numerous interactions and frequent sharing of information. However, under high work-load conditions, constant performance was maintained by a marked reduction in communication ([Kleinman & Serfaty, 1989]). It seems that successful performance of team tasks under high work-load conditions is only possible if team members can correctly anticipate each other's actions and information needs. This may be called *implicit coordination* to indicate that under these conditions there is no opportunity to communicate overtly. The ability to coordinate in this way can only be acquired through training and experience.

In another study of team tasks in a military setting, it was observed that teams are often deliberately designed with redundant capacity and with skills and knowledge distributed redundantly across the whole team. It was found that these redundancies have the function of correcting errors made by team members and providing opportunities to learn from these errors ([Seifert, 1992]). One can imagine that these redundancies probably also function to assist individual team members who are temporarily confronted with peak load or with uncertain and unknown situations. Relating this observation back to supervisory systems, it is probably fair to say that building redundancies into supervisory work teams is a good way to provide both on-the-job training for novices and a capacity for dynamic task allocation. The latter function may be particularly useful in cases of uncertainty or peak load where pre-planned task allocation is difficult.

This brings us to the next observation, related to the technique of *load balancing*. This is a technique for re-assigning tasks to human agents, depending on momentary local loads. In computer networks that are equipped with a network manager, load balancing is already a widely applied technique. In applications in which also human agents participate, load balancing requires accurate assessments of remote environments and requires good user interfaces for interacting with these remote environments. Load balancing may occur automatically or manually. Of course, automatic load balancing must be acceptable to the humans who are affected by it.

An example would be a train traffic control system in which human supervisors are responsible for assigning tracks to trains and for notifying personnel and passengers of locations and times of trains. In these systems some supervisors, especially those at busy traffic terminals, may temporarily be overloaded, in which case load balancing may provide a solution. A study of railway-traffic controllers showed that at some stations they are overloaded more often than not, whereas at other posts they are idle during large parts of their shift ([Neerincx & Griffioen, 1994]).

Another source of observations is provided by the so-called *adaptive aiding* studies. Adaptive aiding involves the automatic assignment of human tasks to the machine (automatic off-loading) if the current situation indicates there is a need for support of the human operator ([Rouse, 1988]). These studies have shown that the availability of aiding improves *unaided* performance if the human agent is in control of the decision to shift the aid to the machine (manual allocation). In contrast, automatic allocation had no impact on unaided performance ([Morris & Rouse, 1986]).

A final observation of the adaptive aiding studies is that, even if users are satisfied with some of their tasks being conducted by the aid, they may not be prepared to leave the allocation decision solely to the aid ([Lehner et al., 1987] ; [Noah & Halpin, 1986]). Finally, these studies show that operators may not be willing to delegate their tasks to the aid if the wider task environment prohibits time being spent on implementing such delegation (e.g., the decision aid may have to be programmed and engaged, which would divert the operator's attention away from other important tasks he has to carry out; see, e.g., [Kirlik, 1993]).

Implications and Theories The reduction in communication observed under high work-load conditions mentioned above seems to indicate the existence of mental models as a basis for anticipating other team members' actions and information needs. It can be hypothesized that the greater the degree of overlap among team members' mental models, the greater team effectiveness ([Cannon-Bowers et al., 1990]).

The observation that humans often are not able to track or redirect the machine agent seems to result from underestimating human information needs (and, perhaps, from overestimating the machine agent's capabilities) and from a lack of knowledge of how to design good user interfaces that can meet these needs. The question how to account for user needs and how to design user interfaces is, of course, a general ergonomic issue which is not typical for multi-agent systems. Nonetheless, it deserves much attention because a failure to answer the question may result in many multi-agent systems not being used, even though they may be well-built from a technical point of view. We will come back to this issue in the conclusions section.

The observations pertaining to redundancies in work teams and load balancing can be related to theories of spontaneous self-organization of group tasks ([Bannon & Schmidt, 1989]) and to theories of how to build learning capabilities into work teams. On the practical side, load balancing needs to be based on accurate assessments and needs to fit the social work organization.

Finally, from the adaptive aiding studies we know that "being in control" is important to users. Users should, as a minimum, be able to overrule any delegation decision made by the aid. In particular, they want to have final responsibility for decisions what they can and cannot do, even though these decisions may favour the machine aid most of the time. These studies also show that a good understanding of the wider task environment of the operator is necessary for determining the usefulness of the aid.

2.4 Cooperative decision making and problem solving

In contrast to supervisory systems, machine resources may be used to support human problem solving and decision making. There is still an application world for which the problem solving or decision making is meant, but this time the human agent acts directly on it (or through some other machine agent). Therefore, the human agent is more the focus of attention than in supervisory systems. Machine support may consist of *assistance with well-defined subtasks* that the machine can perform quicker or better, such as computing and memory management. Many examples of so-called structured decision systems resort under this category of multi-agent systems (e.g., accounting systems, risk analysis systems).

On the other hand, machine support may also consist of *assistance with conceptual parts* of complex problem solving or decision making tasks, for example by providing the user with information that needs to be taken into account during problem formulation or testing solutions. This type of support usually requires a greater degree of interaction between machine agent and human agent and the precise contributions of human and machine are harder to predict in advance. Successful support of this type provides what [Woods & Roth, 1988] call *conceptualization power*.

As an example of a cooperative problem solving system, we briefly discuss Fischer's system for kitchen design ([Fischer *et al.*, 1993]), which is a nice example of what a cooperative system can be like (see Figure 2). It is not a serious application, but it is good enough to illustrate many issues in cooperative systems, without having to explain technical details of the domain, which would be the case if a real CAD application had been used.

The user-interface shows the solution being worked on as a shared object. Both user and system can edit this object and the system can criticize what the user proposes. The user can create a design by selecting objects in the left-hand pane and positioning them in the right-hand side design area. When the system detects a bug in the design, it informs the user by a pop-up window. This is a form of cooperative problem solving known as *critiquing* ([Silverman, 1991]). We take systems for cooperative problem solving by one human and one machine agent as the nominal case of a multi-agent system, as it allows pooling of knowledge and skills in the joint execution of a task.

Observations Sometimes people overestimate or underestimate the capability of the technology. People do not always have good ways to assess this capability, that is, the technology's potential and limitations ([Morris & Rouse, 1986]). It will be clear that technology that is not able to communicate its potential and its limitations may either be trusted too much or too little by its user, provided that this information is not communicated in other ways to the user. User experience and individual differences will determine whether the level of trust is affected one way or the other. The issue of trust is particularly problematic with expert system technology, which often is presented to users as "intelligent" instead of as ordinary tools. As a result, over-confidence in this technology may be the result.

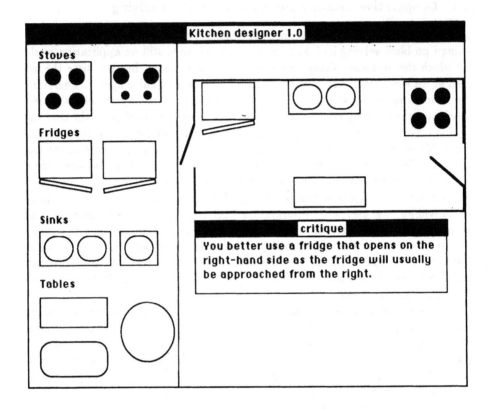

Fig. 2. An example cooperative system

An important observation with respect to the design of problem solving aids relates to *problem solving strategy* in men and machines. Machine aids in interactive decision support systems are often based on a different task model than humans are used to. For example, flight route planning may be considered a linear programming problem and aids can be designed accordingly. However, humans tend to solve planning problems in terms of goal hierarchies, constraint satisfaction and successive refinement of global solutions in a highly dynamic way ([Layton *et al.*,90]). This mismatch of representations and strategies may render cooperative problem solving and decision making ineffective.

The situated and incremental nature of human problem solving makes it also important to design interfaces that allow very flexible human-machine communication. For example, the human must be able to correct the machine in the middle of a problem solving session or provide it with additional information, after which the machine knows how to continue. These so-called *mixed-initiative dialogues* are notoriously difficult to support, however.

Implications and Theories Theories of human-human interaction ([Muir, 1987]) show that human performance in man-machine systems has many determinants. These include psychological conditions such as confidence, trust and being in control. These conditions need to be understood in order to avoid the trust problems mentioned in the previous subsubsection.

General theories and guidelines for designing (intelligent) decision aids with a representation and a solution strategy that match those of the human are still rather rudimentary (but see [Lehner & Kralj, 1988]). As long as these theories and guidelines are lacking, the designer must rely on usability experiments in order to avoid the representation mismatch mentioned in the previous subsubsection.

As cooperative problem solving usually is an iterative process, frequent interaction between user and aid is also important. For example, the machine aid may need to convey solution proposals to the user, the quality of which must subsequently be judged by the human problem solver. For this cycling back and forth between the machine aid and the human agent good interfaces are required.

Two ingredients of interfaces that allow smooth iterative problem solving in cooperative systems include good data abstractions and plan recognition. *Data abstractions* are ways to make the abstract visible, e.g., showing a flight plan in the form of a spreadsheet table with columns representing flight sectors and rows representing height levels ([Layton *et al.*,90]). Such data abstractions facilitate human understanding of machine solutions.

Joint man-machine planning performance may also be improved by equipping the machine agent with the capability to automatically *recognize human intentions*, e.g., interpreting a user pointing at a sector of the flight plan display as a desire to reroute the flight in the direction indicated. In the area of intelligent tutoring systems and on-line information retrieval some progress has been made towards understanding the factors that are involved in plan recognition ([Soloway & Ehrlich ,1984];[Hoppe & Schiele, 1992]).

3 Conclusion and Discussion

MAS technology provides new opportunities to promote and support cooperation amongst humans and machine agents, and to differently organize human work processes. MAS technology facilitates the implementation of various functions which used to be difficult and expensive to realise and it allows novel functions:

- Means for (facilitation of) communication amongst humans that differ from conventional media. Whereas asynchronous communication using person-to-person electronic mail resembles a letter or fax, and whereas news groups or bulletin boards resemble newsletters, the use of shared objects and shared editors in synchronous group-support systems and tele-conferencing tools is unlike any conventional medium.

- Supervisor and supervised system can be geographically separated. This opens opportunities for load balancing between operators in different places as, for example, in applications like railways, power networks and the like.
- Information-technological methods can be employed to support the human decision maker or problem solver. Such aids may be integrated in supervisory systems to compensate for lacking knowledge or capacities on the part of the human operator.

There are many systems, architectures and ideas in the world of multi-agent systems, and these can be assessed using logical criteria, but the final criterion is whether the human can actually profit from such a system. The survey in section 2 shows a number of sociological and social-psychological issues that may prevent successful application. Research in the new field of CSCW has brought to the fore that there is lack of theory about human-human cooperation and lack of knowledge about the conditions under which various support tools are likely to be effective. The most prevalent problem, especially salient in work flow management systems which are based on pre-planned routines as a coordination mechanism, is that in reality even simple office work requires a flexible coordination mechanism to allow for mutual adjustment among co-workers and adjustment to an unpredictable open environment. In work environments with task uncertainty, task allocation and coordination cannot be planned in advance. Allocation and coordination are negotiated and re-negotiated more or less continuously. Not understanding this resulted in the failures of the first generation of office information systems. Research is needed into ways MAS's can support self-organization of cooperative ensembles as opposed to disrupting cooperative work by computerizing formal procedures ([Bannon & Schmidt, 1989]).

Such a MAS would require a language or tool for human-oriented task modeling and cooperation modeling. In this context cooperation does not only refer to the communication of information during task execution, but also to task division and allocation. [Ellis & Nutt, 1988] discuss early attempts to develop languages for multi-agent planning. Work on task-oriented discourse, especially the study of Grosz and Sidner [Grosz & Sidner, 1988], provides insights into a coordination mechanism that may be flexible enough for a complete integration of human and machine work processes: shared multi-agent plans at a meta-level to create, maintain and, if necessary, unshare a shared plan in the application domain. The network of the COORDINATOR shown in Figure 1 is an example of a pre-planned routine at the meta-level. Similar networks may be used for plans at the level of the application domain. To support this flexible coordination mechanism, we need languages for multi-agent plans in the application domain and at the meta-level. Technically it is possible to have one language for both levels. However, this does not solve everything. The model for coordination based on plans at the domain level and protocols at a meta-level allows for mutual adjustment and integration at the level of the group work process, but it does not take into account the necessary informal communication, the human individual work process, or the trade-offs involved in automation.

Many reports on CSCW prototypes mention the need for face-to-face communication. The most successful co-authoring systems, for example, have the group of users sit in one room. [Ellis & Nutt, 1988] regard informal communication as a factor keeping morale or motivation at productive levels, but also as a necessary means to implement the normal distributed problem solving that takes place: no single person or manual contains all procedures completely, therefore these have to be distributed and communicated through informal means. Research is needed into ways to enhance existing systems with opportunities for informal communication and into the required degree and function of such communication in different settings.

Another research issue is the distribution of control. Joint task planning during the configuration of MAS's consists of numerous decisions: *Who* will execute a (sub)task? *When* will this task be executed? *Who* makes these decisions? The adaptive aiding studies discussed in section 2.4 show the importance of humans wanting to be in control in this regard. Exact conditions and required extent of being in control in different settings remain an issue for further research, however.

Many authors stress the importance of transparent information, as cooperative decision making involves a continuous process of assessing the validity of information produced by colleagues. On the other hand, information is not neutral and there are conflicting interests. Therefore, transparency must be bounded ([Bannon & Schmidt, 1989]). The exact conditions and required extent of transparency in concrete settings remain an issue for future research, however. The studies on cooperative problem solving (section 2.4) also show that there is a need for more systematic knowledge about human task representations and solution strategies and about the types of user interfaces that allow smooth communication between machine representations and strategies on the one hand and those of the human on the other.

Developers of new tools tend to overlook sociological, psychological and human factors issues. They seem to depart from the assumption of people as rational agents: an agent has a goal and knowledge about ways to reach this goal, and uses this knowledge to decide about the best way to achieve the goal. This one-dimensional view on the human in a work environment overlooks the multiple needs and the multiple heterogeneous criteria humans actually use in determining their behavior. For example, the study of [Archer, 1990] shows that groups using group-support technology reach the same quality of decisions as groups in face-to-face meetings. On the basis of the criterion of decision quality, the new technology may appear attractive, but when duration is taken into account the group technology appears to take much longer than face-to-face meetings. In a modern business environment, this duration criterion is perhaps even more important than quality of decision making. In general, there are multiple heterogeneous criteria, and new technology will rarely be an unequivocal improvement in all respects.

Apart from sociological and social psychological issues, cognitive ergonomics and HCI issues for the individual human user may explain some of the pitfalls. One of the problems, underexposed in the CSCW literature, but prevalent in cognitive ergonomics, is the human-computer interaction bottleneck. Generally, human-computer interaction is difficult, it involves additional work and constitutes a significant load factor for the human. For example, human-computer dialogue and computer-mediated human-human dialogue often is laborious for the non-skilled typist. Humans are in general highly skilled for communication using an audio channel and this poses little additional work-load for the human. Moreover, audio can convey emotions and informal information much better than typed text.

The effect of the bottleneck depends on the type of application. With control rooms there is a system to be controlled, e.g., a power plant or a railway system, and various sensors provide the control system with a fairly extensive and accurate model of the real world situation. In fact, the control system may be regarded as an intermediary between the humans and the real world. With the still somewhat mythical office automation type of MAS-application, the system depends on human data-entry to obtain a model of the real world situation, but from the point of view of the user there is often little to be gained and a lot of work involved to actually keep the system up to date. The alternative, talking to a colleague on the corridor, on the phone, or perhaps sending e-mail, is probably more attractive. This is only one reason why integrated MAS's for office-type applications cannot be expected to appear anywhere soon. Complete integration may only be achievable in control-room type of applications.

The lack of success of various CSCW tools may also be due to a lack of integration in the work environment. Humans seldom carry out computer tasks in isolation from other tasks. For example, the output of one task often serves as an input for another task, people often have to timeshare between and integrate tasks, and they often need to be able to overrule the agents (automatic or not) who help them with routine or computationally demanding tasks. In addition, in large groups with anonymity, sociological issues such as the free-riding problem come to the fore.

Although in office-type applications integrated multi-agent systems are unlikely to appear soon, humans may benefit from various existing tools for support of communication, information sharing and, in some cases, work flow management, provided that interfaces —perhaps with aiding functions— are well-designed and fit the user's conception of the task and care is taken not to overload the user.

In summary, although we may expect several opportunities from MAS's, we still have to obtain a better understanding of the way people carry out their everyday tasks, even those not directly supported by computers. This understanding may shed light on the ways computers will affect their behaviours, attitudes and performance related to these tasks. Moreover, classical ergonomics issues, such as man-machine compatibility and human overload, are as important for MAS's as they are for traditional (single human – single machine) systems.

References

[Archer, 1990] N.P. Archer. A comparison of computer conferences with face-to-face meetings for small group business decisions. *Behaviour and Information Technology*, 9, 307–317, 1990.

[Bannon & Schmidt, 1989] L.J. Bannon and K. Schmidt. CSCW: four characters in search of a context. In *Proceedings of the first European Conference on Computer Supported Cooperative Work*, London, September, 1989.

[Cannon-Bowers et al., 1990] J.A. Cannon-Bowers, E. Salas, and S.A. Converse. Cognitive psychology and team training: training shared mental models of complex systems. *Human Factors Society Bulletin*, 33(12), 1–4, 1990.

[Carasik & Grantham, 1988] R.P. Carasik and C.E. Grantham. A case study of CSCW in a dispersed organization. In E.Soloway, D.Frye, and S.B. Sheppard, editors, *CHI'88: Conference Proceedings Human Factors in Computing Systems*. New York, ACM: 1988.

[Decouchant et al., 1991] D. Decouchant, V. Normand, and G. Vandome. Application design using the Comandos Distributed Object Oriented System. *Proceedings of the Fourth International Conference on Human-Computer Interaction*, Vol. 1, 359–363, 1991.

[DeGreef et al., 1991] H.P. DeGreef, D. Mahling, M. Neerincx, S. Wyatt, and C.M.M. Hurts. *Analysis of Human-Computer Cooperative Work*. ESPRIT-project 5362 (IMAGINE), Leiden University, 1991.

[Ellis & Nutt, 1988] C.A. Ellis and G.J. Nutt. Office information systems and computer science. In I. Greif (ed.), *Computer Supported Cooperative Work: A book of readings*. San Mateo, CA: Morgan Kaufmann, 1988.

[Fischer et al., 1993] G. Fischer, K. Nakakoji, J. Ostwald, G. Stahl, and T. Sumner. Embedding computer- based critics in the contexts of design. *Proceedings of INTER-CHI '93*, 157– 164. New York: ACM, 1993.

[Gasser, 1986] L. Gasser. The integration of computing and routine work. *ACM Transactions on Office Information systems*, 4, 205–225, 1986.

[Geirland, 1989] J. Geirland. Developing design guidelines for computer-supported cooperative work: a macroergonomic approach. *Human Factors Society Bulletin*, 32(9), 1–4, 1989.

[Greenberg, 1991] S. Greenberg. Personalizable groupware: Accomodating individual roles and group differences. In L. Bannon, M. Robinson, and K. Schmidt, eds., *Proceedings of the Second European Conference on Computer-Supported Cooperative Work*, pages 17–32. Amsterdam, The Netherlands: Kluwer Academic Publishers, 1991.

[Greif, 1988] I. Greif, (ed.). *Computer-Supported Cooperative Work: a book of readings*. San Mateo, CA: Morgan Kaufmann, 1988.

[Grosz & Sidner, 1988] B.J. Grosz and C.L. Sidner. Plans for discourse. In P. Cohen, J. Morgan, and M. Pollack, eds., *Intentions in Communication*. Boston: MIT PRess, 1988.

[Gutek et al., 1987] B.A. Gutek, S. Sasse, and T. Bikson. *The fit between technology and workgroup structure: the structural contingency approach and automation*. Manuscript submitted for publication, 1987.

[Hendrick, 1986] H.W. Hendrick. Macroergonomics: a conceptual model for integrating human factors with organizational design. In O. Brown, Jr. and H.W. Hendrick (eds.), *Human factors in organizational design and management II: proceedings of the second international symposium on human factors in organizational design and management*, 467–478. Amsterdam: Elsevier, 1986.

[Holt et al., 1983] A.W. Holt, H.R. Ramsey, and J.D. Grimes. Coordination system technology at the basis for a programming environment. *Electrical Communication*, 57, 307–314, 1983.

[Hoppe & Schiele, 1992] H.U. Hoppe and F. Schiele. Towards Task models for embedded informationretrieval. *Proceedings of ACM CHI '92 conference on Human Factors in Computing systems*, 173–180, 1992.

[Kirlik, 1993] A. Kirlik. Modeling strategic behavior in human-automation interaction: why an "aid" can (and should) go unused. *Human Factors*, 35(2), 221–242, 1993.

[Kleinman & Serfaty, 1989] D.L. Kleinman and D. Serfaty. Team performance assessment in distributed decision making. In R. Gilson, J.P. Kincaid, and B. Goldiez (eds.). *Proceedings of the Interactive Networked Simulation for Training Conference*, 22–27. Orlando, Fl: Institute for Simulation and Training, 1989.

[Krueger & Chapanis, 1980] G.P. Krueger and A. Chapanis. Conferencing and teleconferencing in three communication modes as a function of the number of conferees. *Ergonomics*, 23(2), 103–122, 1980.

[Lai et al., 1988] K-Y Lai, T.W Malone, and K-C Yu. Object lens: A "spreadsheet" for cooperative work. *ACM Transactions on Office Information Systems*, 6, 332–353, 1988.

[Layton et al.,90] C. Layton, P.J. Smith, E. McCoy, and T. Bihari). *Design concepts for the development of cooperative-problem solving systems*. Technical Report. Columbus, OH: Department of Industrial and Systems Engineering, The Ohio State University, 1990.

[Lee & Malone, 1990] J. Lee and T.W. Malone. Partially shared views: A scheme for communicating among groups that use different type hierarchies. *ACM Transactions on Information Systems*, 8, January 1990.

[Lehner et al., 1987] P.E. Lehner, M.S. Cohen, T.M. Mullin, B.B. Thompson, and K.B. Laskey. *Adaptive decision aiding: interim report*. (Tech. Report 87-3). Falls Church, VA: Decision Science Consortium, Inc., 1987

[Lehner & Kralj, 1988] P.E. Lehner and M.M. Kralj. Cognitive impacts of the user interface. In J.A. Hendler (ed.), *Expert Systems: the User interface*. Norwood: Alex Publishing Corporation, 1989.

[Lyytinen, 1990] K. Lyytinen. Computer supported cooperative work (CSCW)-issues and challenges; a structurational analysis. Technical report, University of Jyvaskyla, Finland, Jyvaskyla, 1990.

[Malone et al., 1989] T.W. Malone, K-C Yu, and J.Lee. What good are semistructured objects? Adding semiformal structure to hypertext. Technical Report #3064.89.MS, Massachusetts Institute of Technology, Cambridge, Massachusetts, 1989.

[Morris & Rouse, 1986] N.M. Morris and W.B. Rouse. *Adaptive aiding for human-computer control: experimental studies of dynamic task allocation*. Tech. Report AAMRL-TR-86-005. Wright-Patterson Air Force Base, OH: Armstrong Aerospace Medical Research Laboratory, 1986.

[Müller, 1986] D.C. Müller. Rational egoism versus adaptive egoism as fundamental postulate for a descriptive theory of human behaviour. *Public Choice*, 51, 3–23, 1986.

[Muir, 1987] B. Muir. Trust between humans and machines. *International Journal of Man-Machine Studies*, 27, 527–539.

[Neerincx & Griffioen, 1994] M.A. Neerincx and E. Griffioen. *Cognitive task analysis: harmonising tasks to human capacities* Manuscript submitted for publication, 1994.

[Noah & Halpin, 1986] W. Noah, and S.M. Halpin. Adaptive user interfaces for planning and decision aids in C3I systems. *IEEE Transactions on Systems, Man and Cybernetics*, SMC-16, 909–918, 1986.

[Rasmussen, 1986] J. Rasmussen. A framework for the cognitive task analysis in systems design. In E. Hollnagel, G. Mancini, and D.D. Woods, eds., *Intelligent decision support in process environments*, 175–210. Springer Verlag, 1986.

[Rice & Williams, 1984] R.E. Rice and F. Williams. Theories old and new: the study of new media. In R.E. Rice (ed.), *The new media*, 55–80. Beverly Hills, CA: Sage, 1984.

[Roth et al., 1987] E.M. Roth, K. Bennett, and D.D. Woods. Human interaction with an "intelligent" machine. *International Journal of Man-Machine Studies*, 27, 479–525, 1987.

[Rouse, 1988] W.B. Rouse. Adaptive aiding for human/computer control. *Human Factors*, 30(4), 431–443, 1988.

[Seifert, 1992] C.M. Seifert. Error as opportunity: learning in a cooperative task. *Human-Computer Interaction*, 4, 409–435, Special Issue on Computer-Supported Cooperative Work, 1992.

[Short et al., 1976] J. Short, E. Williams, and B. Christie. *The social psychology of telecommunications*. New York: Wiley, 1976.

[Silverman, 1991] B.G. Silverman. Expert critics: operationalizing the judgment/decision making literature as a theory of "bugs" and repair strategies. *Knowledge Acquisition*, 3, 175–214, 1991.

[Snellen, 1991] I.Th.M. Snellen. A social network view on information technological networks in public administration. In R. Traunmüller, ed., *Proceedings of the IFIP TC8/WG8.5 Conference on Governmental and Municipal Information Systems*. Amsterdam: Elsevier, 1991.

[Soloway & Ehrlich ,1984] E. Soloway and K. Ehrlich. Empirical studies of programming knowledge. *IEEE Transactions of Software Engineering*, 10(5), 595–609, 1984.

[Winograd & Flores, 1986] T. Winograd and F. Flores. *Understanding Computers and Cognition*. Addison Wesley, Reading, MA, 1986.

[Woods & Roth, 1988] D.D. Woods and E.M. Roth. Cognitive engineering: human problem solving with tools. *Human Factors*, 30(4), 415–430, 1988.

Supporting Collaborative Learning Through the Use of Electronic Conversational Props

R. K. E. Bellamy, E. B. W. Cooper and R. D. Borovoy

Advanced Technology Group
Apple Computer, Inc.
1 Infinite Loop, 301–3E
Cupertino, CA 95014, USA

Abstract. This paper explores the use of electronic 'conversational props' to facilitate collaborative learning. Model-Based Communication (MBC), a technology that links application views, video and text messages — these application views are props for the conversation encoded in the messages — has been applied to the educational domain, the resulting application is called Media Fusion. This paper describes an ethnographic study of Media Fusion, where students in California and Washington D.C. used Media Fusion to explore and collaborate around issues concerning global warming.

Keywords: Conversational Props, Collaboration, Learning, Multimedia

1 Introduction

Support for collaboration is being seen as an increasingly important area for technological innovation in education (e.g. CSILE, 11). This emphasis has arisen because electronic messaging has the potential to support the formation of a community of learners. Such a community is important because knowledge is socially constructed (10). Through collaboration, the community negotiates an understanding of an issue. Although electronic communication offers the potential for supporting collaborative learning, it is still not clear what particular characteristics such systems should embody? We have been investigating one kind of system — the use of conversational props to support asynchronous communication for collaborative learning.

Conversational props are the artifacts that are used to enrich a conversation — e.g. pictures, drawings, video clips. For example an architect might draw a simple sketch to explain the design of a space to a client; the client might point to part of the sketch and ask a question about it, or might suggest an alternative design by grabbing the pen and redrawing the space. In this manner, a rich conversation evolves around the prop (9).

Recognizing the advantages of such props, researchers have developed conversational props to support electronic communication. Early versions of these were very literal in their transformation of 'real-world' conversational props — e.g. the whiteboard from wall to computer. The value added was that participants no longer had to be in the same place to communicate. Later versions, such as the Conversation Board (2), extended the whiteboard concept to support the creation and manipulation of more structured conversational props e.g. lists, geometric objects, graphs, and sketches. Model-Based Communication (MBC) (1) extends the use of conversational props for video and text-based electronic communication in two important directions. Firstly, it enables the same device to function as both a discovery tool and as a conversational prop, eliminating the 'second class' status of conversational props created solely for the purposes of communication, but without the power to do actual discovery (e.g. a slide show overview of one's research). Secondly, MBC enables the use of conversational props to support communication not only between people in different locations, but also at different times.

We have applied MBC to the educational domain in order to provide support for collaborative learning. The resulting application is called Media Fusion. Two features of MBC make it particularly well-suited as a tool to support collaborative learning. Firstly, the linking of discovery tools (data analysis tools) and communication tools (MBC) encourages reflection because it allows students to explore and manipulate the kinds of data that are being used to support opinions presented in messages they receive and it allows them to formulate their own understanding and express these understandings in messages they send. Supporting reflection is important because through reflection, learners can change their knowledge structures which is an important part of coming to understand a subject in depth (3, 5, 8). Reformulating knowledge is not a passive process, but an active one. Research suggests that successful learners actively seek to reorganize their existing knowledge (e.g. 4, 7). They actively seek to prove or disprove their beliefs based on new information they discover in the world. The exploratory nature of Media Fusion supports such active construction of knowledge. Students can explore both the existing messages and the data in any order they wish and at their own pace. Secondly, asynchronous communication with students in different locations permits consideration of messages that have been received, and thoughtful construction of a response. This differs from the kinds of time-pressured responses that happen in traditional conversations.

In the next section we describe the MBC technology. We then show how MBC was customized in Media Fusion for use in an educational setting. Finally we present the results of a ethnographic study of Media Fusion as it was used by students in California and Washington D.C. to study global warming.

2   Model-Based Communication

MBC provides a means of constructing digital video (or text) messages which can contain embedded pointers to various applications. For example, in Figure 1 the top video message titled "MacNeil/Lehrer Global Warming" contains two pointers which are positioned along its scroll bar. As the QuickTime digital video clip plays, the scroll box moves along the scroll bar. When the scroll box "hits" the first pointer, it launches a data analysis application, called Tabletop (6), and configures a pre-specified graph derived from a particular database. All this information (the application, the file, and the various parameters that describe the scatter plot) was encoded into the pointer when the message was created.

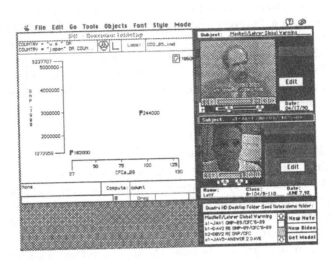

Figure 1: A Media Fusion screen

With MBC capabilities, users can create their own video messages (provided they have a video camera and a digitizing board). Users can also specify various analyses of the data (in Tabletop). These analyses can then be dragged onto the QuickTime digital video. These pointers can be moved around, or deleted. When the user is satisfied that the video message conveys the appropriate message, it can be saved.

It is important to point out that this type of embedding in significantly different from other seemingly similar types of linking. Some applications allow the user to insert bitmap images of other applications, but these are static pictures that do not support exploration. Some applications allow the user to create a "hot link" to another file (possibly opened by another application), but these typically take the user to a fixed document (e.g., a text editor document, or a HyperCard stack).

MBC allows the user to create a narrative that explicates a path of reasoning. A single video message might have several pointers, all perhaps to the same application and the same database file, but each of which shows a different way of looking at the data. In some cases this might mean plotting different fields against each other. In other cases this might mean changing the scales of an axes. In yet other cases this might mean simply highlighting certain data points in one view and others in subsequent views. Collectively these can be used as evidence to support the argument delivered in the message.

The receiver of such a message can not only inspect the graph embedded within a message, but can also manipulate that graph. In this way users come to understand the data not only in terms of the graphical view constructed by the sender of the message, but in their own terms. In turn, the receiver of a message can create their own view of the data (through direct manipulation of the graph that they have received) and can embed their new view of the data in their response. In this way, users can discuss issues shown in the video, use data to augment their reasoning about those issues, and share their findings with others. The collection of messages developed in this manner serves as a history of the community's inquiry and understanding of the issues being discussed.

It is important that messages can be exchanged among users. For this some minimal network is required. This network need not be persistent, but it must support asynchronous communication. In other words, the network may be operational for only a few hours a day.

3   Customizing MBC for Education: Media Fusion

Our work takes a formative approach. Formative evaluation seeks to inform the design of technology by studying the use of initial prototypes in realistic situations. It discovers what is good and bad about the prototype with respect to its initial design goals. This information is then used to inform the subsequent re-design of the technology, which itself is subjected to further study. We recognize that it is not just the technology that is important in determining its usability and usefulness. The context and participants are also an important factor. Thus, our formative evaluation process starts with participatory design (involving researchers, teachers, students, collaborative partners, etc.) of both the technology, AND the situation in which the technology will ultimately be studied. Below we describe how MBC was customized for use in a classroom, the resulting program was Media Fusion. In the following section we describe the formative evaluation of Media Fusion.

Data Analysis Tools Tabletop, a data analysis tool designed at TERC was chosen to be used in Media Fusion. Tabletop is ideally suited for use with Media Fusion because it has been designed specifically for use by school students, with the design goal of enabling authentic inquiry with data. Tabletop provides a simple, non-relational database which is viewable via Venn diagrams and Scatter plots. Such a plot is shown in the left-hand window in Figure 1. Tabletop is highly interactive in that views are constructed via direct manipulation of the interface. For example, a scatter plot is formulated by selecting the variable name specified for the axis and then choosing one of the list of possible variable names that appears on a pop-up menu. Once a change has been made to an axis, the points on the screen do not magically jump to their next position, but gradually reorganize themselves by moving to their new position. In this way the user gets continual feedback on how changing the graphs specification affects the view of the data.

Seed Messages Another component of Media Fusion is seed video and text messages linked to views of the database. We included a clip taken from the MacNeil/Lehrer News Hour because in a preliminary study we found: the authentic issues such a show presents are of interest to students, it treats issues in depth, and it represents an issue from multiple perspectives — a format that invites response. We also included messages made by experts in the field of study.

Databases Databases were designed to serve as a common pool of information from which students could draw in their discussions. One function of the databases was to tie directly into, and expand upon, points presented in the MacNeil/Lehrer News Hour video clip. The databases were not confined to topics presented in the video, they also served to expand upon these topics, giving other types of data pertinent to the topic of the video. A characteristic of the databases is that they consisted of 'real' data. Use of real data makes this unlike the 'storybook' situations sometimes invented for textbooks. Here students are given access to the same kinds of data used by policy analysts and policy makers.

Network In the Media Fusion study, messages were exchange via satellite — through our collaboration with PBS we had access to a VSat connection. Messages were not automatically and immediately exchanged. Rather, this exchange happened overnight and was directed by researchers at each site.

4 Preparing the Situation

Two schools took part in the study; a middle school in Marin County, CA and a junior high school in Washington D.C. In the Washington D.C. school, three teachers (science, social studies and mathematics), and five 7th grade, four 8th grade and four 9th grade students participated in the study. At the Marin County school, two teachers (social studies and language arts), one computer support staff member, and twelve 6th grade students participated.

A few months before the study was due to take place, the teachers took place in a Media Fusion workshop. The purpose of this workshop was to introduce the teachers to Media Fusion from a learners perspective. We provided teachers with the opportunity and time to interact, explore and become sufficiently familiar with the technology to allow them to begin to prepare their students for the user study. The teachers were taught how to use Tabletop and how to make Media Fusion messages.

Following the workshop, we worked with the teachers to develop the Media Fusion curriculum for this study. Our discussions centered around what should be the domain of inquiry and deciding what activities should be part of the user study.

It was important that students at both schools be familiar with the Media Fusion software, in particular the Tabletop component. With this in mind, prior to the user study, teachers involved the students in a number of preparatory exercises. By the time of the user study students had at least an initial familiarity with both the Tabletop and the Media Fusion software — they knew how to make scatter plots and Venn diagrams using Tabletop, and how to compose, read and respond to both text and video messages.

5   The Study

The user study took place over four days, for two hours per day. During that time, students worked at the machines in small groups of three, four or five. The machines were Apple Quadra 700's, each with a 13" color monitor, 20 Meg of RAM, a video digitizing board and a video camera.

The study commenced with the students watching the full MacNeil/Lehrer video from which the digitized video clip had been taken. Following this, the teachers lead a discussion of global warming. Following the discussion, students at both schools worked with Media Fusion for the remainder of the session. They could look at the messages existing in the system — the MacNeil/Lehrer clip and expert seed messages — and compose their first video or text messages. The messages the students composed were exchanged that evening.

For the remaining three days of the user study, students received messages from each other. Each session consisted of a brief discussion, to draw the students back into the Media Fusion activity, followed by the students working with Media Fusion, reading messages that had been received and composing responses or messages on a new topic. As before, all new messages made during the day were exchanged that evening.

A number of different kinds of data were collected during the user study: pre- and post-user study questionnaires, video of students using Media Fusion, pre- and post-participant discussions of global warming, the Media Fusion video and text messages, and interviews with both teachers and students after the user study had finished.

6   Analysis

Analysis of the data led to a number of conclusions regarding how well Media Fusion met the original design goals, these results are discussed below.

The Social Construction of Knowledge Being able to collaborate with fellow learners by sending video and text messages helped the students come to a better understanding of the issues. As one student put it: *"It helps you understand things better, to be able to make a graph and stuff like that and talk to people on the other side of the country about it."*

Altogether we had 8 discussions, these contained between 2 and 10 messages; the average number of messages was 6. There were also two subdiscussions. Out of 66 messages, 61 were messages that were part of a discussion. Much of the discussion centered around alternative interpretations of the data, or discussion of whether the data really supported the argument. In one example, the concept of GNP was discussed in detail because one student made a video message containing a graph that showed the total GNP for a country, and said that the GNP was defined as millions of dollars per person. The students receiving this message noted that this did not really make sense and suggested a different definition of GNP. The original author acknowledge the appropriate definition of GNP, and revised his interpretation of the graph he had made.

Having to negotiate an understanding may have been a factor in students ability to reason about the data. In previous studies of Tabletop, it has been noted that students still held onto their own opinions even in the face of data that seemed to contradict them. This was not evident in this study. Even when a student did state something that was not shown in the graph, other students would pick up on that and correct the view. Students would then in light of the correction re-evaluate what they had said.

All of the teachers emphasized the importance of the audience in motivating the students, for example as one teacher put it: *"...instead of 'let's explain this to the teacher because we have to'. It's 'we want to say something that's valid to these kids, we don't want to look really stupid, so we want to find some interesting information'..."*. Part of the power of collaboration appeared to be increased self-assessment of work because it was being subjected to peer-assessment. Students want both to say something sensible, and also to say it in a manner that looks and sounds appropriate. Typically students would spend a great deal of time deciding what to say in response to a message, and how to say it.

Compared to an isolated individual learner, the community has access to a much more varied and rich pool of information, because all of the members of the community can pool their knowledge and cognitive resources in order to understand an issue. For example, in the discussion about GNP described above, a student found a response to a message he had sent hard to understand. However, he reflected in the post-study interview that this was not a problem because the explanation in a second response was very clear. In fact, when the students who had written the first response were asked about it, they also said that the second response helped them better understand what they had been trying to express. In retrospect however, the amount of knowledgeable available in this study was not as great as it might have been had experts been fully integrated into the learning community. Other studies have shown that experts provide valuable resources to learners when part of a networked learning community, although careful measures must be taken to ensure that expert-student conversations do not detract from the valuable peer-to-peer conversations (12).

Linking Communication and Discovery Tools Supports Reflection

In general, using Media Fusion gave students the opportunity for deeper reflection on issues surrounding global warming and allowed then to understand the power, and meaning of data analysis as a tool for making sense of opinions. Students were really engaged in using the database to understand the issues, and in making graphs to support their views.

In addition to learning about global warming, students also developed a good understanding of what it meant to use data to support a view, and how to investigate hypotheses using the data analysis tools. This is shown in the following protocol taken from the post-study discussion.

> Researcher: *"... if you had both those different graphs, the automobiles with CO2 and the bicycles with carbon dioxide, what would you expect to see?"*
>
> Student: *15: "I'd expect that countries that had a lot of bicycles that those had low CO2 emissions and countries that had a lot of cars would have high CO2 emissions.*
>
> Researcher: *"So the greater the number of bicycles the lower the CO2. And how would it look? Would they look like, the opposite of each other, the graphs, the automobile one and carbon dioxide?"*
>
> Student: *15: "I don't think there would be too much difference because one of them has bikes and CO2 and the other one has cars and CO2, but the one with bikes isn't only bikes in that country, there's also cars giving out CO2."*

In this example, the student is exhibiting an understanding of what the graph actually means. The student argues that there are other variables that can affect the graph, variables that are not shown on the axes — a vital concept in understanding correlations. Media Fusion helps students learn such concepts because when students have to understand other messages containing interpretations of data, and respond to these messages, students are careful and detailed in consideration of the messages they receive and the views of the data embedded in those messages.

Students also developed an understanding of what questions to ask, and how to answer those questions using the database. For example, when trying to respond to a message about a correlation between the amount of CO2 produced and the amount of energy consumed by a country, one student said: *"I think that to find out what CO2 Industry 89, what kind of industry that's based on, you might want to look at cars, transport, population, you might want to look at gas, stuff like that, all those kinds of things... that relate to being industry, and let's see how much that contributes to what is called CO2 89 industry."*

Using someone else's message, the arguments it expresses and the graphs that prove those arguments was central to each group coming to understand more about global warming issues. In this way, the members of the community scaffold each others learning. Students found this one of the most difficult points to grasp, how to have a continued discussion around an issue, refuting, expanding on, and making new arguments based on exploration of the data. There are two reasons why this might have been difficult for students to learn. Firstly, Media Fusion did not provide an adequate model of this We used the expert seed messages to model the kinds of behaviors that we though were important, e.g. using different kinds of graphs to support different points, using text messages to make some points and video messages to make others. However, a surprising result of our study is that the students didn't really look at the expert seed messages. The most likely reason for this, based on discussion with both teachers and students, is that the expert wasn't part of the community — this had been a conscious design decision because we were worried that as part of the community, expert-student conversation would detract from student-student conversations. The teachers conjectured that unless experts are part of the community, their communications are not meaningful to the students.

A second reason that students found it difficult to have an ongoing discussion around an issue was that we provided no structure to the list of messages. This made it very hard for students to see what topic a message was about, because the only cue they had was in the message title. In reaction to the problems students were having finding messages on a particular topic, during the study we reorganized the message browser to structure messages according to discussion topic. Given the time constraints of the study, we did this in the simplest and easiest way possible. The original list of messages showed the contents of one particular 'message' folder. By placing new folders inside this 'message' folder, giving these new folders the names of the discussions and placing the existing messages in the appropriate discussion folder we immediately had a more organized message browser. This reorganization made it far easier for students to find messages, and continue an on-going discussion. When a student responded to a message they were viewing, their response was automatically stored in the same folder as the message they were responding to. Obviously this design has some severe limitations on students ability to organize their discussions, however for the purposes of the study it provided an adequate means of organizing the messages, and future work will investigate browser design.

Asynchronous Communication This study did not let us compare asynchronous with synchronous communication, because the technology we were using could not support synchronous video conferencing. However it did allow us to investigate whether interesting interaction could be supported by asynchronous communication. This is important, because it is unlikely that schools will have facilities for synchronous video communication in the near future, while access to asynchronous communication (at least with text) is more likely in todays schools. We found that the asynchronous nature of the communication in this study was not a problem. In fact, we think it helped structure the students work because they would read messages at the start of the session, decide which ones to respond to and then spend the rest of the time composing their responses.

In fact we suggest that the asynchronous nature of the communication actually provides opportunity for deeper reflection because students are not pressurized to respond immediately to a message.

7 Conclusion

Although there has been much attention paid in the literature to video as a communication device, little attention has been paid to the integration of video with conversational props, or to the use of such video as an aid to learning. This study has shown that Media Fusion has the potential to become a tool that can support such activities. However, although the study spanned days — a longer time than many studies of technology-use — a longer study needs to be carried out to more fully assess the potential of this technology for use in a classroom. It should also be noted that we studied school children in one particular educational setting, further studies are required to see whether the results described in this paper generalize to adults, and other learning situations.

This study suggests that sending and receiving video and text messages supports the social construction of knowledge. The study also suggests that linking video to data analysis supports reflective learning because through exploration and interpretation of the data students can actively construct an understanding of the opinions presented in received messages, and formulate their own understanding and express them in messages they compose and send to others. Finally, in this study, asynchronous communication tools were found to be adequate support for communications that support collaborative learning.

We also discovered certain aspects of Media Fusion that need to be redesigned so that it better supports learning. In particular, future versions of Media Fusion should provide more appropriate support for the organization and retrieval of messages. We are currently working on a concept of dynamic viewers to address this issue. A second important area of on which our redesign work concentrates on the integration of experts into communities of learners. We have realized that a community of learners needs to contain experts who can provide important insights to novices. Future studies will fully integrate experts into the Media Fusion Community.

From a formative evaluation perspective, this study has shown the importance of designing not just tools, but also tasks and situations. Much of the effort in this study was placed on designing the situation of use for the technology. This was important because it enabled us to go beyond a purely technological focus to incorporate details about supporting materials and social issues in our evaluation. We think that expanding the design space beyond how the tools support learning to look at the tools in the context of the task and the situation is an important aspect of this work. It is critical when designing tools that are to be placed in organizations such as schools that have pre-existing entrenched approaches to the use of educational support materials.

Acknowledgments

We would like to thank Charles Kerns, Jacqui Celsi, Wayne Grant and Steve Adams for their help in running the Media Fusion user study. We would also like to thank PBS, MacNeil/Lehrer and TERC (Technology and Education Research Center) for their support of this work.

References

1. Borovoy R. and Cooper, E. Model-Based Communication. Apple Patent Pending.
2. Brinck, T. and Gomez, L. M. A Collaborative Medium for the Support of Conversational Props. In *Proceedings of CSCW'92, the Conference on Computer-Supported Cooperative Work*, pp. 171–178. New York: ACM.
3. Bruner, J. The Process of Education. Harvard University Press: Cambridge MA.
4. Chan, C. and Burtis, J. Level of Constructive Effort, Prior Knowledge and Learning. Presented at *The Symposium on Constructive Effort in Learning, Annual Meeting of the American Educational Research Association*, New Orleans.
5. Greeno, J. G. A Perspective on Thinking. IRL Report #IRL88-0010.
6. Hancock, C., Kaput, J. J. and Goldsmith, L. T. Authentic Inquiry with Data: Critical Barriers to Classroom Implementation. In *Educational Psychologist*.
7. Lave, J. and Wenger, E. Situated Learning: Legitimate Peripheral Participation. Cambridge University Press: Ny, NY.A
8. Norman, D. *Things that make Us Smart* Addison-Wesley:Reading, MA.
9. Pea, R. Augmenting the Discourse of learning with Computer-Based Learning Environments. In E. de Corte, M. C. Linn, H. Mandl, L. Vershaffel (Eds.) Computer-Based Learning Environments and Problem Solving. pp. 313-340. Springer-Verlag: Heidelberg, Germany.
10. Roschelle, J. and Clancey, W. Learning as Social and Neural. Presented at AERA Symposium, Implications of Cognitive Theories of hoe the Nervous System Functions for Research and Practice in Education, Chicago.
11. Scardamalia, M., Bereiter, C., McLean, R. S., Swallow, J. and Woodruff, E. Computer-Supported Intentional Learning Environments. *Journal of Educational Computing Research*, 5(1), pp. 51-68.
12. Woolsey, K. and Kerns, C. The Ross Bulletin Board. Apple Internal Report.

A Knowledge-Based Authoring System for Hypermedia-Based Learning Environments

Doris Nitsche-Ruhland

University of Stuttgart
Department of Computer Science
Breitwiesenstr. 20-22
D-70565 Stuttgart
phone: ++49 711 7816 404
fax: ++49 711 7816 340

Keywords: Hypermedia systems, educational systems, authoring systems, critic, learner/system control, learner modelling, semantic networks, browsing tools.

Abstract: The use of hypermedia in educational systems requires a new type of literacy from learners and authors. In this paper some issues of hypermedia-based educational systems such as learner control, the database structuring and browsing tools will be discussed, which results in an architecture of an educational system. To build such an educational systems, the architecture of the authoring system CADYS is presented. For learning benefits an author who builds a hypermedia-based educational system has to observe other design criteria than in tutorial or instructional systems. Since authors usually are no design experts for hypermedia systems, the authoring system supports the author during the design process. A critic supervises this process in order to support the author.

1   Introduction

Over the last years, hypermedia has commonly been used in educational systems. Its efficiency has not been established until now, especially if the learner is responsible for the access and sequencing of information.

New problems arise with the use of hypermedia. Both learner and author have to acquire a new type of literacy to benefit from hypermedia. Since the author is not supposed to be an expert in designing an educational hypermedia system he needs support for this task.

In section 2, the requirements for educational hypermedia systems will be discussed. In section 3 the authoring system CADYS[1] will be presented which supports the author in designing educational hypermedia systems with respect to the requirements of section 2.

---

[1] Critic-Authoring System for Designing Hypermedia-based Learning Systems

2 Requirements for Educational Hypermedia Systems

The database of a hypermedia system can be conceptualized as a network of nodes with links connecting the nodes. The nodes consist of chunks of text, graphic, video, or other information [4]. One striking characteristic of hypermedia is the user control. The learner is responsible for the access and sequencing of information in hypermedia-based systems for learning. Thereby hypermedia motivates informal, individualized, and content-oriented strategies for information seeking and exploration.

The associative structure contained in a hypermedia database supports the associative thinking during information seeking. Usually, browsing systems do not support the creation of nodes and links by the learner. However to build his own information model, the learner has to build own information structures. He must have the ability to create nodes and links in order to organize and structure the information according to his interests. So hypermedia systems appropriate for learning should support the active processes "building an information model" and "information seeking".

2.1 Learner Control Versus System Control

Learning benefits from using hypermedia systems if the learner chooses the appropriate strategy. It is evident [8] [10] that this is not always the case. Especially for average and below-average learners, control by the learner does not generally support learning. They regularly learn less than with adaptive, instructional systems.

Therefore it is useful to have a mixed control. This requires a user model to adapt the control to the learner. A novice will be guided through the hypermedia network by the system ("guided tour"). It offers the learner appropriate paths for browsing. The more familiar a learner is with the domain the more he gets control and becomes responsible for the access and sequencing of information [1].

This method reflects the different use of a hypermedia system. A novice will use the system for knowledge acquisition; so guiding the learner through the network is useful. An expert will use the system to look up or search special information. It is not necessary to guide him, but it is necessary to offer him query mechanisms for efficient information retrieval [7].

2.2 Structured Versus Unstructured Hypermedia

Structured and unstructured hypermedia can be distinguished. In unstructured hypermedia two nodes are connected because one node contains a reference to the other node. Thereby the network does not necessarily have a general conceptual structure [8]. On the other hand, structured hypermedia contains an explicit organization of the nodes and links and is suitable to represent several conceptual structures. Typed nodes and links show the structural interrelations of the database. In learning environments hypermedia should be structured and typed in order to represent the authors conceptual model of the subject domain and to support the learning process "building an information model". Further well structured hypermedia supports navigation and reduces the problem of disorientation.

2.3 Browsing-tools for learning

Both learner and author need appropriate browsing tools for analyzing the structural interrelations contained in the hypermedia database and for easier navigation. Graphical browsing tools such as global and local maps [20], as well as fisheye views [11] are helpful to show the structure of the database and the meaning of a node in its context.

Maps have to be dynamic, not static. Only dynamic maps are able to show changes of the database. Further, dynamic maps simplify the interactive editing of the network.

To avoid disorientation problems ("Lost in Hyperspace") a history and a backtrack [12] facility should be available, to show the learner the path he went. A bookmark facility is important for marking interesting nodes and task stacking [4].

As Halasz claims in [6], an index and query mechanism should be available to support the search of special information and thereby especially the work of an expert user.

In order to follow the points discussed, an educational hypermedia system must have, in addition to the hypermedia database and the hypermedia management-system, a hypermedia editor for enabling the learner to create own nodes and links, several browsing tools to support different navigational strategies as well as different types of users, a user model and a component containing the knowledge necessary to adapt the control to the learner, which is defined by the interaction of the user model and the hypermedia database.

3 The Architecture of the Authoring System CADYS

The authoring system CADYS can be seen as a critic expert system supporting the author in designing a hypermedia-based system for learning outlined in 2. In the authoring system of Ottmann [13] the author has to fill predefined frames in order to create a hypermedia node. The author does not have to make any design decisions.

In CADYS the author himself is responsible for these decisions, but is supervised and supported by a *critic*. If an action or decision seems to be suboptimal or wrong, the critic intervenes. It contains different knowledge bases about designing the different components of the educational system and is a fundamental component of the authoring system.

Besides the critic, the system includes *tools for editing* the hypermedia database, several *browsing tools*, a *library containing predefined node formats*, a *library with predefined user interfaces*, a special component called *control specification*, the user modelling component MODUS [15], and a *user interface builder* (Figure 1).

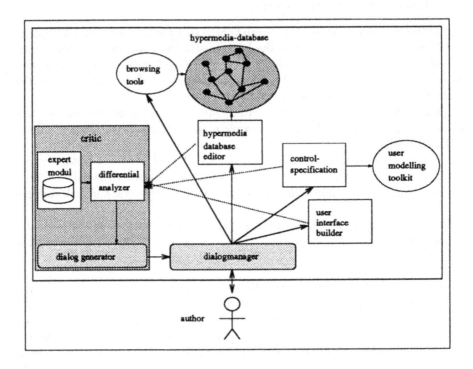

Fig. 1. The authoring system architecture

3.1 Hypermedia Database Editor

One of the most important tasks in the design process is the creation of the hypermedia database. The author has to impose his conceptual structure of the learning domain on the hypermedia database. The hypermedia database editor should support him in this task by several tools which can be divided in two groups. The first group supports the creation and editing of the nodes with their content, the second group containing the tool STRUKTOMAT supports the structuring of the network.

A node has two representations. The internal representation describes the logical structure of the nodes content and the links to other nodes in the markup language HTML [21]. The external representation is computed from the internal representation together with a style format, when a node is accessed in the educational system. The author can specify this style format or he can select it from a library. The divison in content and layout has the advantage that the layout can be changed in an easy way and that documents in HTML as offered in the World Wide Web can be included. To support the creation of textual nodes in HTML and style formats for text two editors are available [3]. The HTML-editor for textnodes simplifies the creation of HTML-tags. With the style-format editor[2] the layout of the HTML-tags can be defined with a style sheet (Figure 2). Both are easy to use also for unexperienced authors.

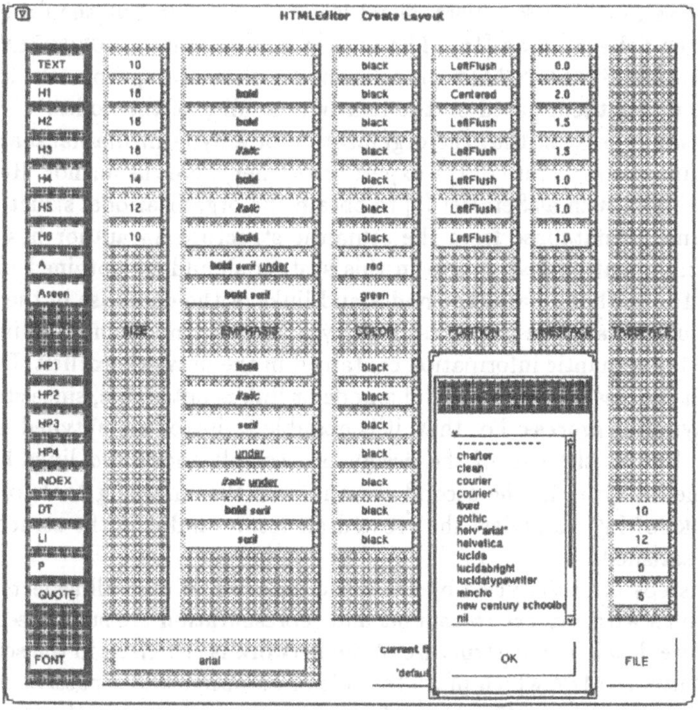

Fig. 2. The style-sheet with a dialog view to choose the text font

The global and local maps of the browsing tools help the author to keep the graphical overview and see the nodes in their context in order to control the depiction of his conceptual model on the hypermedia database. The tool STRUK-TOMAT permits the author to edit the structure and offers him feedback about structural properties of the database. STRUKTOMAT has knowledge about the importance of link types and uses metrics for hypertext networks [2][14] to iden-

---

[2] HTML is based on SGML. The layout of a SGML-document is defined by a DSSSL specification (Document Style Semantics and Specification Language), which is unsuitable for authors

tify hierarchies, calculate the relativ depth of the nodes and the compactness[3] of the network.

The editing of the whole structure as well as the editing of nodes and links is supported in an easy way by STRUKTOMAT and the maps. The editors for the nodes can be accessed from them.

There are several restrictions for the design of the hypermedia database the author has to observe:

- In addition to the associative links a hierarchical structure has to be imposed on the network. Thereby, hierarchical views are possible. The simpler cognitive model makes hierarchical views more attractive than other global maps or fisheye views [16]. The author can consult STRUKTOMAT to find hierarchies. STRUKTOMAT proposes nodes that are appropriate for a root. It calculates them based on the relativ centrality of the nodes.
- Jonassen [9] states, that the organization of a hypermedia database reflects the semantic structure of the expert or teacher, here the author. He suggests to use tools such as SemNet [5] to obtain the organizational structure of the hypermedia database from the semantic structure an author has in mind. The organizational structure in this system should be obtained in another way. The author creates the nodes and links of the database in the first step without any aid. He has to assign a type to every node and link in order to make the semantic information contained in the network explicit. During the design process often the type of a node or link is not stable, since structuring is a dynamic process. For that, it is possible to introduce untyped nodes and links. But at the end of the design process all nodes and links have been assigned a type. In the second step he uses the browsing tools or the tool STRUKTOMAT to review the created structure and edit the structure until he is satisfied.

Both steps are supervised by the critic. In the first step all aspects of nodes and links with respect to content and representation are supervised (see 3.4 for more details). The structure of the network is criticized in the second step by STRUKTOMAT which plays the role of an active and a passive critic. The author can activate STRUKTOMAT at every time during the construction of the database, the system activates it automatically when the database is saved.

3.2   *Control-specification* Component

As discussed above, mixed control together with a user model seems to be useful for hypermedia-based systems for learning. The specification of the knowledge needed for the mixed control is achieved by the control-specification component. The user model is built with the user modelling toolkit MODUS [15]. MODUS supports the construction and management of individual dynamic user models.

---

[3] The compactness of a network is a value between 1 and 0. In a network with compactness 1 every node is connected with all other nodes, in a network with compactness 0 there is no connection at all.

The author has to define the attributes the user model represents. These attributes model the different aspects of the user the author is interested in. Based on the attributes stereotypes and classification rules which assign a stereotype to a user have to be defined. Typical stereotypes for learning purposes could be novice, beginner, intermediate and expert. During a learning session the system as well as the learner enter information in the user model from which additional knowledge can be infered. To use the knowledge of the user model selection rules have to be declared. They connect the application with the user model.

Special attribute/value pairs are assigned to all nodes of the hypermedia database [1]. For learning purposes attributes about the degree of difficulty or necessary pre-knowledge are appropriate. Possible values of the attribute degree of difficulty are mundane, simple, advanced, complex and esoteric. From these attibute/value pairs and the user model the selection rules can compute appropriate paths for the learner which the system suggests him. The task of the author is to specify the control-specification, that means the assignment of attribute/value pairs to the nodes, the attributes be stored in the user model, the stereotypes and classification rules and the selection rules of the user model.

3.3 User Interface Builder

The author creates the user interface with the user interface builder. If the author does not want to design the user interface, he can select a predefined user interface from a library. Otherwise he has to modify a template from the library or design one. Then he must decide for example, which kind of nodes can be displayed at the same time, which buttons and functions are available, which color the background should have, etc.

3.4 Critic

The critic supervises the creation of the hypermedia network as well as the overall design, including the design of the user interface and the control-specification. It is connected to all tools of the authoring system. Based on the architecture of critiquing systems in [18] the critic has an expert-modul, a differential analyzer and a dialog generator (see Figure 1).

The expert modul contains several knowledge bases according to the different design tasks. A knowledge base contains either application dependent or application independent rules, therefore two knowledge bases can be assigned to the same design task. For each design task and the corresponding knowledge the differential analyzer contains an analyzing modul. This is based on the different analyzing strategies for the different design tasks. The critic components responsible for the structuring process of the network are the same as for STRUKTOMAT (see 3.1).

The application independent knowledge base connected to the editors for the nodes and style-sheets includes rules which take special media characteristics into consideration. For nodes containing text, there are rules about fonts to be used, the text size, the emphasizing of anchors of links etc. For example there is a rule that a "good" text-node contains between 4 and 80 lines of text [17]. In addition rules for the uniform representation of nodes with the same media type are contained. If an author has emphasized the anchor of links in a text by a different font and now uses a different color, he will be pointed to this inconsistency by the critic.

STRUKTOMAT test the structural properties of the database. It contains two knowledge bases. The application independent knowledgebase contains rules about the reachability, centrality and depth of nodes and the compactness of the network. The analyzing modul therefore can find unreachable nodes and can test if there is a hierarchical structure imposed on the database. If there is none it can propose possible root nodes. If the compactness is very high, it can point the author to the fact, that an extremly connected network is not appropriate for learning purposes. The application dependent knowledge includes rules about the importance of link types. If the author wants to remove some links STRUKTOMAT can propose him the links that are semantically and structurally not so important. Further it comprises rules which test whether special node types are allowed to be connected by special link types. For example, if the hypermedia database should have an argumentative structure as described in [19], it is not allowed to connect two nodes of type "claim" by a link of type "so".

Two further knowledge bases contain all rules about the user interface design [17] and the control-specification. The knowledge about the user interface is application independent. It cares for example about the number of used colors, the size of buttons, and if an user interface is suitable for color as well as for monochrom displays. It has shown that user interfaces developed on a color display often are unusable on a monochrom display because the contrasts were bad and the labels were unreadable. The authors who worked with the critic environment approved it when the critic points them to this weakness. Rules dealing with the control-specification are application dependent. For example, they have to take care that a novice in the teaching domain is guided first through all basic concepts and not through advanced concepts.

The critic records every step done by the author but the points it intervenes the design process to criticize special decisions are different. In our example about emphasizing anchors of links in a text, it intervenes as soon as it recognizes that the author uses a different color. Structural restrictions are tested by the system not until the creation of the nodes and links of the database (step 1 in 3.1) is finished. The rules of the critics knowledgebases can be inspected by the author and he has the possiblity to turn them off separately, if the criticism of some rules gets annoying.

4 Summary and Outlook

The architecture of the authoring system presented here is designed to support the author in the creation of *good* hypermedia systems for learning. The author is free to design the hypermedia network and the entire system as he likes, but is supervised and supported by a critic. The main focus in this system is the creation of a hypermedia database. The fundamental question is, how a hypermedia database should be structured in a meaningful way to support the intended learning process best. The testing of structural properties and semantic restrictions as descibed here is a first step in this direction.

At the moment the structuring of hypertext databases for learning programming languages and technical documentation is examined. The prototype of the authoring system is implemented in Objectworks\Smalltalk. Detailed evaluation of CADYS is in progress. First result concerning the editors and the critic for the user interface were achieved.

Acknowledgement

For the fundamental discussions about the ideas and the design I acknowledge Professor R. Gunzenhäuser.

References

1. Böcker, H.-D, Hohl, H., Schwab,T.: *HypAdapter-Individualizing Hypertext.* Proceedings of INTERACT'90, IFIP Conference on Human-Computer-Interaction; 1990
2. Botafogo,R. A., Rivlin, E.,Shneiderman, B.: *Structural Analysis of Hypertexts: Identifying Hierarchies and Useful Metrics.* ACM Transactions on Information Systems, Vol. 10, No. 2, 1992
3. Brehm, V.: *Ein Editor für Hypertext Dokumente.* Studienarbeit Nr. 1285, Fakultät Informatik der Universität Stuttgart, 1994
4. Conklin, J.: *Hypertext: An Intoduction and Survey.* IEEE Computer, Vol. 20, No. 9, 1987
5. Fisher, K., Faletti, J., Thronton, R., Patterson, H., Lipson, J., Spring, C.: *Computer-based knowledge representation as a tool for students and teachers.* Annual meeting of American Educational Research Association, New Orleans, April, 1988
6. Halasz, F. G.: *Reflection on NoteCards: Seven Issues for the next generation of Hypermedia systems.* Communications of the ACM, Vol. 31, No. 7, 1988
7. Jerke, K.-H. et al.: *Combining Hypermedia Browsing with Formal Queries.* Proceedings of INTERACT'90, IFIP Conference on Human-Computer-Interaction, 1990
8. Jonassen, D. H., Grabinger, S. R.: *Problems and Issues in Designing Hypertext/Hypermedia for Learning.* Designing Hypermedia for Learning, Proceedings of the NATO Advanced Research Workshop on Designing Hypertext/Hypermedia, Springer, 1989
9. Jonassen, D. H.: *Semantic network elicitation: tools for structuring hypertext.* Hypertext: State of the Art, Blackwell Scientific Publications, 1990
10. Marchionini, G.: *Evaluating Hypermedia-Based Learning.* Designing Hypermedia for Learning, Proceedings of the NATO Advanced Research Workshop on Designing Hypertext/Hypermedia, Springer, 1989
11. McAleese, R.: *Navigation and Browsing in Hypertext.* Hypertext: Theory into Practice, Blackwell Scientific Publications,1989
12. Nilson, J.: *The Art of Navigation.* Communications of the ACM, Vol. 33, No. 3, 1990

13. Ottmann, Th.: *Elektronische Kurse - Kritische Bilanz und Konsequenzen für die Werkzeugentwicklung.* Informatik und Schule, Springer, 1991
14. Rivlin, E., Botafogo, R., Shneiderman, B.: *Navigating in Hyperspace: Designing a Structure-Based Toolbox.* Communications of the ACM, Vol. 37, No. 2, 1994
15. Schwab, T. : *Methoden zur Dialog- und Benutzermodellierung in adaptiven Computersystemen.* Dissertation, Fakultät Informatik der Universität Stuttgart, 1989
16. Shneiderman, B., Kearsley, G.: *Hypertext Hands-On.* Addison-Wesley Publishing Company, 1989
17. Shneiderman, B.: *Designing the User Interface.* Addison-Wesley Publishing Company, 1992
18. Silverman,B. G.: *Survey of Expert Critiquing Systems: Practical and Theoretical Frontiers.* Communications of the ACM, Vol. 35, No. 4, 1992
19. Streitz,N. A., Hannemann, J., Thüring, M.: *From Ideas and Arguments to Hyperdocuments: Travelling through Activity Spaces.* Hypertext '89 Proceddings, 1989
20. Utting, K., Yankelovich, N.: *Context and Orientation in Hypermedia Networks.* ACM Transactions on Information Systems, Vol. 7, No. 1, 1989
21. World Wide Web. On Line Documentation, CERN, Geneva

Explanatory Visualization in an Educational Programming Environment: Connecting Examples with General Knowledge

Peter Brusilovsky

International Centre for Scientific and Technical Information,
Kuusinen str. 21b, Moscow 125252, Russia
E-mail: plb@plb.icsti.su

Abstract: Explanatory program visualization is a name for program visualization extended with natural language explanations. Explanatory visualization can seriously increase students' understanding of program behavior. This paper gives the rationale and background for explanatory visualization and introduces our work on using explanatory visualization in educational programming environments. In particular, we present first experimental results on using explanatory visualization and provide a fine-grained description of the implementation of adaptive explanatory visualization in our ITEM/IP-II system. This system employs student model to adapt the visualization to the student knowledge level.

1 Introduction

Intelligent programming environments for novices (Brusilovsky, 1993a) attempt to bridge the gap between Intelligent Tutoring Systems for programming and novice programming environments. An Educational Programming Environment (EPE) is a set of tools supporting the student in the process of learning introductory programming. Some of these tools support students' activities in program design and debugging, other tools support teachers' activities such as presenting new material or evaluating students' programs. Good examples of tools provided by an EPE are program visualization tools and intelligent program debuggers. A program visualizer is a tool that provides the student with an animated representation of program execution and makes some of the hidden aspects of program behavior visible to the programmer. A program visualization tool is an important component of a learning environment for programming. Such a tool enables the student to build a clear mental model of virtual (notional) machine behavior (du Boulay et al, 1981), as well as understand the semantics of programming language constructs and the behavior of algorithms. There are a number of systems and environments that employ program visualization (see McGlinn, Britt & Woolard, 1989; Sanders & Gopal, 1991 for a good review and reference list). Traditionally program visualization is comprised of flow of control visualization and data structure visualizations on different levels. The traditional role of program visualization is to enhance the understanding of the semantics of programming constructs and algorithms and to support learning through exploratory programming.

For a number of years we have been working on EPE problems. In 1985 we designed the ITEM/IP environment (Brusilovsky, 1992) to support an introductory programming course for first year students at Moscow University. The course was based upon the visual, educational mini-language Turingal (Brusilovsky, 1991), which is a combination of a Turing machine language with Pascal control structures.

ITEM/IP consists of several modules that support student and teacher activities. Two important modules are the visual interpreter for Turingal and the evaluation module. The interpreter produces flow of control and action visualizations: each statement is marked before being executed and the machine head moves along the tape and replaces symbols as the corresponding statement is executed. The interpreter also produces some visual effects while evaluating conditions in ``while'' and ``if'' statements. The evaluation module checks the student's solution of a programming problem. The module applies a simple, but effective test-based method. Each programming problem presented to the student has a prestored model solution and a set of input tests. The evaluation module compares the results produced by the model solution to the results produced by the student solution for each test. If the results differ for one of the tests, the test is called ``faulty'' and the student program is considered to be wrong in some way, otherwise it is considered to be correct.

The visualization tool was widely used by the tutoring module in the explanation and debugging stage. First, visual examples were used to explain the semantics of programming language constructs to the student. Second, the system provided debugging assistance by visually executing the student program on the ``faulty'' test found by the evaluation module, thus visually demonstrating student errors. Our first experience with ITEM/IP in 1985 showed that the use of the visual interpreter for explanation and debugging significantly increased students' understanding of both language semantics and of their own bugs. However, more experience with ITEM/IP in 1986-1987 showed that program visualization is sometimes a less effective tool than it is expected to be.

We have revealed an interesting phenomenon - quite often weak students (and sometimes average students) simply cannot make sense of the visualizations. They look at the visualized piece of code but ``do not understand'' what is happening on the screen. For example, if an important loop in a buggy program is always skipped due to an incorrectly written condition (the cause of the error), the students sometimes cannot understand why the flow of control pointer passes this loop? They will run the program again and again on the same faulty test with no changes. The interview showed that they really do not understand why the loop is passed. At the same time, most of the students can answer questions about the semantics of the loop correctly. Thus they have good general knowledge, but often fail to apply it to a specific example.

Our ``first aid'' to such students was to explain in words how the given construct behaves in the given example. For example, the following explanation can be presented by an assistant when checking the condition of a ``while A'' statement: ``The condition `A' of the while statement is false because the tortoise stands on letter `B' which is not `A'.'' On the next step of the execution the assistant might say: ``Since the condition of the while statement is false, we jump to the statement after `endwhile', and do not execute the body of the loop.'' Such natural language explanations complement regular visualization and appear to provide very effective instructional help. Our assistants were often working in exactly this way, as ``explainers'' of what the program is doing, often repeating the same explanations.

The above experience motivated our current research and development work on explanations in program visualization. The preliminary results of this work are presented in this paper. We provide a brief summary of research on example explanation in programming, then we introduce our work on (what we call) explanatory visualization in a new ITEM/IP system and present the first experimental results which support our hypotheses and design decisions. The second part of the paper is devoted to a fine-grained description of the implementation of explanatory visualization in the ITEM/IP-II system.

Background: Example explanations in teaching and learning programming.
The most relevant research on using explanations of examples in teaching programming was performed by the group of Peter Pirolli. Their ideas were based on previous research into the role of examples in programming (Pirolli & Anderson 1989) and on findings about the role of self-explanations in the domain of physics problem solving (Chi at al, 1989). Investigating student self-explanation strategies in the programming domain (Pirolli & Bielaczyc, 1989), Pirolli, et al. found that the self-explanations students made while studying instructional materials correlated with the corresponding problem solving performance of those students. Students showing good performance not only generated more self-explanations than students showing poor performance, their explanations were qualitatively different. In particular, the following two effective self-explanation strategies were identified: connecting ideas in the texts with their instantiations in the examples (and vice-versa), and determining the meaning of LISP code presented in the examples. Good performers generated almost an order of magnitude more explanations connecting portions of the example solution to concepts introduced in the text.

Such findings can be used to produce better learning support systems. The first idea is to make a meta-cognitive tool that supports self-explanations by providing students with the ability to make written comments about both provided examples and their own programs. Unfortunately, such tools that have been designed recently (Recker & Pirolli, 1992; Linn, 1992) do not appear to be very effective. Many students consider such commenting activity as a waste of time.

From our point of view, the educational role of self-explanations is to provide a way for the student to relate their general knowledge about a subject with situational knowledge represented in a particular example. Using Clancey's terms (1987), self-explanations establish the links between general models and situation-specific models of an example. There is, however, another way - the instructional materials provided by the system can be extended with special example explanations that connect the problem examples with general knowledge. System-provided explanations are not as effective as self-explanations, but they can be easily provided and are very beneficial for the students, as was shown by Recker and Pirolli (1992). They designed a hypermedia-based system that contained a set of examples. These examples were annotated with explanatory elaborations (accessed via mouse clicks), that explained how programming principles were implemented within a concrete model. The idea of representing examples augmented with explorable explanations has also been implemented in other systems, such as Molehill (Singley & Carrol, 1992) and

Explainer (Redmiles, 1993). These tools were also effective, but their implementation was inspired more by experience of the authors than by cognitive considerations.

The work of Pirolli and his group gives more support to our hypotheses about our problems with understanding visualization. Weak students often cannot understand the visualization, because they do not relate the behavior of a particular construct in an example with their general knowledge about the semantics of the construct. An assistant's explanations bridge the gap between the example and general knowledge and enable the student to understand the example. Stronger students, or the students with more experience, have well established connections between general knowledge and situational knowledge that control the interpretation of examples, so they require example explanations much less frequently.

Interestingly, a similar phenomenon was reported in a related domain - algorithm visualization (Stasko, Badre & Lewis, 1993). It appears that novices and weak students benefit much less from algorithm visualization than was expected. Based on our experience and the ideas of Pirolli, we can explain this phenomenon: novices didn't relate their general knowledge of algorithms with the animation of a particular case on the screen. We think specific system-provided explanations bridging this gap can be of significant help here.

2 Explanatory Visualization: First Experience

Once our experience has shown that example explanations are helpful to resolve student problems with understanding visualization, the next step was to design a tool that can generate such explanations for the student. We have designed such a tool as a component of our recent ITEM/IP-II system that was designed to support a part of ``the computer literacy'' course for 14--16 year-old students of Moscow schools. ITEM/IP-II is similar in its architecture to ITEM/IP and uses a similar mini-language called Tortoise.

One of the new features of ITEM/IP-II is what we call "explanatory visualization". In addition to standard visualizations, the visual interpreter uses a special window to explain all the steps of the executed program in the same way that human assistants sometimes do when working with ITEM/IP. Note that our explanatory visualization tool differs from the tools suggested by Pirolli and other authors. First, all existing example explanation tools are applied to examples of program design, while our tool deals with examples of program behavior. Second, all other tools use static explanations of examples, provided by a course designer beforehand; our tool is able to generate explanations for any given example, either contained in the course, or suggested by the student. In this sense, our system is similar to the SCENT (McCalla, Greer, et al, 1992) program understanding system, which can explain the role of particular lines in a recursive student program in terms of standard recursion techniques. An ability to generate explanations requires expert knowledge to be represented in the tool - in our case, knowledge about language semantics.

Last year we completed the first classroom study of the ITEM/IP-II system. One of our goals was to measure the role of explanatory visualization in program debugging. The subjects in this study, 30 students from Moscow Lyceum of Information

Technologies, were divided into two groups. The students were 15--16 years old and most of them had never had any programming experience. The subjects were presented with a course of introductory programming based on the Tortoise mini-language. A course contains 14 lessons of 40 minutes each. Six lessons were spent presenting new material and solving some problems in a blackboard classroom. Each of these lessons was followed by a lesson in the computer classroom where the subjects used the ITEM/IP-II system to solve a sequence of related problems. The students used the structure editor and the visual interpreter to prepare solutions and called the evaluation module to check a solution when they thought it was ready. The solution was checked on a sequence of tests. If the solution appeared to be correct, then the student was presented with the next problem. Otherwise the evaluation module determined the ``faulty'' test and beeped to call one of the assistants to the student's computer for a short ``interview''.

The role of the assistant was to test several kinds of tools aimed at helping the student to understand the source of the error. At the beginning of the ``interview,'' and again after trying each tool, the assistant checked to determine whether the student understood the location and the source of the bug. If the student claimed that the error was understood and explained it correctly to the assistant, then the case was recorded and the student was permitted to correct the program. Otherwise, the next tool was applied. The first tool presented to the student showed the unequal results produced by the student solution and by the model solution on the ``faulty'' test. Then the student was presented with a standard, computer-generated visual execution of his or her incorrect solution on the faulty test. Next the assistant, with the use of the computer, formally simulated a standard explanatory visualization, as it is implemented, and then gave an adaptive explanatory visualization. Finally, the assistant applied his or her own intelligence to explain the error until the student understood it.

We utilized simulated vs. automatic explanatory visualizations because we wanted to obtain some feedback on our explanation methods, and because explanatory visualization was not well-tested enough to be used in a real classroom. However, all of the assistants were carefully instructed to produce standard explanatory visualizations as they were implemented in our system. Adaptive explanatory visualizations were produced less formally than standard visualizations, but more formally than ad-hoc assistant explanations. We found one very interesting result of the experiment was that sometimes ``assistant explanations'' were just the same explanatory visualizations given in an earlier step, but adapted to the student in two ways: the better the particular student's knowledge, the less detailed the explanations were, and at the same time, the closer the explanation was to the source of an error, the more detailed it was. It was about in the middle of the experiment that we formalized the rules of adaptive visualization and started counting it as a separate case (so the effect of adaptive visualization is probably even bigger than the data show). Up to six assistants were employed to work with each of 15 students in a group. They processed 167 interviews. The following table presents the proportion of students that understood the error after the corresponding tool was applied to the ``faulty'' test.

Table 1. The results of experiment

Tool	Interviews	%
Before all tools were applied	10	6.0%
Demonstrating results	32	19.0%
Standard visual execution	64	39.0%
Simulated explanatory visualization	34	20.0%
Simulated adaptive visualization	11	6.5%
Assistant explanations	16	9.5%
Total	167	100%

The results confirm our hypotheses that visualization is really a good tool for program debugging. We also found that explanatory visualization can significantly increase the effect of visualizations, leaving only 16% of errors uncovered, and that adaptive visualization provides further improvement. Measuring the role of visualization was not the only goal of the experiment. However, we obtained encouraging results as well as some new ideas about how to improve the visualization. Of course, even formally simulated explanatory visualization is not the same as computer generated visualization. First, human assistants cannot be as rigid as a computer, even if instructed. Second, simulated visualization was presented in a spoken way, i.e. in a different modality than the computer-generated visualization. Both aspects make simulated visualization more effective than computer-generated visualization. We plan to study the role of explanatory visualization (including adaptive visualization) more formally in the next studies.

3 Adaptive Explanatory Visualization in ITEM/IP-II

The results of the experiment gave us some idea about how to improve explanatory visualization in ITEM/IP. The current version of ITEM/IP-II includes not just explanatory visualization, but also adaptive explanatory visualization. At present we have implemented automatic adaptation of generated explanations for various student knowledge levels. This kind of adaptation was investigated by us previously (Brusilovsky, 1992a) for the case of regular visualizations. With adaptive program visualization the level of detail given in the visualization of a programming construct is made dependent on the differences in the students' knowledge about this construct. Adaptive visualization appears to be a very useful feature. For explanatory visualization adaptation is even more important. Explanatory visualization produces large amounts of text, so students may get lost in this stream of explanations and miss the important piece of the explanation.

There are 13 constructs in the Tortoise mini-language having from 1 to 4 degrees of visualization. The current state of visualization is determined by the visualization status vector which consists of 13 integers. This vector is formed using the central student model in the system. Each component of the vector determines the level of visualization for one of the constructs (level 1 - concept is new or poorly studied - maximum degree of visualization; level 2 - concept is understood better -

visualization is less detailed; ...; 4 - concept is understood well enough and does not need to be visualized). For each construct a template with stop points was developed. For example, consider the operator "IF < condition > THEN - ELSE - END_IF". This operator has five potential stops (figure 1) for stepwise execution mode. At each stop the corresponding part of the operator is pointed out and an appropriate message is displayed in the explanation window.

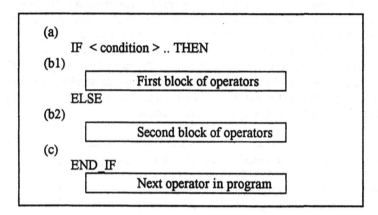

Figure 1. A construct template with visualization stops

Examples of comments for several degrees of visualization are given bellow.
1-st degree of visualization:
(a)   - Operator "IF < condition > THEN - ELSE - END_IF" consists of one
            condition and two branches - "THEN - ELSE" and "ELSE - END_IF".
            First we shall check the condition: true or false. (Here a visualization of
            checking the condition can follow).
(b1(b2))   - Condition is true (false)- control is passed to the "THEN - ELSE"
            ("ELSE - END_IF") block of operators.
(c1(c2))   - The "THEN - ELSE" ("ELSE - END_IF") block of operators has been
            executed - go to the operator following END_IF.

2-nd degree of visualization:
(a)   - Operator "IF". Checking if the condition is true or false. (Here a
            visualization of checking the condition can follow).
(b1(b2))   - Condition is true (false) - control is passed to the THEN (ELSE) block
            of operators.
No visualization and no stop at points (c1, c2).

3-rd degree of visualization:
(a)   - just stop without any explanation message
(b1(b2))   - Condition is true (false) - control is passed to the THEN (ELSE) block
            of operators.
No visualization and no stop at points (c1, c2).
4-th degree of visualization:

operator "IF" is well understood, we shall not explain it, however the silent stop is kept at (a).

All text displayed in the visualization window is stored in a file in an easily modifiable format (figure 2). This was specifically done to provide the teacher with the ability to represent pedagogical knowledge about the required behavior of the visualizations. An example of the explanation message representation is given in figure 3. The role of the teacher is important for the explanatory visualization mechanism. Actually, it's the knowledge and the experience of the teacher that should determine when and how to use explanatory visualization. The system provides the teacher with a great deal of control over the use of visualization. The teacher can change the vector of parameters of visualization, the number of visualization degrees for any concept, the number of break points (stops), and the content of all visualization messages for every degree of visualization.

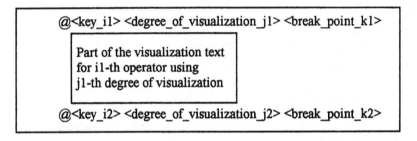

```
@<key_i1> <degree_of_visualization_j1> <break_point_k1>

    Part of the visualization text
    for i1-th operator using
    j1-th degree of visualization

@<key_i2> <degree_of_visualization_j2> <break_point_k2>
```

Figure 2. Representation of teacher's knowledge about visualization

```
@if 2 1
Operator "IF". Checking the condition true or false.
@if 2 2
Condition is true (false) - control is passed
to the THEN (ELSE) block of operators.
@if 2 3
NIL      . . . . .
```

Figure 3. An example of explanations for operator "IF" (translated from Russian). If the word "NIL" is stored, instead of text , then there is no stop for the given degree of visualization at this point.

4 Student Modeling for Adaptive Explanatory Visualization

The vector of visualization parameters is constructed as a dynamic projection of the central student model. According to our general approach to student modeling (Brusilovsky, 1993b), the central student model keeps the history of student interactions with system components, with the domain model concepts clearly indicated.

For the case of the visualization module, the central student model stores the number of its executions for each level of visualization separately for each construct (table 2).

Table 2. Individual parameters for student modeling

	regular non-stop execution	regular stepwise execution	executed with visualization of 1st degree	executed with visualization of 2nd degree	...
number of repetitions	X_1	X_2	X_3	X_4	...
weight	a_1	a_2	a_3	a_4	...

$X_1, X_2, X_3, ...$ - how many times a construct was executed in different conditions;
$a_1, a_2, a_3, ...$ - weights to calculate the cumulative amount of visualization.
For example: $a_1 = 0.1$, $a_2 = 1$, $a_3 = 5$, $a_4 = 4$, $a_5 = 3$, $a_6 = 3$, $a_7 = 2$.

When projecting the central student model onto the vector of visualization parameters, first the cumulative amount Y of the visualization the student has received for a construct is calculated.

$$Y = a_1 \cdot X_1 + a_2 \cdot X_2 + a_3 \cdot X_3 + ... + a_i \cdot X_i ;$$

The weights (a_1, a_2, ...) are specific to each student (table 2). They are stored in a file, and may be changed by the teacher. The visualization parameters for a construct are determined from Y using thresholds R_1, R_2, R_3 and R_4 for the 1-st, 2-nd, 3-rd, and 4-th degrees. If Y falls within segment $[R_{i-1}, R_i]$, then the i-th degree of visualization is assigned.

Thus the historic content of the central student model is currently projected into the vector of visualization parameters and used to control the visualization granularity. If the student is not satisfied with the degree of visualization, the vector of visualization parameters may be modified by the student or the teacher for better comprehension. More details about student modeling for adaptive visualization can be found in (Brusilovsky, 1992a, 1993b).

5 Conclusion

We have presented some ideas about explanatory program visualization. We describe the technique of adaptive explanatory visualization developed for a mini-language and provide some experimental results for its effectiveness. We consider two directions of further work on explanatory visualization. First, a more formal study should be conducted to carefully measure the contributions of both adaptive and standard explanatory visualization. Second, a similar approach can be used to support other parts of teaching programming. A particularly interesting area to support is the production of adaptive explanatory visualization at the level of algorithms. We think that such an explanatory visualization can solve some of the problems with algorithm visualization reported by Stasko, Badre and Lewis (1993). Eisenstadt et al. (1992) also suggest some good ideas regarding the application of knowledge about plans and algorithms to dynamic algorithm visualization. In addition, some of the existing approaches to program understanding and plan recognition can be used to evaluate the student knowledge about plans and to update the student model.

References

1. du Boulay J.B.H., O'Shea T., Monk J. (1981) "The black box inside the glass box: Presenting computing concepts to novices", International Journal on the Man-Machine Studies, v.14, 237-249.
2. Brusilovsky P. (1991) "Turingal - the language for teaching the principles of programming", Proc. EUROLOGO-91 conference, August 1991, Parma, 423-432.
3. Brusilovsky P. (1992a) Adaptive visualization in an intelligent programming environment. In: J.Gornostaev, (ed.) Proceedings of the East-West International Conference on Human-Computer Interaction, EWHCI'92, St.Petersburg, 4-8 August, 1992. - Moscow, p.46-50.
4. Brusilovsky P. (1992b) "Intelligent environment, tutor and manual for introductory programming", Educational Technology and Training International, v.29, n.1, 26-34.
5. Brusilovsky P.L. (1993a) Towards an intelligent environment for learning introductory programming. - In: E.Lemut, B.du Boulay, G.Dettori (eds.) Cognitive models and intelligent learning environments for learning programming. Springer-Verlag, p.114-124.
6. Brusilovsky P. (1993b) Student as user: Towards an adaptive interface for an intelligent learning environment. - In: P.Brna, S.Ohlson and H.Pain (Eds.) Proceedings of AI-ED'93, World Conference on Artificial Intelligence and Education, Edinburgh, 23-27 August 1993, AACE, Charlottesville, p.386-393
7. Chi M.T.H, Bassok M., Lewis M.W., Peiman P., Glaser R. (1989) Self-explanations: How students study and use examples in learning to solve problems. Cognitive Science, 13, 145-182.
8. Clancey W.J. (1988) The role of qualitative models in instruction. In J.Self (ed.) Artificial intelligence and human learning. Chapman and Hall, London, 49-68
9. Eisenstadt M., Price B.A., Domingue J. (1992) Software visualization vs. ITS: a better way forward In Brusilovsky P. and Stefanuk V. (eds.). Proc. East-West Conference on Emerging Computer Technologies in Education, Moscow, April 1992, 111-115.
10. Linn M.C. (1992) How can hypermedia tools help teaching programming. Learning and instruction, 2, 119-139.
11. McCalla G.I., Greer J.E et al (1992) Granularity hierarchies. International journal of computers and mathematics with applications, 23, 363-376.
12. McGlinn R.J., Britt M., Woolard L. (1989) APEX1, a library of dynamic programming examples. SIGCSE bulletin, v.21, n.1, 98-102.

13. Pirolli P. and Anderson J.R. (1985) The role of learning from examples in the acquisition of of recursive programming skills. Canadian Journal od Psychology, 39, 240-272.

14. Pirolli P. and Bielaczyc K. (1989) Empirical studies of self-explanations and transfer in learning to program. Proc of 11th Annual Conference of the Cognitive Science Society. Lawrence Erlbaum, Hillsdale, 450-457.

15. Recker M.M. and Pirolli P. (1992) Student strategies for learning programming from a computational environment. In: Proceedings of Second International Conference, ITS'92, LNCS N.608, Springer-Verlag, Berlin, p.499-506.

16. Redmiles D.F. (1993) Reducing the variability of programmers' performance through explained examples. In Human factors in computing systems. Proceedings of INTERCHI'93. Amsterdam, 67-73.

17. Sanders I. and Gopal H. (1991) AAPT: Algorithm animator and programming toolbox. SIGCSE bulletin, v.23, n.4, 41-47.

18. Stasko J., Badre A. and Lewis C. (1993) Do algorithm animations assist learning? An empirical study and analysis. In Human factors in computing systems. Proceedings of INTERCHI'93. Amsterdam, 61-66

Cultivating and Harvesting Semantic Coherence in SMIsC Hypertext Networks

Valery M. Chelnokov and Victoria L. Zephyrova

MosCHI, State Scientific and Technical Center for Hypertext
Information Technology (SSTC-GINTECH)
52/16, Zemlyanoy Val, Moscow, 109240, Russia
Phone: (095) 915-7004, 915-7620, 287-2968
Fax: (095) 915-7531

Abstract. This paper describes a hypertext system called System of Meaning Integrities structural Creation (SMIsC). The central component of this system is the macrocontrol subsystem. Its purpose is to overcome the Navigation Problem in hypertext by assisting users to blaze semantically coherent trails. These semantically coherent trails are meaning integrities. To construct the subsystem, we used discourse analysis and psycholinguistics and this is explained in detail in our previous paper [3]. The present paper deals with other aspects of SMIsC. Although not the central component, these other aspects of the system directly contribute to the general "coherentist" (holistic) orientation of SMIsC. We discuss the working of the micro level of the database network with respect to newly incoming nodes and links. We also discuss the monitoring of the emergence of large coherence clusters at the macro level in the network. We emphasize the close analogy between these events and the self-creation of meaning in synergetics [7]. Harvesting coherence is described as "catching" the clusters in the network for using them as global navigational contexts and a source of grounding materials and goal structures.

1 Introduction

In our previous paper [3], we dealt with the coherent navigation problem in hypertext environments: how to assist users moving within a network (of nodes with internally coherent contents and internode links of local coherence) so that the sequence of nodes visited in a session can be treated as a meaning integrity at the level above a node --- as a globally coherent discourse on the theme specified by the sequence's initial node.

Supporting a user moving within a network in this manner offers a solution to the general Navigation Problem. It allows users to perceive their current position in the network, thus reducing their feeling of getting lost in hyperspace (disorientation). In addition, the system's assisting mechanism selects, at each current node, the links for the next step, discarding the distracting ones, thus reducing the cognitive overhead of link choice.

Therefore, each navigation session dealing with a single initial thematic node, should result in the user's extracting some unity of meaning from the network, hence the name *System of Meaning Integrities structural Creation*, or *SMIsC*. The term 'structural' refers to the specificity of the macrocontrol subsystem, the system's assisting mechanism.

In developing the mechanism described in our previous paper, we had recourse to the well-known psycholinguistic models of discourse comprehension and production [10, 6, 13, 14]. According to these models, the global or thematic coherence of a discourse is revealed through the derivation of a *macrostructure* from the discourse's propositional content. The macrostructure of a discourse is a hierarchy of propositions in which the propositions are ordered at each level. At the lowest level of the hierarchy is the propositional sequence forming the discourse itself. At the apex is a proposition expressing, in it's most condensed form, the discourse theme. In general, the hierarchy is derived by upward, level-by-level application of the principle that a parent proposition is semantically entailed by each of its children propositions or by their joint set. This derivation process is such that a given level's propositional sequence gives a *summary* of the discourse [6, pp. 203, 218]. We deal with the particular case where all *macrounits*, the propositions at levels higher than the bottom, can in fact be borrowed from this last, i.e., from the set of the original discourse's propositions (microunits).

No integral macrostructure is possible for a discourse having a disconnected *microstructure*, the interpropositional linkage of local coherence. But the connectedness is not sufficient for the macrostructure's existence. Without submitting its course to what it should be about globally, even a connected sequence of propositions can go astray and arrive at a disunity of meaning. It is said that, to produce a semantically coherent discourse, the progress of its propositional sequence must be put under the *macrocontrol* [6, p. 150]. In this case, where some microunits act additionally as macros, it is the macrocontrol that directs, while in discourse production the user is blazing a trail through the meaning space in such a way that a macrostructure unfolds together with the micro.

Since it is based on the semantic relation of entailment among propositions, and hence involves propositions' reference to the facts of some possible world, the proper macrocontrol can operate only on the basis of world knowledge. Naturally, the last should underlie any correct inference that a proposition from a pair of interlinked propositions has a higher *macrostatus* than another, and is able to function as its parent in a macrohierarchy. Attempts to provide the system with the ability to make proper entailment inferences are beyond our intentions .

We use what we regard as indirect evidence of the macrostatus instead. For this purpose, we model discourse production as a linearization of a suitable fragment of a sufficiently large propositional network, in which a pair of node-propositions forms a link every time a discourse is possible whose microstructure could include the link. The linearization process is a genuine form of coherent navigation.

In the previous paper [3], we formulated an open set of if-then rules to macrocontrol this process at each current node. The rules, or strategies, are based on an accounting of a node's macrostatus in terms of the structural importance of the node's position within the network's graph. Navigationally, they support a depth-first traversal, allowing only macrostatus-dropping link followings and seeking to observe the Levelt's principle of minimal effort [14] which minimizes the stack of "unfinished" choice points. Though the subset *NEXT* of the node's links returned by the strategies' link filtering at a current node may contain more than one element, thus keeping hypertextuality alive, any choice from it would maintain the coherence from the macrocontrol's viewpoint.

A discourse generated in this way (we call such discourses 'canonically ordered') inherits its microstructure from the mother network, which acts as a supernetwork of its microstructure and creates its factual context helping to evaluate the macrostatus of its propositions. The traversal's tree allows the macrostructure to be easily reconstructed. It gives a *semantic outline* of the discourse and specifies a set of mutually embedded summaries of the discourse. One may note that our approach can be viewed as a contribution to what van Dijk and Kintsch termed 'a formal theory of linearization strategies in discourse production' [6, p. 276].

Coherence networks, the type of hypertext networks that SMIsC supports, are similar to propositional (super)networks, because the links in them connect entities like paragraphs as wholes, and in fact express the local coherence relations among the main ideas of the entities. This is why the above strategies constitute the core of SMIsC's macrocontrol subsystem. What we have said above shows that the macrocontrol is content-independent and it only deals with storing the network's graph and computing its structural characteristics (this explains the term *structural* in the system's name). Since we only consider large graphs, the enormous calculation complexities make this work the kind that computers, and only computers, are good at.

The present paper is concerned mainly with the aspects of SMIsC that are complementary to pure navigational ones. Some of them refer to coherence cultivation, i.e., preparation and working on the network in order that regions (node clusters) of meaning integrity could emerge in it, while others are related to coherence harvesting, i.e., gathering and using the results of this emergence. It seems to us that a far reaching analogy exists between the appearance of such coherence regions and the processes of coherent spatio-temporal structures' formation in physical systems open to influx of matter, energy and information --- the subject of modern physics of instability and of synergetics. It is not excluded that similar processes are involved in arising holistic mental forms like Gestalts, and this should not be indifferent for hypertext as 'a computer-based medium for thinking and communication' [5].

2 Coherence Cultivation in SMIsC

2.1 On SMIsC Functioning

Fig. 1 shows four sectors of user-SMIsC interaction. Each of them lists particular points of activity distinguishing the sector. We hope to clarify the matrix content in what follows.

	STATICS (Being): Stationary DB Network	DYNAMICS (Becoming): Evolving DB Network
MICRO-STATE: The Network's Node-Link Structure	Sector 1: Micro-Statics • Investigating adjacent nodes of a particular node • Random browsing in the network	Sector 3: Micro-Dynamics • Preparing texts of new nodes • Keyword profiling of new nodes • Linking a new node with nodes in DB by means of an information-filtering subsystem
MACRO-STATE: Thematic Clusters of Nodes	Sector 2: Macro-Statics • Learning of the current macrostate indicators • Thematic prestructure and cluster generation • Coherent navigation under the system's macrocontrol • Discourse-like trails and summaries • Tree-like semantic/goal structures (outlines)	Sector 4: Macro-Dynamics • Observing the dynamics of macrostate indicators • Detecting trends and sudden changes in the indicator values

Fig 1. Matrix of user-SMIsC interaction.

For a better understanding of the system's functioning, the following remarks will be useful.

An essential quality of SMIsC is its openness to new nodes and links. This invites us to look more closely at the dynamic aspect of the database coherence network, its microstructure's evolution, resulting from the gradual addition of nodes and links to the database. At each current moment, the microstructure, or the "microscopic" state, of the database is represented by a set of numbered nodes of information and a collection of the nodes' adjacency lists, each comprising the nodes linked with a given node. Adding a new node may have no serious influence upon the structural parameters being consumed by the macrocontrol subsystem. But it is also possible that the previous additions have so "prepared", or "destabilized", the microstructure that the node's arrival becomes "the last straw" resulting in a significant reordering of the parameters' values causing emergence of new large coherent clusters of nodes. Such global events, abruptly changing the "macroscopic" state of the database, noticeably contribute to the real flavor of SMIsC.

The influx of nodes and links acts upon the database network in a nonspecific fashion, in the sense that it is not (and cannot be) organized so that all structural events it causes are pre-planned ones. A new incoming node establishes local coherence relations with all relevant nodes in the database, and what these will be and how structural parameters, e.g., between-node distances, will react is far from being fully predictable in large networks. The reason for this is that fitting a new node into the network is associated with making all relationships between ideas explicit (the work that is never done in texts) and that the structure is very complex in general.

Because of this nonspecificity, the emergence of the nodes' collective state, such as a large node cluster traversable with our macrocontrol subsystem, can be equated with the act of *self-creation of meaning*, the term used by Hermann Haken in describing the subject of synergetics to refer to the emergence of new qualities at a macroscopic level in an open system of any nature [7, p. 23].

We also find a close analogy between occurrence of such global events within our network and the process of emergence of coherent macroscopic spatio-temporal structures in open systems in conditions far from thermodynamic equilibrium, as this process was described by Nobel laureate Ilya Prigogine. The network undergoes local perturbations at the microscopic level in the form of local modifications of the microstructure due to the entrance of new nodes and links. The stability of coherent clusters in the network is thus constantly being explored, and eventually a perturbation can occur leading to a significant redistribution of their size and hence driving the network to a significantly new macroscopic state. The network's behavior is a stochastic or chance phenomenon, because its macroscopic evolution is decided by which one of the possible critical perturbations occurs first. The Prigogine's scheme of this 'order through fluctuation' mechanism of self-organization [16, p. 39], in our case, takes the form of Fig. 2. By association with Prigogine's book *From Being to Becoming*, one may say that, in SMIsC, being and becoming of the database network should constitute two complementary aspects of the users' subject of interest.

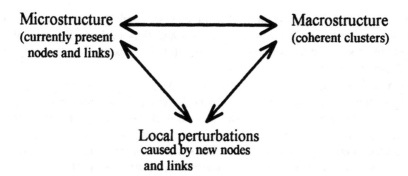

Fig 2. The self-determining sequence of network evolution in SMIsC.

2.2 Working at the Micro Level: Entering New Nodes and Links

Let nodes be produced as paragraphs; links then represent local coherence relationships among the node-paragraphs' main ideas (propositions). The relationships denote relations between facts in some possible world. They may denote conditional relations between facts or indicate a semantic function, such as comparison, information-adding, giving an example, explanation, generalization, specification, etc. [6].

When a series of nodes is produced in the process of "shredding and threading" of one linear text, i.e., converting the text into a non-linear document by means of its explicit presentation as a set of mutually interconnected ideas [2], a part of the links can be found as indicated by the text's surface structure cohesive devices, while the remaining part is to be derived on the basis of world knowledge. In the case of diverse sources of nodes, the same methods should be used in different proportions.

In fact, the linking process, if it is to be implemented properly, inherently includes human judgments. For this reason, searching the database network for all relevant nodes, to which a new incoming node is to be linked, becomes a more and more time-consuming task as the network becomes larger. Human crafting of links in a large network turns out impractical.

This problem of linking nodes in large hypertext systems has been indicated by various authors, e.g., [9, 18]. It is this problem that is to be mentioned when answering the question 'Where are the big systems?' [19]. Naturally, attempts are being made to automate the linking.

All the attempts can be interpreted as a passage from one model of memory trace to an alternative one. The first model represents the trace as a localized node or set of nodes in a semantic network. According to the second model, the trace is a pattern of activity distributed across memory cells and it tends to be reinstated only by the probes (retrieval cues) that are similar to it. For example, the work [9], relying on this model explicitly, uses traces in the form of binary attribute vectors where an individual element is one if the attribute is present and zero, otherwise. Now, if we maintain a set of attributes (terms, features, descriptors, keywords, or the like), then a hypertext node acquires a vector profile in that set, and the computer could calculate the similarity between any two profiles and thus evaluate the semantic proximity of the nodes and the possibility of their automatic linking. The human part of the work shifts to the task of indexing of nodes.

This approach to linking, in its simplest form, is well known in psychology for a long time as the associative principle of similarity: ideas (propositions) whose referents are similar tend to become associated to each other [20]. However, this principle can provide only a first approximation to recognition of local coherence links, for such coreference is neither a sufficient nor a necessary condition for such a link but is only a frequent concomitant property of its existence [6, 10]. The same should be true for the whole passage from the first model of memory traces to the second.

Being aware of these limitations, we nevertheless exploit in SMIsC a semi-automatic linking based on the principle of similarity, for it is unclear whether an essentially different approach could be operationalized. To link a new incoming node with nodes in the database, the node is indexed by hand and its keyword profile is used as a retrieval cue. The system returns a set of candidate nodes ranked by the number of keywords matched, and the user approves a subset of them. We are going to consider the possibility of using a tree-like outline hierarchy for the linking. This outline is the output of a navigation session and creates a context in which a new node is to be fit into the network. (The systems described in [9, 18] do not use explicitly coded links at all; rather, the activation of a part of a current node's profile defines the retrieval cue taking the user automatically to the node whose profile is the closest to the cue --- one may say that linkage is deferred until the link is required.)

It is noteworthy that a fully automatic linking would undermine the very idea of hypertext. As Patricia Ann Carlson recalls [1], hypertext, from its early times, is associated with a prethreaded body of information, a web of links and nodes, synonymous with an expert's knowledge, in passing, having a commercial value. From this viewpoint, it seems to be misleading to use, like Murray [15], the term 'computed hypertext links' for a full-text search specified by pointing at one or more words in an electronic text. The human supervised indexing phase cannot be removed from hypertext authoring, for, otherwise, there would be little to distinguish the hyperbase from a full-text-retrieval system [19].

2.3 Prenavigational Computing: Clusters' Automatic Generation and the Network's Macro State Monitoring

Prestructures and Clusters. In SMIsC, a navigation session begins with the selection of a node in the database network to specify the session's theme; from this node, the coherent sequence of nodes (discourse trail) will start. Immediately after selection of the node, the system generates a so called *prestructure*, consisting of only those nodes and links that can take part in the navigation, from the macrocontrol subsystem's "point of view" [3]. The prestructure is a hierarchy that has the thematic node (t) as its apex and a group of nodes being i links distant from t, as its ith level, $i=1, ... , l=l(t)$; formally, this is a $(l+1)$-partite graph. Generating this prestructure is equivalent to doing in advance some of the work associated with directing the navigational depth-first search; having this precursory work done permits the system to react quickly when the user selects a link during navigation. The collection of nodes included in the thematic prestructure generated for a given node is called the *thematic cluster* associated with the node.

The generation of a prestructure follows an algorithm for searching through the network's graph, namely one implementing a breadth-first search or spreading activation, with the given thematic node as the starting point ("source of activation"). The specificity of our algorithm is such that, when the search is at a particular node, only those of its adjacent nodes which have a macrostatus lower than its own are visited --- that is, only macrostatus-dropping links are open or "conductive" from the current node. As a result, only those nodes that a top-down path of a special kind can reach can enter the prestructure (cluster) --- the macrostatus must monotonically decrease along that path.

Naturally, the question is: given a link, how does the system infer that the link is open in one and not another direction? how does it use the macrostatus to compare the link's two nodes?

Modeling macrostatus dropping. Given a link, we assume that one of its two nodes, j, has a higher macrostatus than another, k, --- that k entails j --- iff the following two conditions are simultaneously satisfied. The first condition is related to the theme, while the second is independent of the theme:

- the distance from j to the thematic node, measured as the shortest path between them in the network's graph, is less than that from k, implying that the former node is in a closer semantic proximity to the theme than the latter;
- an event $E(j,k)$ takes place, modeling the abstract part of entailment.

By definition, the last event happens if, independently of the theme, knowing of the occurrence of the fact expressed by the content of k gives us a certain knowledge of the occurrence of the fact expressed by the content of j.

Two schemes are used for E recognition, one is deterministic while the other is less rigid, it is probabilistic. Both refer to the structural parameters known as node centralities in graph theory. Of the centrality's three forms discussed in [3], in this paper we consider only one, namely the centrality function r. Given a graph, the value of r at a node is equal to the sum of distances between the node and all other nodes of the graph; the less the r of a node, the more central the node.

Let $P[j,k]$ denote the probability of the event.

Deterministic scheme

If an expert indicates the event with full certainty ($P[j,k]=1$), then $E(j,k)$ takes place and $E(k,j)$ does not. Otherwise, if $r(j)<r(k)$ then the event takes place.

Probabilistic scheme

Is used when $P[j,k]$ is evaluated as p, $0 < p < 1$. Two cases are possible. In the first, p is indicated by an expert. In the second, when such indication is absent, it is

assumed that $p = \dfrac{r(k)}{r(j)+r(k)}$. The system uses a random number generator, a subprogram calculating pseudo-random numbers uniformly distributed in the range $(0,1)$. When a number x is generated, such that $x < p$, then the system simulates that $E(j,k)$ has occurred.

Network's Cluster Size Vector. For a node in the network, the thematic cluster can be determined by the system at any moment. One practical benefit is associated with merely knowing in advance the cluster sizes.

Let G be the network's graph, $V=\{j\}$ the set of its nodes, $F(j)$ the automatically generated cluster for j, $j \in V$, and $f(j)=|F(j)|$ the cluster size.

Vector $f(G)=\{f(j), j \in V\}$ describes an important aspect of the current state of the database. The user can consult it, as well as the node content's keyword index, when choosing a thematic node. The vector is to be recalculated immediately after each node-entering session.

The Macro State Monitoring through Thematic-Cluster Covering. A node-entering session is followed by the system finding the family of thematic clusters $\{F(j), j \in V\}$. A subfamily of the family of thematic clusters is called a *thematic-cluster covering* of the network, if each of the network's nodes enters at least one cluster from the subfamily.

Among all possible coverings of a current network, the following ones have a remarkable practical utility for users. A covering $\Phi=\Phi(G)=\{F(j), j \in W \subset V\}$ is said to be a *minimal thematic-cluster covering* of the network, if $\varphi=|\Phi|=|W|$, the number of clusters it includes, is minimally possible for the network's graph. The problem of finding Φ and φ is a case of the 'set covering problem', a classic problem in combinatorics and in graph theory, and algorithms for it are well known (see, e.g., [4]).

The number φ and the set W characterize a current macroscopic state of the database (network). They inform users about the "real thematicity" of the database at a current moment, and indicate the database's "degree of coherence", which are hidden by the apparent multiplicity of nodes as potential themes. If the number φ is comparable with $|V|$, the total number of nodes, then the network is hardly interesting, from the coherent-navigational viewpoint, and needs further "cultivation". On the other hand, the case when φ is very close to 1 may be regarded as not very interesting, as well, because of its "totalitarian" character. The number $\varphi=\varphi(G)$ may be called the *coherence index* of the network G.

Being aware of which nodes constitute the set W, the user becomes informed about the shortest series of thematic journeys (coherent discourses) such that, after its completion, no node of the network remains unvisited. Due to the mentioned qualities of the set *NEXT*, given a thematic node, the system is able to produce one of several possible coherent sequences of nodes in an automatic mode [3], i.e., to make any thematic journey autonomously, so the full series, or a part of it, can be completed in that mode, too.

At the level of the network's evolution, a sudden change in φ's value, after a node-entering session, indicates an event of "self-creation/destruction of meaning" within the database network.

3 Harvesting Coherence in SMIsC

3.1 Non-Confusing Navigation

As noted above, one part of the answer to the question 'Where are the big systems?' should refer to the problem of linking nodes in large hypertext systems; undoubtedly, another part of the answer to this question must address the Navigation Problem [3]. Preventing users from getting "lost in hyperspace", being selective to avoid swamping users with irrelevant links --- the provision of this will be of crucial importance in any sufficiently large hyperbase [19]. It seems to us that in SMIsC, the cultivation of "coherentism" allows to attain such a provision, at least to the degree to which the macrocontrol model [3] is workable.

Figuratively, the navigation harvests the results of the large "number-crunching" work that the system does in advance to make sure that the user's journey in the database is not confusing, does not overload the user, and does not last for an indefinitely long time. In fact, this precursory work makes the user's load, while navigating on a specific theme, almost independent of the network size or, at most, depend on the network size in a linear fashion only.

We'd like only to enumerate what the "fruits" are. The system:
- gives the user a general ("coherentist") view of the database through informing him/her about the macro state;
- informs the user about the maximal duration of navigation (journey) on that or another theme through the thematic cluster size vector;
- performs the extraction and thematic stratification of the database's relevant region through automatic generation of a prestructure (thematic cluster); in this way a global context is created for the navigation;
- reduces the number of link options presented to the user at a current node (and even prioritizes them);
- converts each navigational move into a step in explicit building a hierarchical tree-like outline, thus helping the user to account for his/her current location;
- produces a summary of the trail already blazed, at any moment of navigation;
- makes it possible, at the end of a session, to have not only the final coherent sequence of nodes, but also its full semantic outline and a crop of its summaries;
- is able to blaze (autonomously and coherently) its own trails, to continue and complete trails unfinished by users, and obtain the same output as the one just mentioned.

3.2 Intertextuality

In essence, what SMIsC practices (or pretends to) can be viewed as a kind of intertextuality, a phenomenon conceptualized in linguistics and literary criticism [8]. This is done by dealing with the database network as a package of interlaced coherent texts, where each one is a mosaic of quotations from others. Each of the "texts" can be drawn out by its initial thematic node, together with it's a semantic outline, and may serve as a backbone for a linear document. The principal moment is the "stochastic" or "chance" formation of thematic node clusters; many of the "texts" that arise are not something pre-planned, rather they are sudden synergetic effects of the interaction of semantic meanings of source texts underlying the database content.

It may also be said that SMIsC realizes a 'reuse strategy', according to which previously written material can be recycled in the generation of new written material [17].

3.3 SMIsC as a Belief System

Belief is an assent to or acceptance of the truth of propositions, statements or facts; belief, as a cognitive notion, belongs to the main topic of epistemology (as well as the notion of understanding with which SMIsC foundations are related) [11]. Beliefs are involved in theoretical discussions because of the problem of their justification: what is the proper manner one must use to explain why one thinks what one says is true [12, p. 9]. Philosophers, who defend so called coherence theories of justification, argue that all beliefs may be justified by their relations (of coherence) to others, that "justification is like a house of cards: the edifice of justification stands because of the way in which the parts fit and support each other" [ibid, p. 15].

According to some views, a belief must cohere with other beliefs through the relation of entailment, while others maintain that the kind of coherence required for justification is explanatory coherence and it is those beliefs whose justification seems most adequate that both explain and are explained [ibid, pp. 157, 159, 162]. However, the difference between entailment and explanation is vague. For example, given two propositions, 'X is a machine' and 'X is a computer', one may say that the second both entails the first and explains it. As a first approximation, we may refer to entailment and explanation interchangeably.

Now, let's remember that navigation in SMIsC is organized in such a way that each effective (leading to a new node) step in the navigation that is made along a macrostatus dropping link, models just entailment. This is why the coherent node sequence, generated as a result of a navigational session in SMIsC, may be proposed as an explanation of why the statement expressed by the thematic node is true --- as a justification of the belief contained in the node based on the support giving by the beliefs contained in other nodes of the cluster.

Therefore, one may view a "text" or "discourse" generated in SMIsC as a kind of grounding material; this kind of material is one demanded at both personal and organizational levels. In the next paragraph, we consider a special form that such a material can take.

3.4 Goal Structures

The output of a navigation session in SMIsC includes a semantic outline of the generated sequence of nodes, in the form of a hierarchical tree built from the same nodes, with the thematic node as its apex. If a goal statement can be associated with the content of a node, such a tree may be viewed as a goal structure, in which the main goal occupies the topmost position, and, at each lower level, subgoals are arranged into groups of siblings in such a way that within a group a subgoal entails, or contributes to explanation of, the group's common parent goal. In this hierarchy, the children (subgoals) of each parent (goal) are presented in a strict order, as a subsequence of the sequence, and so a depth-first traversal is uniquely defined on the structure that converts it back into the coherent "text" associated with the sequence. The previous section gives a "justification" of the structure, and makes it "well-grounded". This same justification may be applied to purposeful activity based on the structure.

4 Conclusion

We have described here those aspects of SMIsC which are complementary to ones presented in [3]. What we have tried to show here is the following:

- global semantic coherence grows or emerges within SMIsC hypertext networks as a quality associated with some discourse-like sequences of nodes, or clusters of nodes where such sequences unfold. The macro events of global coherence appearing occur as a consequence of local coherence relations underlying the hypertext links;
- the system practices coherence-cluster recognition through a semantic interpretation of the database network's node-link structure;
- global coherence is cultivated in SMIsC through the network's macrostate monitoring and the user's concentration on improving a specific cluster or the macroscopic "degree of coherence" of the network as a whole;
- global coherence is harvested in the system through "catching" and "removing" the discourse-like sequences and the thematic clusters during navigation sessions. These sequences are used as grounding materials and linear-document backbones. By "catching" rather than "removing", a cluster creates a global context helping to make the navigation non-confusing.

We emphasized that it is important for the user to pay attention not only to the exploration of the network's informational content in statics but also to the macroevents' dynamics while the network is evolving. In fact, users are invited to try working in a rather unusual mode that is entirely SMIsC-specific --- when the focus of attention is kept more on the network's "becoming" than on its "being", that is on discovering macroevents ("anastrophes") while the network is evolving rather than discovering the nodes' content while browsing the network. It may be said that, when an influx of new nodes is maintained, SMIsC functions in this mode as a *situation detector* --- implying that situations are coherent configurations of facts.

We'd like only to add that SMIsC itself is in not so much a state of being as a state of becoming, from both conceptual and implementational viewpoints.

References

1. P.A. Carlson: Square books and round books: cognitive implications of hypertext. *Academic Computing*, April 1990, 16-19, 26-31.
2. P.A. Carlson: Virtual text and new habits of mind. In: H.Maurer, ed., *New results and new trends in computer science; Lecture Notes in Computer Science*, Vol. 555. Berlin: Springer-Verlag, 1991; 25-53.
3. V.M. Chelnokov, V.L. Zephyrova: Coherent navigation in hypertext environments: the SMIsC conception. In: L.J. Bass, J. Gornostaev and C. Unger, eds., *Human-computer interaction (EWHCI'93 selected papers); Lecture Notes in Computer Science*, Vol. 753. Berlin: Springer-Verlag, 1993; 298-317.
4. N. Christofides: *Graph theory: an algorithmic approach*. New York: Academic Press, 1975.
5. J. Conklin: Hypertext: an introduction and survey. *IEEE Computer*, 20(9), 1987, 17-41.
6. T.A. van Dijk, W. Kintsch: *Strategies of discourse comprehension*. New York: Academic Press, 1983.
7. H. Haken: *Information and self-organization: a macroscopic approach to complex systems*. Berlin: Springer-Verlag, 1988.
8. C.H. Holman, W. Harman: *A handbook to literature* (6th ed.). New York: Macmillan, 1992.
9. M.R. Kibby, J.T. Mayes: Towards intelligent hypertext. In: R. McAleese, ed., *Hypertext: theory into practice*. Norwood, NJ: Ablex, 1989; 164-172.
10. W. Kintsch, T.A. van Dijk: Towards a model of text comprehension and production. *Psychological Review*, 85(5), 1978, 363-394.
11. A.R. Lacey: *A dictionary of philosophy*. London: Routledge and Kegan Paul, 1979.
12. K. Lehrer: *Knowledge*. Oxford: Oxford University Press, 1978.
13. W.J.M. Levelt: The speaker's linearization problem. *Philosophical Transactions of the Royal Society of London*, B-295(1077), 1981, 305-314.
14. W.J.M. Levelt: Linearization in describing spatial networks. In: S. Peters and E. Saarinen, eds., *Processes, beliefs, and questions*. Dordrecht: D. Reidel, 1982; 199-220.
15. P.C. Murray: Documentation goes digital. *BYTE*, 18(10), September 1993, 121-129.
16. I. Prigogine, P.M. Allen, R. Herman: Long term trends and the evolution of complexity. In: E. Laszlo and J. Bierman, eds., *Goals in global community (A report to the Club of Rome)*, Vol. 1. New York: Pergamon Press, 1977; 1-63.
17. R. Rada, M. Mhashi, J. Barlow: Hierarchical semantic nets support retrieving and generating hypertext. *Information and Decision Technologies*, 16(2), 1990, 117-135.
18. K. Ray, J.R. Driscoll: New directions for microcomputer-based hypertext systems. *DATABASE*, August 1990, 60-64.
19. C.F. Reynolds, J. Robertson: Navigation requirements in large hypertext systems. *Journal of Document&Text Management*, 1(1), 1993, 7-23.
20. R. Siiter: Associationism. In: *The encyclopedic dictionary of psychology* (4th ed.). Guilford, CT: The Dushkin Publishing Group, Inc., 1991.

1.1   Defining characteristics of kiosks

Within the HCI community, some defining characteristics of hypertext-based kiosk systems have begun to emerge. For example:

- Hypertext-based kiosk systems are intended to be used by wide-ranging audiences, often spanning different age groups and levels of computing sophistication.

- The primary function of hypertext-based kiosk systems is to provide reference information. They are intended for information retrieval. They do not offer authoring opportunities.

- Hypertext-based kiosk systems are appropriate to hypertext, because the information they contain is not linear. It may incorporate a variety of structural inter-relations. The materials do not have a single starting and ending point, but consist of many separate packets of information. Furthermore, there are many potential informational associations among the contents of different entries. For example, in an encyclopedia, items may be related both by alphabetical order and by content-based connections.

- Hypertext-based kiosk systems, because of their intended use as public access systems, may use pointing or touching devices for input, rather than more traditional keyboards. For example, Shneiderman (1987) reports that at Disney World's Epcott Center, only touchscreens were durable enough for kiosks in the park.

- Hypertext-based kiosk systems require effective search mechanisms. The typical use of kiosk is walk-up and users have little time or patience for difficult or painful search. However, because kiosk systems often use non-keyboard input devices, search mechanisms often involve other strategies than simple electronic searching of strings.

- Hypertext-based kiosk systems often include sound, graphics, and animation integrated into the text.

1.2   Challenges for the designers of kiosks

These characteristics lead to a number of challenges to the designer. These challenges fall into three categories. User Characteristics and Capabilities, Presentation of Information and Searching. Each of these is discussed below.

User Characteristics and Capabilities.

Challenge 1: Because kiosks are walk-up systems, it is not reasonable to expect their users to participate in extensive training. While previous studies have shown that training does improve performance with hypertext or multi-window applications, kiosk users operate in a minimal training environment (Tombaugh, Lickorish and Wright, 1987; Mynatt, Leventhal, Instone, Farhat, and Rohlman, 1992; Leventhal, Teasley, Instone, Rohlman, and Farhat, 1993). Kiosk designers are challenged to develop systems that can be readily used, with little training. Instone, Teasley and Leventhal, (1993) provide some evidence that effective interface design and high visibility of tools can reduce the need for training in hypertext information retrieval systems.

Challenge 2: Kiosks users often have widely-varying demographics. Leventhal, Teasley, Instone and Farhat (1994) have demonstrated that child users of a hypertext-based library card catalog sometimes use different search strategies that adults users. Marchionini (1989) found a similar result among children whose ages differed by only a few years. Kiosk designers are challenged to develop systems that are usable by a diverse audience with diverse problem-solving approaches.

Presentation of Information.

Challenge 3: Many authors have found that the simple fact of presenting text electronically does not guarantee that users will be able to effectively comprehend the information, particularly when compared to comprehension of text from traditional media (e.g., Dillon, to appear; Mynatt, Leventhal, Instone, Farhat and Rohlman, 1992; Leventhal, Teasley, Instone, Rohlman and Farhat, 1993). Kiosk designers are challenged to develop systems that afford good comprehension of textual information.

Challenge 4: Several authors have reported difficulties in effective use of graphics, embedded in hypermedia systems. (e.g., Instone, Brown, Leventhal and Teasley, 1993). Little is known about extraction of information from integrated animation and sound. Designers are challenged to develop systems in which integrated multimedia provides usable and enhancing information.

Searching.

Challenge 5: Because kiosk systems often use pointing input devices, rather than keyboard entry, searching is not necessarily based on user-entered strings and string searching. In kiosk systems where the input devices do not include keyboards, it is likely that searching is accomplished by choosing alternatives from a list, selecting a potential group or category from a menu, linear traversal of the database, or linked traversal, via hypertext links. There are challenges to any of these search strategies. Menus and lists provide a set of choices; however, the user has to know the correct choice. If the user is searching for information that is not explicitly specified in the list, searching will likely be quite hard, of course. Even if the user knows the target alternative, they will have to recognize it from the list. Landauer and Nachbar (1985) have demonstrated that when the database has a regular and familiar organization, such as the alphabetical organization of a telephone directory, hierarchical menus directing the search can be effective. Providing an organized list of search choices works less well when the list is unorganized and less structured (e.g., Dumais and Landauer, 1984). Previous work has suggested that on-line keyboards, with data entry through a pointing device is tedious and difficult, regardless of the configuration of the on-line keyboard (e.g. Leventhal, Mynatt and McKeeby, 1991).

Challenge 6: Kiosks often are constructed with sophisticated display hardware, in addition to pointing devices. This environment makes it possible to search and navigate using non-text based and visual direct manipulation. Designers are challenged to provide effective search techniques that take advantage of the hardware.

Challenge 7: Because kiosk systems contain integrated graphics, animation, and sound, new, search techniques to search for non-text objects will be required. Designers are challenged to develop search strategies for non-textual objects.

Some preliminary design guidelines have emerged for designing public access systems (e.g., Heller, 1987). However, as the above challenges suggest, there are many unanswered design questions. In this paper, we focus on Challenge 5: non-keyboard-based search mechanisms for text. We describe a comparative study of three search mechanisms for a hypertext-based kiosk system, *InfoBooth*.

2   The InfoBooth

An interactive, hypertext, kiosk system, called the InfoBooth, was specially created for the 1989 ACM CHI'89 conference. The InfoBooth was intended as a public-access kiosk system, and ran on a HyperCard platform on the Macintosh computer.(Salomon 1990a and 1990b).

The InfoBooth was divided into four sections: Kiosk Information, Presentation Information, Austin Information and the Attendee Yearbook. The Kiosk information described the system. The Austin Information gave information about the site of the conference (Austin). The Presentation Information gave information about the papers, panels and posters from the conference. The Attendee Yearbook gave information about the attendees of the conference. The focus of our study was on the Attendee Yearbook.

2.1   Attendee Yearbook

To be entered into the Attendee Yearbook, people at the conference had their pictures taken at a special photo booth. They answered a small number of questions about human-computer interaction. The pictures and answers to the questions were then entered into the Attendee Yearbook during the conference.

Typical of a hypertext kiosk system, all navigation through the InfoBooth's elements was via mouse clicks on buttons. There were no facilities for keyboard entry or searching on strings, and there were no menus.

The Attendee yearbook included three types of cards:

- Attendee Yearbook Card. This card was the starting point of the Attendee Yearbook

- Person Cards. These were the data cards that contained information about persons in the Yearbook. They included personal information and a picture. From this card, users could follow a hypertext link to information about papers, posters, and panels, if the person was an author.

- Index Cards. These were alphabetical lists (by first name or last name) of the persons in the Yearbook.

All of the three types of cards had a search tool on the side that included buttons for *First Name*, *Last Name*, and the letters of the alphabet. The Attendee Yearbook card and Person Cards also had a button for *Show Names*.

3   Our Study

The focus in our study was *Challenge 5*: the effective, non-keyboard-based searching of the database. The study was an empirical evaluation of different search mechanisms in the Attendee Yearbook. It compared the original search mechanism with two variations. We were interested in the impact of the different search mechanisms on both accuracy and speed of information retrieval. To vary the search mechanisms, we varied the functionality of the search tools in the Attendee Yearbook. However, the appearance of the cards was held constant.

3.1   Three Search Methods

In the Attendee Yearbook, the information is organized in two ways: hierarchically and linearly. Hierarchically, the Attendee Yearbook Card is on top. At the next level are the Index Cards. At the bottom level are the specific Person Cards. To search hierarchically, one would traverse the Person Cards by searching from the Index Cards.

The Attendee Yearbook is also organized linearly because the Person Cards are organized in alphabetical order, by both first names and last names. To search linearly, one would traverse the Person Cards in alphabetical order, similar to page turning in a paper book.

The three search variation that were considered were:

• A hierarchical search, based on the Index Cards.

• A linear search, based on alphabetic traversal of the Person Cards.

• A mixed mode that was based on combined use of the Index Cards and the Person Cards.

3.2   (Hierarchical) Index Search Mode

In the Index Search mode, the search tools lead the user to follow a hierarchical search strategy. In this mode, when users enter the Attendee Yearbook at the Attendee Yearbook Card, they click on a letter from the Alphabetic Palette (on the right portion of the screen). This letter takes them to the Index Card that corresponds to the letter. From the Index Card, they either 1) Click on a name, which takes them to the corresponding Person Card or 2) Click on another letter which takes them to another Index Card or 3) Move to the next or previous Index Cards, via the arrows. If they go to a Person Card they either 1) Click on a letter which takes them back to the Index Cards or 2) Click on the next or previous arrows, which takes them linearly to the next or previous Person Card.

When users select a letter from the Alphabetic Palette in this mode, they are always taken to the Index Cards, regardless of their current card.

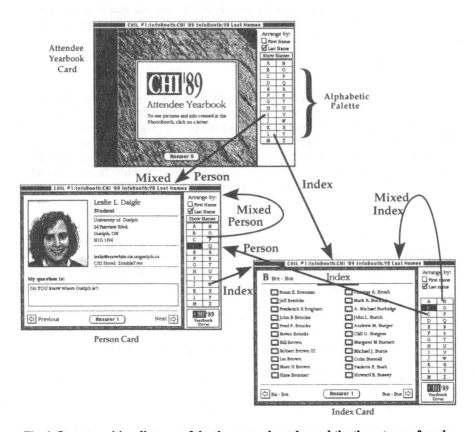

Fig. 1. State-transition diagram of the three search modes and the three types of cards. Notice that all of the arrows labeled "Index" always point to the Index Card; in Index search mode, selecting a letter from the Alphabetic Palette always takes the user to an Index Card. Compare that with the arrows labelled "Mixed," which point to both the Person Card and the Index Card.

3.3 (Linear) Person Search Mode

In the Person Search mode, the search tools encourage a linear search strategy. When users enter the Attendee Yearbook Card, they click on a letter in the Alphabetic Palette. The letter click takes them to a Person Card. From the Person Card, they then may 1) Move up and down the alphabet with the *next* and *previous* buttons. 2) Go to another Person Card by choosing *Last Name* or *First Name* and then specifying a letter or 3) Go to an Index Card by selecting *Show Names*. If they go to an Index Card, they either 1) Move up and down the alphabet with the *next* and *previous* buttons. 2) Pick a particular name and go to the corresponding Person Card or 3) Pick a letter of the alphabet which takes them to the first Person Card that corresponds to the selected letter.

In the Person search mode, selecting a letter from the Alphabetic Palette always takes the user to the first person in that letter.

3.4 (Original) Mixed Search Mode

The search mode that was included in the original InfoBooth was a mixed mode of searching, encouraging both linear and hierarchical searching. In this Mixed method, the user initiated a search at the Attendee Yearbook Card. The user may either select a letter for *First* or *Last Name*, or they may ask for a list of names with the *Show Names* button. If they select *Last Name* and then select a letter, they will see the Person Card that corresponds to the first person in the database whose last name began with the selected letter. The response is similar if they select *first name*. If they select *Show Names*, they go to the Index Card for the letter that they have selected. If they go to a Person Card, they may 1) Move up and down the alphabet with the *next* and *previous* buttons. 2) Go to another Person Card by choosing *Last name* or *First Name* and then specifying a letter or 3) Go to an Index Card by selecting *Show Names*. If they go to an Index Card, they either 1) Move up and down the alphabet with the *next* and *previous* buttons. 2) Pick a particular name and go to the corresponding Person Card or 3) Pick a letter of the alphabet which takes them to the Index Card for that letter.

We called this search mode "Mixed" because the interface has mixed or different reactions to selections from the Alphabetic Palette, depending on which type of card is current. If the user selects a letter from either a Person Card or the Attendee Yearbook Card, they go to a Person Card. However, if they select a letter from the Index Card, they go to another Index card. It is also mixed in the sense that both the Index Cards and the Person Cards are central to searching.

Figure 1 illustrates the three search approaches.

Salomon (1990a) collected usability data about the InfoBooth at the CHI'89 Conference. She reported that users had difficulties finding the *Show Names* button and hence, did not use the Index Cards. Specifically, she reported that 74% of users selected a letter when they entered the Attendee Yearbook and went to a Person Card. It appears from her data that the Mixed Search method was not successful because subjects could not effectively distinguish or use hierarchical and linear searching.

3.5 Materials

We developed a series of 10 questions that could be answered from the Attendee Yearbook. Table 1 shows the questions and their characteristics.

3.6 Procedure

Subjects were presented with the Attendee Yearbook Card and a booklet of the information retrieval questions. The questions were completely randomized across the subjects. Subjects were instructed to find the answers to the questions, using the Attendee Yearbook.

3.7 Subjects

There were 30 subjects, with 10 subjects per search mode condition. These subjects were faculty members and graduate students. These subjects were chosen because we felt that they were similar to the intended audience of the InfoBooth.

QUESTIONS	INTERESTING CHARACTERISTICS
What is Cindy's title?	There is only one "Cindy" in the database and Cindy is a first name. This question can be answered from a Person Card.
What country is Saila from?	There is only one "Saila" in the database and Saila is a first name. However, it is not a common first name for Americans. This question can be answered from a Person Card. The user must click on the "Author of" button to find the correct answer.
Was Tom Moher's paper about adaptive user interfaces?	"Moher" is toward the end of the "M's". There are many "M's" and a linear search through the "M's" would be quite lengthy.
You have to pick up Blaine Price and Arnie Lund for dinner. If they are staying at the same hotel, you can leave a little bit later. Are they both staying at the same hotel?	Need information for two entries. This question can be answered from Person Cards.
What city does Ms. Daigle live in?	"Daigle" is the first "D" in the last names that begin with "D". This question can be answered from a Person Card.
How many people named "Brown" are in the yearbook?	This question can be answered from an Index Card or from the Person Cards.
Does Stuart Zweben wear glasses?	"Zweben" is the final last name in the database. This question can be answered from a Person Card.
You heard a presentation entitled "Whither CHI in the 1990s?" but can only remember that the author's last name was something like "Nilson". What is his full name?	This question can be answered from the Person Cards. The user must click on the "Author of" button to find the correct answer.
You remember meeting a man named "Allan" (unsure of the spelling) who works for Apple. What is his full name?	This question can be answered from a Person Card.
Is Mr. Shneiderman in the yearbook?	This question can be answered from an Index card or from the Person Cards.

Table 1. The questions used in the experiment and relevant characteristics of each

3.8 Experimental Design

Each subject received one of the three versions of the attendee yearbook. Each subject answered the ten questions. We collected three types of data: accuracy on the questions, time to answer the questions, and number of cards viewed for each question.

4   Results

4.1   Accuracy

Each question was scored 0 for incorrect or 1 for correct and an average score for each subject was calculated. Overall, subjects in all conditions did quite well. The average score across all subjects was 0.95 (s.d. = .07). There were no significant differences in score by type of search tool (F < 1). It appears that subjects were able to answer nearly all of the questions, regardless of search mode.

4.2   Time to Answer Questions

We measured the time, in seconds, to answer questions, for each subject. The means were 91.3 (s.d. = 15.7) seconds for Index, 101.3 (s.d. = 50.5) seconds for Person, and 122.8 (s.d. = 56.2) seconds for the Mixed. The differences in times were not significant.

Nine of the twenty subjects who had either the Person or Mixed search mode did eventually find an Index Card and did figure out how to do Index-based searching within their own search mode. We were interested in determining whether discovery of the Index Card affected the time to answer questions for these subjects. For these two groups, the mean times before and after discovery of the index card were 111.6 (s.d. = 77.5) seconds and 47.1 (s.d. = 77.5) seconds, respectively. This difference was highly significant (F(1,18) = 9.1, p < .01). For these subjects, discovery of the Index Card reduced search times immensely. These results point up an unexpected result: the subjects who did not have the Index mode, but who found the Index Cards, were much faster than the subjects who did have the Index mode (compare means of 91.3 seconds to 47.1 seconds). We speculate that the subjects who did not have the Index mode had plenty of opportunities to read through some of the Person Cards in the database. When they found the Index Cards, we believe that they spent no more time perusing the contents of the database. The Index group on the other hand, were forced to see little of the database. We feel that they probably spent more time reading the Person Cards that they did encounter, throughout all of their 10 questions.

4.3   Number of Cards Visited

In addition to time to answer questions, we also measured the number of cards that each subject visited to answer each question. While this measure is closely related to time to answer question, it also gives some indication of the efficiency of the subject's search. Unlike the time to answer questions, this variable is independent of reading time. It is desirable that searching in a kiosk system should be efficient and effective; otherwise users may give up on their search. In a highly efficient search, subjects should visit few cards. In the Index mode, for example, each search for an individual person should have involved about two cards: the Index Card and the Person Card. If it was necessary to view extra Index Cards, the number of cards would be increased slightly. However, in the other modes, the number of visited cards is likely to be somewhat higher, particularly if the subject is perusing the database linearly. There was only one exception. For the question, "What city does Ms. Daigle live in?," either the Mixed or Person modes will find this card, by selecting the "D". This question, for those subjects should require only one card.

The mean number of cards visited for each question was 17.5 (s.d. 15.5). This number seems astonishingly high until one breaks up the subjects by search mode. The means by search mode are Index(M=5.8, s.d. 2.0), Person (M=22.2, s.d. 14.0) and Mixed (M=24.6, s.d. 18.3). This difference is highly significant (F(2,27)=5.9, p<.01). Planned comparisons showed that the differences between the Mixed and Person modes were not significantly different.

As with search times, finding the Index Cards had a profound effect on the numbers of cards visited for subjects with either the Mixed or Person mode. The difference in number of cards for these subjects before and after is highly significant (F(1,18)=28.7, p<.0001) with means of 27.2 (s.d. 17.1) cards before finding the Index and 4.8 (s.d. 5.7) cards after finding an Index Card. In other words, even when the use of the Index Cards was not encouraged by the search method, once subjects found the Index, they continued to use it.

5   Summary

One of the challenges facing designers of hypertext-based kiosk systems is to identify effective, non-keyboard based searching. In the CHI'89 InfoBooth, the original searching mechanism encouraged a mixture of hierarchical and linear searching. It was found, in practice, to be quite awkward (Salomon, 1990). We were interested in identifying reasons why the mixed-mode searching did not work. Did it fail because it did not fully support hierarchical searching or because it did not encourage linear searching? Which search mechanism was more appropriate for the informational organization of the InfoBooth?

From our study, we demonstrated that subjects were quite accurate in answering questions in any of three search modes: hierarchical, linear or mixed. However, in terms of speed and minimizing the number of cards visited, the hierarchical approach was far superior.

In general, we believe that the hierarchical was superior because the tool mimicked the structure of the information. The information in the InfoBooth was intended to be used hierarchically, starting from the Attendee Yearbook Card, to the Index Cards, to the Person Cards. The database is only rarely navigated linearly. However, the original search tool provided support for only partial hierarchical navigation. The mixed mode searching encouraged users to hierarchically find the first name in a group and then navigate linearly from that point. The fact that the Person and the Mixed mode were equally bad further suggests that users need a hierarchical search tool for hierarchical data.

Our original motivation for this study was to determine how a designer of a hypertext-based kiosk system should approach the searching in the situation when searching is not based on keyboard-entered strings. We conclude that as a general rule, designers should provide a tool which matches the search pattern. In the case of multiple patterns, we recommend providing multiple, non-ambiguous tools.

Acknowledgments
    The authors would like to thank Lisa Weihl and John Beck for their assistance on this project. This research was supported by funds from an Ohio Board of Regents Academic Challenge Grant.

References

Dillon, A. (1993) Reading from paper versus screens: a critical review of the empirical literature. *Ergonomics*.

Dumais, S.T. and Landauer, T.K. (1984) Describing Categories of objects for menu retrieval systems. *Behavior Research, Methods, Instruments, and Computers*. 16. 242-248.

Landauer, T.K. and Nachbar, D.W. (1985) Selection from alphabetic and numeric menu trees using a touch screen: breadth, depth, and width. In *Proceedings of CHI '85 Human Factors in Computing Systems*. New York: ACM.73-78.

Leventhal, L.M., McKeeby, J.W. and Mynatt, B.T. (1991) Screen Keyboards: An Empirical Study of the Effects of Shape and Character Layout. In Bullinger, H.-J. (ed.) *Human Aspects in Computing: Design and Use of Interactive Systems and Work with Terminals*. New York, Elsevier Science Publishers B. V. 108-112.

Instone, K., Leventhal, L.M., Teasley, B.M., Farhat, J. and Rohlman, D.S. (1992) What do I want? and How do I get there?: Performance and navigation in information retrieval tasks with hypertext documents, Proceedings of the *East–West International Conference on Human-Computer Interaction*. St. Petersburg, Russia, August 4-8, 1992. 85-95.

Instone, K., Brown, E., Leventhal, L. and Teasley, B. (1993) The challenge of effectively integrating graphics into hypertext. In L.J. Bass, J. Gornostaev, C. Unger (Eds.). *Human-Computer Interaction: Third International Conference, EWHCI '93*. Moscow, Russia, August 1993. Lecture Notes in Computer Science, Springer-Verlag. Vol. 753. 290-297.

Heller, R.S. (1991) Computing Access in Public Spaces: Design Lessons Learned. In Bullinger, H.-J. (ed.) *Human Aspects in Computing: Design and Use of Interactive Systems and Work with Terminals*. New York: Elsevier Science Publishers B.V. 699-703.

Instone, K., Teasley, B., and Leventhal, L.M. (1993) Empirically-based re-design of a hypertext encyclopedia. *Proceedings of INTERCHI'93 Human Factors in Computer Systems*. Addison-Wesley Publishing Company: Reading, MA.

Leventhal, L.M., Teasley, B.M., Instone, K., Rohlman, D.S. and Farhat, J. (1993) Sleuthing in HyperHolmes: Using hypertext vs. a book to answer questions, *Behaviour and Information Technology*. 12 (1).

Leventhal, L. M., Teasley, B. M., Instone, K. and Farhat, J. (1994). Age-Related Differences in the Use of Hypertext: Experiment and Design Guidelines. *Hypermedia*.

Marchionini, G. (1989) Information-seeking strategies of novices using a full-text encyclopedia. *Journal of the American Society for Information Science*. 40(1). 54-66.

Mynatt, B.T., Leventhal, L.M., Instone, K. Farhat, J. and Rohlman, D.S. (1992) Hypertext or Book: Which is Better for Answering Questions? *Proceedings of CHI'92. Human Factors in Computer Systems*. Addison-Wesley Publishing Company: Reading, MA. 19-25.

Shneiderman, B. (1987) *Designing the User Interface. Strategies for Effective Human-Computer Interaction.* Addison-Wesley Publishing Company: Reading, MA.

Salomon, G. (1990a) Designing casual-use hypertext: The CHI '89 InfoBooth. *CHI '90 Proceedings.* 451-458.

Salomon, G. (1990b) How the look affects the feel: Visual design and the creation of an information kiosk. Proceedings of the Human Factors Society 34th Annual Meeting. 277-281.

Time Warner Interactive Group (1993) *The New Family Bible: From the Garden to the Promised Land.* Burbank, CA.

Tombaugh, J., Lickorish, A. and Wright P. (1987) Multiwindow displays for readers of lengthy texts. *International Journal of Man-Machine Studies.* 26(5). 597-615.

Author Index

Springer-Verlag
and the Environment

We at Springer-Verlag firmly believe that an international science publisher has a special obligation to the environment, and our corporate policies consistently reflect this conviction.

We also expect our business partners – paper mills, printers, packaging manufacturers, etc. – to commit themselves to using environmentally friendly materials and production processes.

The paper in this book is made from low- or no-chlorine pulp and is acid free, in conformance with international standards for paper permanency.

Lecture Notes in Computer Science

For information about Vols. 1–798
please contact your bookseller or Springer-Verlag

Vol. 835: W. M. Tepfenhart, J. P. Dick, J. F. Sowa (Eds.), Conceptual Structures: Current Practices. Proceedings, 1994. VIII, 331 pages. 1994. (Subseries LNAI).

Vol. 836: B. Jonsson, J. Parrow (Eds.), CONCUR '94: Concurrency Theory. Proceedings, 1994. IX, 529 pages. 1994.

Vol. 837: S. Wess, K.-D. Althoff, M. M. Richter (Eds.), Topics in Case-Based Reasoning. Proceedings, 1993. IX, 471 pages. 1994. (Subseries LNAI).

Vol. 838: C. MacNish, D. Pearce, L. Moniz Pereira (Eds.), Logics in Artificial Intelligence. Proceedings, 1994. IX, 413 pages. 1994. (Subseries LNAI).

Vol. 839: Y. G. Desmedt (Ed.), Advances in Cryptology - CRYPTO '94. Proceedings, 1994. XII, 439 pages. 1994.

Vol. 840: G. Reinelt, The Traveling Salesman. VIII, 223 pages. 1994.

Vol. 841: I. Prívara, B. Rovan, P. Ružička (Eds.), Mathematical Foundations of Computer Science 1994. Proceedings, 1994. X, 628 pages. 1994.

Vol. 842: T. Kloks, Treewidth. IX, 209 pages. 1994.

Vol. 843: A. Szepietowski, Turing Machines with Sublogarithmic Space. VIII, 115 pages. 1994.

Vol. 844: M. Hermenegildo, J. Penjam (Eds.), Programming Language Implementation and Logic Programming. Proceedings, 1994. XII, 469 pages. 1994.

Vol. 845: J.-P. Jouannaud (Ed.), Constraints in Computational Logics. Proceedings, 1994. VIII, 367 pages. 1994.

Vol. 846: D. Shepherd, G. Blair, G. Coulson, N. Davies, F. Garcia (Eds.), Network and Operating System Support for Digital Audio and Video. Proceedings, 1993. VIII, 269 pages. 1994.

Vol. 847: A. L. Ralescu (Ed.) Fuzzy Logic in Artificial Intelligence. Proceedings, 1993. VII, 128 pages. 1994. (Subseries LNAI).

Vol. 848: A. R. Krommer, C. W. Ueberhuber, Numerical Integration on Advanced Computer Systems. XIII, 341 pages. 1994.

Vol. 849: R. W. Hartenstein, M. Z. Servít (Eds.), Field-Programmable Logic. Proceedings, 1994. XI, 434 pages. 1994.

Vol. 850: G. Levi, M. Rodríguez-Artalejo (Eds.), Algebraic and Logic Programming. Proceedings, 1994. VIII, 304 pages. 1994.

Vol. 851: H.-J. Kugler, A. Mullery, N. Niebert (Eds.), Towards a Pan-European Telecommunication Service Infrastructure. Proceedings, 1994. XIII, 582 pages. 1994.

Vol. 852: K. Echtle, D. Hammer, D. Powell (Eds.), Dependable Computing – EDCC-1. Proceedings, 1994. XVII, 618 pages. 1994.

Vol. 853: K. Bolding, L. Snyder (Eds.), Parallel Computer Routing and Communication. Proceedings, 1994. IX, 317 pages. 1994.

Vol. 854: B. Buchberger, J. Volkert (Eds.), Parallel Processing: CONPAR 94 – VAPP VI. Proceedings, 1994. XVI, 893 pages. 1994.

Vol. 855: J. van Leeuwen (Ed.), Algorithms – ESA '94. Proceedings, 1994. X, 510 pages.1994.

Vol. 856: D. Karagiannis (Ed.), Database and Expert Systems Applications. Proceedings, 1994. XVII, 807 pages. 1994.

Vol. 857: G. Tel, P. Vitányi (Eds.), Distributed Algorithms. Proceedings, 1994. X, 370 pages. 1994.

Vol. 858: E. Bertino, S. Urban (Eds.), Object-Oriented Methodologies and Systems. Proceedings, 1994. X, 386 pages. 1994.

Vol. 859: T. F. Melham, J. Camilleri (Eds.), Higher Order Logic Theorem Proving and Its Applications. Proceedings, 1994. IX, 470 pages. 1994.

Vol. 860: W. L. Zagler, G. Busby, R. R. Wagner (Eds.), Computers for Handicapped Persons. Proceedings, 1994. XX, 625 pages. 1994.

Vol: 861: B. Nebel, L. Dreschler-Fischer (Eds.), KI-94: Advances in Artificial Intelligence. Proceedings, 1994. IX, 401 pages. 1994. (Subseries LNAI).

Vol. 862: R. C. Carrasco, J. Oncina (Eds.), Grammatical Inference and Applications. Proceedings, 1994. VIII, 290 pages. 1994. (Subseries LNAI).

Vol. 863: H. Langmaack, W.-P. de Roever, J. Vytopil (Eds.), Formal Techniques in Real-Time and Fault-Tolerant Systems. Proceedings, 1994. XIV, 787 pages. 1994.

Vol. 864: B. Le Charlier (Ed.), Static Analysis. Proceedings, 1994. XII, 465 pages. 1994.

Vol. 865: T. C. Fogarty (Ed.), Evolutionary Computing. Proceedings, 1994. XII, 332 pages. 1994.

Vol. 866: Y. Davidor, H.-P. Schwefel, R. Männer (Eds.), Parallel Problem Solving from Nature - PPSN III. Proceedings, 1994. XV, 642 pages. 1994.

Vol 867: L. Steels, G. Schreiber, W. Van de Velde (Eds.), A Future for Knowledge Acquisition. Proceedings, 1994. XII, 414 pages. 1994. (Subseries LNAI).

Vol. 868: R. Steinmetz (Ed.), Multimedia: Advanced Teleservices and High-Speed Communication Architectures. Proceedings, 1994. IX, 451 pages. 1994.

Vol. 869: Z. W. Raś, Zemankova (Eds.), Methodologies for Intelligent Systems. Proceedings, 1994. X, 613 pages. 1994. (Subseries LNAI).

Vol. 870: J. S. Greenfield, Distributed Programming Paradigms with Cryptography Applications. XI, 182 pages. 1994.

Vol. 871: J. P. Lee, G. G. Grinstein (Eds.), Database Issues for Data Visualization. Proceedings, 1993. XIV, 229 pages. 1994.

Vol. 873: M. Naftalin, T. Denvir, M. Bertran (Eds.), FME '94: Industrial Benefit of Formal Methods. Proceedings, 1994. XI, 723 pages. 1994.

Vol. 874: A. Borning (Ed.), Principles and Practice of Constraint Programming. Proceedings, 1994. IX, 361 pages. 1994.

Vol. 875: D. Gollmann (Ed.), Computer Security – ESORICS 94. Proceedings, 1994. XI, 469 pages. 1994.

Vol. 876: B. Blumenthal, J. Gornostaev, C. Unger (Eds.), Human-Computer Interaction. Proceedings, 1994. IX, 239 pages. 1994.